The Albanian Operation
of the CIA and MI6,
1949–1953

The Albanian Operation of the CIA and MI6, 1949–1953

Conversations with Participants in a Venture Betrayed

NICHOLAS BETHELL

Edited by Robert Elsie *and* Bejtullah Destani

McFarland & Company, Inc., Publishers
Jefferson, North Carolina

All photographs courtesy Centre for Albanian Studies, London, unless otherwise noted.

LIBRARY OF CONGRESS CATALOGUING-IN-PUBLICATION DATA

Names: Bethell, Nicholas, 1938–2007, author. | Elsie, Robert, 1950– author. | Destani, Bejtullah D., author.
Title: The Albanian Operation of the CIA and MI6, 1949–1953 : conversations with participants in a venture betrayed / Nicholas Bethell ; edited by Robert Elsie and Bejtullah Destani.
Description: Jefferson, North Carolina : McFarland & Company, Inc., Publishers, 2016 | Includes bibliographical references and index.
Identifiers: LCCN 2016006266 | ISBN 9781476663791 (softcover : acid free paper) ∞
Subjects: LCSH: Albania—History—1944–1990. | Subversive activities—Albania. | Espionage—Albania—History—20th century. | Spies—Interviews. | United States. Central Intelligence Agency—Biography. | Great Britain. MI6—Biography. | Albania—Relations—Great Britain. | Great Britain—Relations—Albania. | Albania—Relations—United States. | United States—Relations—Albania.
Classification: LCC DR977 .B468 2016 | DDC 327.12410496509/045—dc23
LC record available at http://lccn.loc.gov/2016006266

BRITISH LIBRARY CATALOGUING DATA ARE AVAILABLE

© 2016 Robert Elsie, Bejtullah Destani and John Bethell. All rights reserved

No part of this book may be reproduced or transmitted in any form or by any means, electronic or mechanical, including photocopying or recording, or by any information storage and retrieval system, without permission in writing from the publisher.

Front cover *clockwise from top left:* Vasil Andoni (1901–1994); David Smiley (1916–2009); Albanian landowner Ihsan Toptani (1908–2001); Abdyl Sino, an Albanian anticommunist fighter in exile; Queen Geraldine (1915–2002) (courtesy Centre for Albanian Studies, London)

Printed in the United States of America

McFarland & Company, Inc., Publishers
Box 611, Jefferson, North Carolina 28640
www.mcfarlandpub.com

Table of Contents

Introduction 1

THE INTERVIEWS

Alan J. Adams 7
Julian Amery 10
Vasil Andoni 22
James J. Angleton 26
Sam Barclay 26
Zbigniew Bobinski 34
Michael Burke 35
Ramazan Cenaj 44
Terence Cooling 51
Ramazan Dalipi 56
Sali Daliu 57
Rodney Dennys 60
Lawrence De Neufville 61
Jani Dilo 61
Abas Ermenji 64
Queen Geraldine of Albania 71
Bardhyl Gerveshi 74
Adem Gjura 80
Gaqi Goga 86
Dino Gregory 90
Sir Reginald Hibbert 92
George Jellicoe 102
Robert Joyce 104
Peter Kemp 105
Said Kryeziu 107
Bido Kuka 109
Safet Malushi 112
Billy McLean 114
Sefër Muço 124
Halil Nerguti 127
Anthony Northrop 131
Lord St. Oswald 140
Abdyl Sino 141
Colonel David Smiley 147
Moy Smiley 157
Cyrus Sulzberger 158
Ihsan Toptani 159
Sali Toptani 162
Kevin Walton 163
Patrick Whinney 165
Sir Richard White 169
Martin Whitworth 171
Gratian Yatsevitch 175

Bibliography 181
Index 184

Introduction

Kim Philby (1912–1988), a high-ranking British intelligence officer and, at the same time, a spy for the Soviet Union, is one of the most fascinating figures in the murky history of twentieth-century espionage. He was at war with the British establishment, of which he was himself an integral part. Among his victims, in very concrete terms, were hundreds of Albanians.

This book provides insight into the so-called Albanian Operation, carried out by the British and American secret services in the years 1949–1953 to infiltrate communist Albania and topple the hermetic Stalinist regime that had seized power there. It focuses on conversations and interviews with the people who actually took part in the operation in one way or another: British and American officials, and Albanian fighters who infiltrated Albania and escaped alive.

The Historical Background

Albania, a small country in southeastern Europe, had gained its independence from the Ottoman Empire in 1912. In 1939, the realm of King Zog, its autocratic ruler, was invaded by Italian forces. The Albanian king fled abroad and the country became part of Mussolini's new Roman Empire. With the capitulation of fascist Italy on 8 September 1943, Nazi Germany occupied Albania to ensure that the country did not fall into the hands of the British. Throughout the period of Italian and German occupation, the Albanians were very divided in their loyalties. Many thought it best to submit and adapt to the new situation; others called for armed resistance. Even within the resistance, there was deep division, with the presence of three rival resistance groups: the communist partisans under Enver Hoxha (1908–1985) and Mehmet Shehu (1913–1981), the anticommunist *Balli Kombëtar* (National Front) under Midhat bey Frashëri (1880–1949), and the smaller royalist *Legaliteti* (Legality) movement under Abas Kupi (1892–1976). The German Foreign Office endeavored to revive an independent Albanian state to safeguard German strategic interests in the Balkans. A new administration was formed in Tirana, but it was not able to exert much authority over the country, which was now enmeshed in a bloody civil war. When German troops withdrew from Albania at the end of November 1944, the communists under Enver Hoxha took power and subsequently set up the People's Republic of Albania.

Once in office, the new regime took immediate measures to consolidate its power.

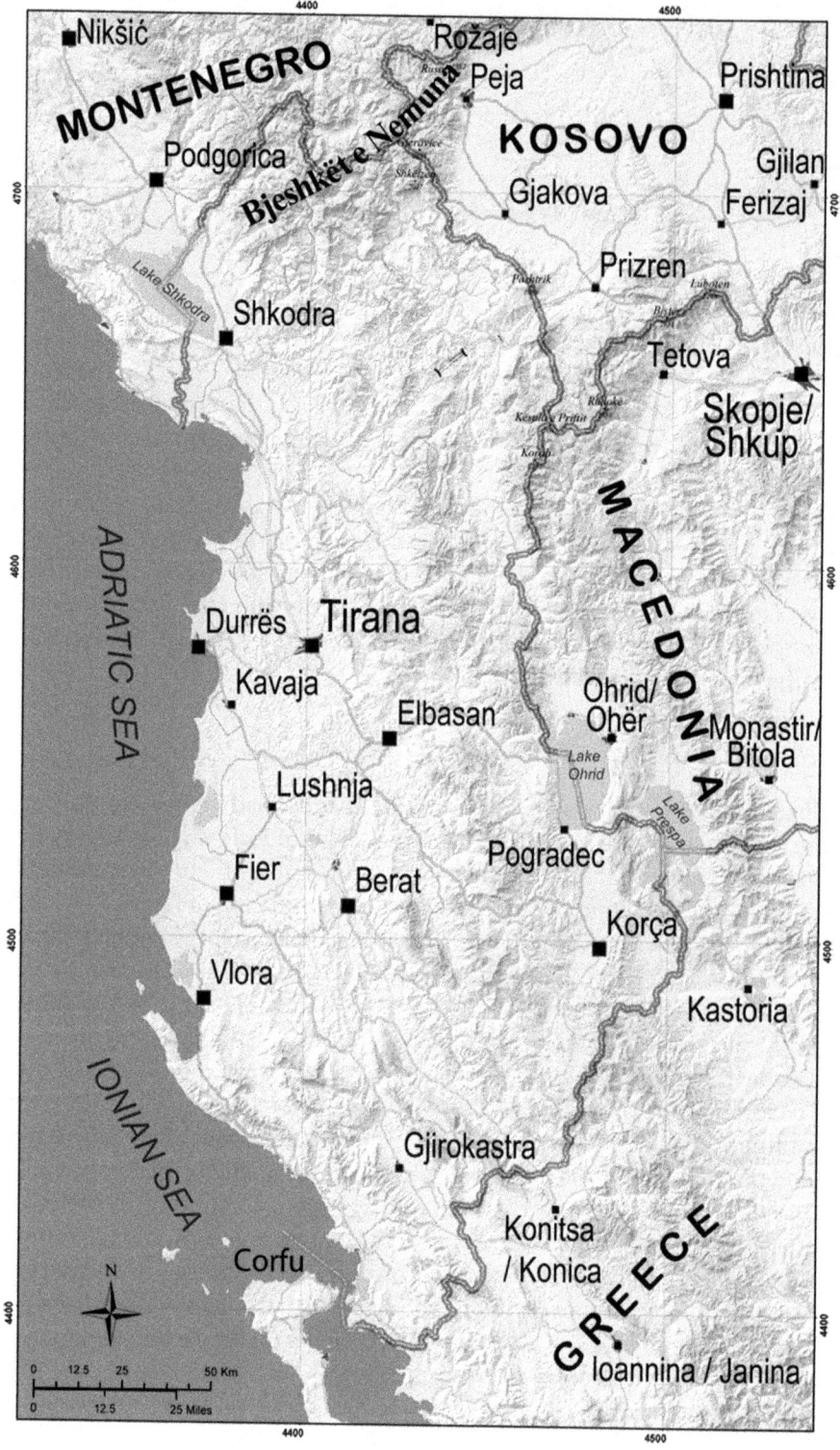

Map of Albania, by Ismajl Gagica (Prishtina).

Introduction

In January 1945, a special people's court was set up in Tirana under Koçi Xoxe (1917–1949), the new minister of the interior from Korça, for the purpose of trying "major war criminals." This tribunal conducted a series of show trials which went on for months, during which hundreds of actual or suspected opponents of the regime were sentenced to death or to long years of imprisonment. In March, private property and wealth were confiscated by means of a special profit tax, thus eliminating the middle class, and industry was nationalized. In August 1945, a radical agrarian reform was introduced, virtually wiping out the landowning class which had ruled the country since independence in 1912. At the same time, initial efforts were undertaken to combat illiteracy, which cast its shadow over about 80 percent of the population. Apart from a shattered economy and anticommunist uprisings in the north of the country, the new regime had a number of major foreign policy problems to deal with. Greece still considered itself in a state of war with Albania, relations with the United States had declined dramatically, and ties with the United Kingdom were severely strained after the so-called Corfu Channel incident of October 22, 1946, in which two British destroyers hit mines off the Albanian coast.

The communist leadership in Albania, always plagued by factional division, had split into two camps shortly after it took power. One side, represented by poet Sejfullah Malëshova (1901–1971), in charge of cultural affairs, contended that Albania should conduct an independent foreign policy, maintaining relations with both East and West, and more moderate domestic policies to encourage national reconciliation. The pro-Yugoslav faction, led by minister of the interior Koçi Xoxe, advocated closer ties with Yugoslavia and the Soviet Union, and insisted that more radical social and economic policies be introduced and coordinated with those being implemented by Belgrade. Xoxe and his Yugoslav advisors won out, and in February 1946, Malëshova was expelled from the Politburo and condemned as a "right-wing opportunist." Enver Hoxha himself seems to have maintained a tactically vague position, lying low and waiting for a chance to eliminate his opponents for good. Relations with the United Kingdom and the United States worsened, and in July 1946, Enver Hoxha signed a treaty of friendship, cooperation and mutual assistance with Yugoslavia following a visit to Belgrade. This was envisaged as the first step towards the union of the two countries and Albania was to remain a virtual Yugoslav colony until June 1948. During this period, Koçi Xoxe, as minister of the interior, made ample use of his powers over the security apparatus and police to eliminate all potential rivals and enemies. These witch hunts, known euphemistically in official party history as the period of Koçi-Xoxism, resulted in the execution or imprisonment not only of political figures but also of numerous talented writers and intellectuals.

The rift between Tito and Joseph Stalin in 1948 gave Enver Hoxha a Soviet ally with whose support he could now act to preserve his own position, and he soon managed to eliminate his rivals. Albania became the first Eastern European country to denounce Yugoslavia after the latter's expulsion from the Cominform, i.e., the Soviet bloc, on June 17, 1948, and all Yugoslav advisors were expelled from the country without delay. Albania had entered the Soviet fold. The series of show trials and purges which ensued were similar to those that took place elsewhere in Eastern Europe in the late 1940s and early 1950s. At its first congress of 8–22 November 1948, the purged Albanian

Communist Party was renamed the Albanian Party of Labour. Koçi Xoxe's own reign of terror came to an end when he was convicted of treason in May 1949 and executed on June 11 of that year. For the people of Albania, the late 1940s were a period of blatant terror. Even those who had supported the communists in 1944 realized that the ideals of socialism and equality had become a farce. Nowhere in the eastern bloc were people more oppressed, more terrified into submission than in Albania.

Albania's alliance with the Soviet Union had several advantages. The Soviets offered much food and economic assistance to replace the losses caused by the interruption of Yugoslav aid. They also gave the Hoxha regime military protection both from neighboring Yugoslavia and from the West at a time when the Cold War was at its height.

By 1947, the Western world and the Soviet Union, one-time allies against Nazi Germany, were embittered rivals in a Cold War that was played out in the Balkans primarily in Greece. The Powers had divided the spoils of Europe in advance during the war. The major Balkan countries: Yugoslavia, Bulgaria and Romania, were to go to the Soviet bloc whereas Greece was to be part of the West. No specific provision was made for Albania. Greece, however, descended into a bloody civil war between the Greek Communist Party, supported by the Soviet Union and the communist countries of the Balkans, and anti-communist government forces, supported by Britain and the United States.

The Albanian Operation

The postwar Albanian Operation was one of the first Western attempts to subvert a country behind the Iron Curtain. It was devised initially around 1946 by officials of the British Secret Intelligence Service (SIS) who believed, rather naively, that if they could parachute a few well-trained agents into Albania, they could bring about a mass uprising against the communist regime. By 1949 the CIA was heavily involved in the project, too. The British liaison officer for the project in Washington was none other than Kim Philby. The venture was facilitated by the large numbers of Albanian refugees languishing in camps in Italy and Greece. When contacted, with the intercession of their exile leaders, they were more than willing to be recruited. The volunteers were given brief and vastly insufficient training, primarily in Malta and southern Germany, and were sent into Albania by boat, overland from Greece, and by parachute drop, in small groups, mainly from the second half of 1949 to Easter 1952. Most of them were captured and shot the moment they arrived. The communist security forces had seemingly been informed in advance of their arrival. The Albanian fighters had thus been betrayed. In all, about 300 agents and civilians are thought to have been killed in the operation—probably a conservative estimate.

It has been suggested that the Albanian Operation, promoted by Britain and later by the United States, was intended not so much to overthrow the Hoxha regime, but to weaken communist forces fighting in Greece. If this is true, the Albanian fighters who returned to liberate their country and perished in doing so were betrayed twice over. They were mere pawns in a larger game.

The Albanian Operation was eventually abandoned and hushed up. For Britain and the United States, it was a humiliating disaster about which they did not want the

Introduction

world to know, in particular because they still did not understand the exact reason for its failure. It was only years later, with the defection of Kim Philby to Moscow, that the full extent of his treachery became apparent.

The full story of the disastrous Albanian Operation was first pieced together by Nicholas Bethell in his book *The Great Betrayal: The Untold Story of Kim Philby's Biggest Coup*, published in London in 1984. Lord Bethell based his book on conversations and interviews recorded with those involved in the project at the time, among them being some of the Albanian fighters who survived and managed to escape from Albania. The interviews, which were conducted over a three-year period from May 1981 to August 1984, were not themselves published at the time. It was Lord Bethell's wish to edit them and make them available to the public domain. However, suffering from Parkinson's disease in later life, he passed away before he could realize this intention. We are grateful to the Bethell family for providing this first-hand material to the Centre for Albanian Studies in London for publication. The present edition of the conversations and interviews on a venture betrayed will, we hope, throw new light on what actually took place.

**Lord Nicholas Bethell (1938–2007)
(courtesy Bethell estate).**

Robert Elsie
Berlin, Germany

The Interviews

Alan J. Adams

Alan J. Adams (b. ca. 1930) was a British military figure and intelligence officer. He joined the intelligence corps and was posted to Malta in July 1949 to work on security duties for the Albanian fighters training there.

I joined the army for 18 months National Service at the beginning of 1949, went into the Royal Corps of Signals in Catterick, and was posted to the intelligence corps in Maresfield for a field security course. At the end of the course, they asked for volunteers for a special posting of a very secret nature. They said it was in Malta, which sounded reasonably attractive, so six of us volunteered. We flew out to Malta from Blackbushe Airport in Surrey in July 1949.

After a short time, we were all rather disappointed, to tell you the truth. We thought that it was going to be an exciting assignment, whereas all it really involved was general duties around the camp. We realized that we would have had a much more interesting time in a field security unit in Germany or Hong Kong.

We were known as the Fourth Pioneer Training and Disposal Unit and the Albanians with us were known as "pixies." Looking back, it seems to me to have been a sloppy and halfhearted operation. It cannot have been easy to maintain security in a place like Malta, which was full of British service personnel, but within a short time there were all sorts of rumors flying about over what we were up to. It would have been better to have it somewhere more remote, perhaps even on Gozo, Malta's offshore island.

There was "Blondie" Stover, a cook from the army Catering Corps, and George Odey, who was the armorer although he had no training as an armorer, and Corporal Topliss, who was the clerk. Our only qualification was one of security. The secrecy of the operation was emphasized to us again and again. We felt, however, that, in the circumstances, it would have been better to do the training in a more secluded place. There was no need for us to have towns and bars and cinemas within easy reach. On the contrary, all this made it more likely that the purpose of the operation was going to leak out. And there were plenty of people in Malta, army and civilian, who came across us and figured out that there was something queer going on.

There was one day, Albanian national day, when everyone in the camp got completely drunk on ouzo, British as well as Albanian. Stover took a 15-cwt truck out of the gate across the moat, round the bend to the left and then round the bend to the right. Only this last bend was too much for him and he took the truck straight through a wall and into the field. Everyone fell about laughing. The whole camp was paralytic.

There was no guardhouse, no permanent guard on the gate. Anyone who was sufficiently bold could have wandered straight in. It is true that Fort Bin Jema was in a remote part of the island up a windy road, but from there to Valetta was only a 25-minute drive. We all used to go into town to have a drink or go to the cinema, including the Albanians, although they were always under supervision. There were occasions when Albanians were picked up by the military police. They couldn't speak in English and someone had to go down from the camp to spring them. I remember some of them being arrested for wearing tennis shoes with uniform.

We kept our vehicles mechanically sound, but there wasn't the backup to wash them and keep them looking good. They looked terrible sometimes. The "Red Caps" used to stop me and ask to see my worksheet. Only I hadn't got a worksheet. So we had dirty vehicles, no worksheets, men from the camp not speaking English and wearing tennis shoes with uniform. It was all very mystifying to the military police. Eventually they were told to turn a blind eye to what went on at our camp. In the end, I remember, they arranged a party for us and the military police, so that we could get to know one another. The MPs had got so angry about stopping us, taking us in and having us sprung. It was thought advisable to bring us together.

David Smiley lived in the Phoenicia Hotel for a while, then in married quarters at Slima. His batman was a chap from the Horse Guards called Ron Little, who later became a policeman.

The Albanians did their own maintenance and cooking. Stover cooked for the British. We had a very efficient clerk, Corporal Topliss, he was from Nottingham way, a regular soldier. And when regulars saw what was going on, they weren't very happy. George Odey was in charge of the armory. Then there was another clerk, Pat Woods from Sale, Manchester.

I shepherded the Albanians about, took them swimming. I would drive the truck and somebody else would be there to make sure they didn't stray away. Then I would go into town to collect the mail from the Auberge de Castille, which was HQ Valetta. We also collected ice for the married quarters from the RAC stores. There were no fridges, only insulated iceboxes. The married quarters were in M'tarfa, where there was a military hospital.

There were around about 20 British in the camp. There was Colonel Smiley, Major Howard, Alastair Grant, Captain Zaehner, who left before I did—a super guy but very, very strange, freakish really, drank too much. He was much older than we were, a larger-than-life character with huge pebble-rim glasses and a squeaky voice. He spoke very quickly, like a mad professor.

They had a firing range in the moat and we were down there one day with some small arms, playing around, aiming at these targets that dropped down from the moat's sides. We really should have been supervised. We also dropped a couple of grenades down into the moat just to hear them go off—not the sort of thing that happens in a well-run camp. The moat was 15 or 20 feet deep and about as wide. They had brick walls or buttresses with targets that dropped out from behind them. There was a steel ladder screwed to the wall just by the drawbridge for us to get into it. But I was a driver and should not really have had anything to do with guns.

Albanian fighters in Malta around 1949.

We were a family in a way, but I don't know if we were happy. We were most reluctant soldiers. We couldn't see any end result of what was happening. It didn't seem for the greater glory of Europe or man or anything. It was a bit unreal. We couldn't really believe that these chaps were going to be dropped. If it had been run on more disciplined lines, it might have got home to us more, but I was only 18 and it seemed like a holiday atmosphere almost. Perhaps the older people realized the seriousness of it, but we didn't.

I remember an enormously fat American. Another officer, Captain Rollo Young, came over but didn't stay very long. He was an Englishman but somehow tied up with this American. I think he stayed at the Xara Palace Hotel. The Albanians were a very cheerful, affable bunch of blokes. There wasn't one of them you could say was unpleasant. They were happy, smiling types, small, sturdy, wiry.

The English soldiers from Maresfield were myself, Pat Woods, a chap called Denham from Newcastle, Robson, Odey. A year later we were demobbed at intervals of a fortnight or a month.

It wasn't very arduous. There was a lot of swimming. It was boring. I suppose that was the main complaint. We'd finish about four or five and there was really little else to do then. Swimming was quite a way away, an afternoon occupation. We could commandeer a truck and get into town for the evening. I got very friendly with Major Howard and we used to play Mah Jong three or four times a week at his house, with his wife. There wasn't a gap between the officers and the men and in that respect it was a good atmosphere. I got to know Zaehner and Grant quite well. It was almost as if we were a family and the babies were the Albanians. We had to look after them. I suppose they must have picked up a bit of English, but they were never any trouble at all. They kept themselves to themselves. They might wander into our barrack room and have a cigarette, but the language problem meant that we couldn't make friends easily. There was no NAAFI or canteen.

We went to Athens once to collect some Albanians, about January 1950. We flew to Athens in a Dakota and didn't leave the airport, just picked them up and brought them back. We were told not to greet them, because we weren't supposed to know them. I said hallo to one of the Albanians I knew and was immediately stopped short. It seems strange that I was picked for such a job, but then, I suppose it would not have been easy to find any Albanian-speaking British soldiers.

We had to have civilian cars, since it was a secret operation, a Humber shooting brake, like something out of a gangster film, and an old Ford V8 that we thought was marvelous.

We approached the whole thing rather lightheartedly, I am afraid, but then we were only 18 and we didn't know anything. In the first place, they needn't have had married officers. Or the officers' wives needn't have been in Malta, with them. It would have been far better if the officers had stayed in the fort with everyone else. It would have tightened things up considerably. As it was, the officers left in the early afternoon and I can't honestly remember who was in charge of the shop. Smiley, Howard, Grant and Zaehner all knocked off at five o'clock and went home.

Major Alf Howard was the one we called "Q." Apart from Colonel Smiley, he was the only professional soldier among us. He was ex–Scots Guards, commissioned through the ranks to the Pioneer Corps. He used to wring his hands when he saw some of the things that went on. He realized that it could never be a thoroughly correct military establishment, but it could have been a lot better than it was. It was obvious that some of the things he saw went against years and years of military training.

Interview conducted February 19, 1983

Julian Amery

Harold Julian Amery (1919–1996) was British military officer and writer. He was educated at Eton and Balliol College, Oxford. He was a war correspondent in the Spanish civil war and worked as press attaché at the British Embassy in Belgrade in 1939. He was asked, in late April 1940 during World War II, to help in preliminary work to organize an Albanian resistance movement and was then recruited directly by the Special Operations Executive (SOE) to foment anti–Italian resistance in Albania. Amery was dropped onto the Biza plateau in central Albania on 20 April 1944 with Billy McLean and David Smiley, and spent seven months in the mountains, where he maintained close contacts with Abas Kupi and the royalist Legality movement.

He was evacuated in late October 1944 with Billy McLean, but without Abas Kupi, who was denied passage by the SOE. After the war, Amery was closely involved in the Albanian operation, in particular through the training of the Albanian fighters in Malta in 1949–1953, and then embarked on a political career. He was Conservative member of parliament for Preston North in 1950, minister of aviation in 1962–1964, minister of state for public buildings and works in 1970 and for housing in 1970–1972. Amery was particularly influential during the administration of Sir Harold Macmillan, who was his father-in-law. In 1992, he was made a life peer as Lord Amery of Lustleigh. Julian Amery's memoirs of the period appeared in Sons of the Eagle: A Study in Guerrilla War, *London 1948; and* Approach March: A Venture in Autobiography, *London 1973.*

[NB]: You were outraged by the treatment of the non-communist Albanian guerrillas?

[JA]: It was partly a sense of outrage, partly a sense of tragedy that the decision was taken to let the communists win in Albania. It meant inevitably that the anti-communist resistance leaders would be ditched. I thought we could have handled the thing more honorably by arranging for their evacuation, good people fighting alongside of us with our encouragement. I thought just to abandon them was completely wrong. In point of fact when they escaped, they arranged their own escape, were not abandoned and were looked after to a greater or lesser extent. The majority of them managed to emigrate to Europe or America in due course.

We arranged for debts to be paid, travel papers secured and for some of the younger ones to emigrate to Australia. As they were great personal friends we saw a good deal of them in France, Italy or Greece. Many of them were in refugee camps for two or three years. Some were very difficult to resettle. Luckily some had good friends who looked after them. Abas Kupi had friends in Italy, a rich merchant of Albanian extraction who looked after him so he didn't have to stay in a refugee camp. But Muharrem Bajraktari and Said Kryeziu and others

Julian Amery (1919–1996) and Ihsan Toptani (1908–2001) in Albania during the Second World War.

were a year or two in camps. Said got out quite early and then he got a job in Rome as well as a small pension from us and later he emigrated to America.

But we kept in touch with them and were pretty convinced that the situation wouldn't stabilize in Albania and these people would still be needed as friends of our country and would serve us abroad.

[NB]: You wrote that in your view the communists were using crude destabilizing methods in various countries, like Greece, and that you felt justified in doing the same.

[JA]: Yes, I think any student of guerrilla war will know that a guerrilla is practically invincible if he has a safe harbor to which to retreat. The left-wing guerrillas in Greece survived as long as they did because when hard pressed they nipped back across the border to Albania, or Yugoslavia or Bulgaria where they rested and were supplied with weapons. And it was very much the same with Vietnam; as long as the Chinese border was open, there was no possibility of the French, and later of the Americans, really suppressing the Vietcong. So it was a natural military deduction, that the only way to counter what the Soviets were engineering in Greece was to do it back to them. And there was a further objective in my mind. The Straits of Taranto were a very important geographical checkpoint and if one could successfully take Albania out of the Soviet bloc, which it was then firmly in, this would be an important step forward for the West in the Cold War which was then approaching its height.

[NB]: And you presumably felt that the Albanians had the right to elect their own government.

[JA]: Oh, certainly. And also a central obligation to one's old friends and allies, who had been, I won't say betrayed, but let down by the British policy of letting the communists win. So there were two Albanian objectives, first of all the right of the Albanians to self-determination and also a certain central obligation to old friends and comrades in arms.

[NB]: Who thought up this idea?

[JA]: I never came across anyone who was thinking about it independently until we floated it. What one met everywhere—you went to the military missions in Greece, and British military missions on the border—was we can't win this war so long as they find a safe harbor on the other side of the border and get themselves supplied. I went to northern Greece on more than one occasion up to Janina, which is very close to the border place in the Grammos mountains, which was a stronghold of the ELAS communist guerrillas.

I think I wrote some letters on it to some political leaders in our own party and of course I had friends in the intelligence service and discussed it with them at great length. I don't remember a written document, but there may have been one. But certainly I had several talks with friends in the intelligence service about the desirability of doing this and I think certainly one meeting in the Foreign Office.

In 1949 we went to Alexandria to see the king and then to Athens and Rome. I have a feeling that I was in Greece in 1948, paid my first visit to the north in 1948. In 1949 there was an actual operation designed to convince the Greeks of the need to help Albanian guerrillas if they were to escape into Greece. That was when I communicated with Papagos who was commander-in-chief of the army, a virtual dictator. They had a martial law system and the commander-in-chief ran the entire country. I didn't see him on that occasion, though I did subsequently. I was in touch with him through Bodsaki, the great arms king in Greece in those days.

[NB]: As a result of this, you got the impression that Papagos approved the idea?

[JA]: Yes. I think the Papagos connection and contact was after the committee had been formed. After it had been decided to form it, to the best of my recollection. We went first to Alexandria to try and get the king's blessing. We may have gone on to Cairo on our own but the king was living in Alexandria. Then we had meetings with different groups of Albanian refugees in Rome and in Athens. Then one of the things we were asked to try and do was to see if we could get the cooperation of the Greek government.

The Greeks at that period were still very much in favor of annexing northern Epirus. And it was more than any political leader's life was worth to take on any commitment and go back on that ambition. That was why there was no direct approach to Papagos. We talked to Bodsaki at great length explaining that without abandoning their commitment to northern Epirus, which was still the heart of Greek politics in those days, it would still be in their interest to encourage counter-operations in Albania, because it could only help to relieve the pressure on them. Billy McLean was at that meeting. This was communicated to Papagos. And if the answer was "yes," we'd get twelve bottles of brandy, if the answer was "no," we'd get one. Rather picturesque. And we got the twelve, not very good brandy either. So no details, just a straight "yes."

The most important thing was that guerrillas who were dropped into Albania and failed to find a footing could get through to Greece and were looked after at the Greek end; otherwise they might easily have been shot down.

[NB]: Your task was entirely political?

[JA]: Yes, I had no connection with the military side of it. That was Smiley and Hare, who were on the strength of MI6 at the time. We were picked out as old friends of the Albanian leaders to form a committee which was to be the umbrella. You couldn't expect the Albanians to go and risk their lives or find any support unless they went in the name of some organization. And as the judgment was that neither the king nor the Balli Kombëtar could by themselves provide the necessary umbrella, the committee had to form such an umbrella out of the royalists, Balli Kombëtar and well known independents. We managed to put them together, but they weren't very keen at first.

[NB]: I don't suppose the king was very keen on a committee where he was not head?

[JA]: No, he took a view: "I won't oppose you and I won't denounce you and I'll let Abas Kupi join." In his view it was a mistake. The argument was over legitimacy. He had been the last legitimate ruler of Albania and therefore we ought to go back to that, although he was quite prepared to undertake to submit his own future to a referendum. It never came to a disagreement because the committee, after all, was a committee not a government and there was no reason for the king to abandon the throne. The committee was no substitute for him. He could still say: "I'm icing and have got nothing against the committee." It wasn't a provisional government.

The king acquiesced unenthusiastically but he was very friendly. We had long discussions every couple of days. I think he probably was the most impressive man I ever met, with an absolutely unerring ability to sum up into a single sentence a crucial point. He was the son of a highland chief. Then the chief rebelled against the sultan of Turkey and the sultan took the boy hostage for the father's good behavior after the plot had been exposed, and he was made a page at the imperial court. He stayed there until he was 16, 17 or 18. He must have been a pretty precocious boy and he got to know all the young Turks very early in life. He got a sophisticated understanding of Balkan politics. Then the Balkan War came and the Turks sent him back to raise his tribe. He was made a colonel in the Ottoman army at a young age. Then Albania was declared independent.

Then World War I came along and the Austrians invaded Albania in the course of their fight against the Serbs and made him a colonel in the Austrian army with his army working alongside the Austrians. But he was a hotheaded chap in those days and some Austrian officer shot a couple of Albanians on what he thought to be preposterous grounds and he said, "I'm not having any of this rot," and he took three Austrian officers and had them shot himself. The Austrians didn't know what to do about this, so they made him an ADC to Franz Joseph in Vienna, where he saw again all the intrigues of the Hapsburg court at first hand. Then after the war, the collapse of Austria, he came back to Albania and embarked on his political career.

Zog didn't speak English. He spoke good German and a French of his own. The first time I met him I attempted to speak to him in German, but my German is not all that good. We talked for about an hour, then I came across some phrase I couldn't express so I tried it in French in the hope that he would follow and he did, so after that we more often spoke in French. But I saw a lot of him again in later years; he helped to organize the Egyptian group that might have taken over if Nasser had left Cairo in 1956.

In my talks with Zog, part of the time Billy and I were alone, part of the time with Bob Low and George Young, if I remember right. Either George Young or a fellow called Perkins, who played some part in this. Typically, the Americans on the whole inclined to the Balli Kombëtar. Partly because it was Republican and partly because the Albanians in the United States were more that way inclined. We were rather more inclined to Abas Kupi and the royalists.

I don't think there was any chance of getting the Balli Kombëtar, or indeed the Kryezius, to work under the king. Zog's sister had married Kryeziu's brother, and then Zog had murdered him. So there was a blood feud there. And the Balli Kombëtar were staunchly Republican and anti-king.

We came back from this tour, and I think we had these intelligence people from MI6 with us all the time. They approached us to form the committee so they were in on that. We also had the Foreign Office's blessing. My memory is that Dick Brooman-White is the man who first approached me about it, then George Young and Alan Hare.

The most effective Balli person was Abas Ermenji. He was the one who mattered. I remember a very jolly scene. The committee was formed in London and I had them all down to lunch at a house in the country. After lunch we went for a walk in the garden and Abas Kupi saw a snake and with great peasant skill he managed to pick it up and chased Midhat Frashëri around the garden. Frashëri wasn't at all sure Abas Kupi wouldn't let it strike. I can't remember offhand who was at the lunch, but certainly Abas Kupi and Said Kryeziu and Ermenji and Frashëri and Ali Klissura. He was sort of co-president with Frashëri.

In January 1950, I got married and won the election for Preston, so I was then in the House of Commons. It was fairly soon indicated to me that it wasn't at all suitable for a serving MP, particularly one belonging to the opposition, to be actively engaged in these matters. Subsequently, I did intelligence jobs as a Member of Parliament. But it can be used politically against the party concerned or against the government. I think the left-wing Labour people would have been horrified if they'd found out the truth. George Young communicated with me. Naturally, we were interested in what was going on and asked questions and had lunch with our friends from MI6 and said, "What's happening, do give us a call."

[NB]: You have no doubt that the main objective was achieved of preventing the people in the north from helping the Greeks, Albanians and Yugoslavs?

Midhat Frashëri (1880–1949), head of the Balli Kombëtar movement (1942) and later of the National Committee for a Free Albania (1949), speaking here to the BBC in London.

[JA]: Yes, it made an important contribution to easing the pressure on the Greeks. Even more critical, I think, was that it influenced Tito who had already broken with Moscow, but whose attitude was still pretty uncertain. He hadn't moved as far away from the Russians as he later did. Tito must have said, "Look here, we've got to watch out, we can see what the West are up to in Albania and they might pull it off, so we'd better lay off the Greeks." And I deduce that he was the first of the three countries to desist. He stopped Yugoslav help to Marcos. He closed the pipe lines and supply lines, I think as a result of what we did. Once Yugoslavia was not prepared to cooperate, a logistic problem arose of how to help the Greek communists through Albania. At the Bulgarian border there wasn't a great deal to be done. Then there was an isolated Albania, cut off by Yugoslavia from the main Soviet bloc, taking responsibility for the guerrilla war in Greece with the western powers aiming at destabilizing Albania.

I had hopes that Tito might be helpful, because the classical way of taking power in Albania was Zog's way, which was to raise forces in Kosovo and then go into the country from the north with the assistance of the Yugoslavs. I did it myself on a much smaller scale in 1940. I got the Yugoslav authorities to turn a blind eye and we infiltrated arms, while Yugoslavia was still neutral—arms, propaganda and agents.

Interview conducted February 2, 1982

* * *

[JA]: The intelligence people cut us off in early 1950, after I was elected to the House of Commons. I never had any contact with ministers. My information, I think, was fed into the FO through Orme Sargent and perhaps Harold Caccia. They consulted me and then asked me to go on this grand tour.

My contact with Bodosis Athenisiades, known as Bodasaki, was with a Turk called Lutfi Tozan, a private arms dealer who had been with SOE during the war. Bodasaki was a very big arms dealer in those days, before Onassis and Niarchos had got going some of the richest men in Greece.

I also had talks with Greek politicians, indicating to them that instead of making territorial demands on northern Epirus, they ought to be stirring up trouble for the Albanian government, which was providing bases for Greek communist rebels. All their talk about northern Epirus was counter-productive, I told them. The two main ones I saw were Sophoulis and Gonotas, the leaders of the Venizelos party, known as the "venereal diseases." Sophoulis must have been about 90. I also met Papagos's political adviser, a Greek boy from Manchester whose name began with "M." The object of these meetings was to persuade the Greeks to drop the idea of northern Epirus and take up retaliation instead.

As for the clandestine side, I only mentioned that to Bodasaki. Billy McLean and I had lunch with him at a taverna outside Athens and we put it to him, adding that it was essential to have Papagos's agreement. Bodasaki promised to ask Papagos and to indicate his reply by a delivery of brandy to my hotel room. Twelve bottles would mean yes, one bottle no.

Zog was by far the cleverest Albanian in exile. He was probably the cleverest man I ever met. But neither the Ballists nor the Kryeziu people would have him.

I had all the committee members to lunch at my aunt's house in Kent. It belonged to old Lord Harding, the Viceroy. Her name was Sadie Rodney. It was the lunch where they chased each other round the garden with a snake. Peter Kemp had big problems getting them through customs because they all had guns on them. Abas Kupi had two, even at the lunch table. Albanians usually carry guns, because life in that country tends to be nasty, brutish and short. The address was Oakfield, Penshurst, Kent.

Many of our meetings on Albania were in this house. I had a flat on the top floor and my father lived in the rest of this house.

Interview conducted December 7, 1983

* * *

[JA]: Let's look at the problem from the top end of the scale and from the bottom end of the scale. The bottom end of the scale was to make so much trouble in Albania that it would stop the Albanians nourishing the Greek communist revolt. At the middle end of the scale was the concept that the Albanians, who had been my friends, with whom I had worked, ought not to be left under the Soviet heel. At the top end of the scale was a feeling that the settlement reached at the end of the war was wrong from the point of view of the interests of Europe and of the West. And it would be a healthy thing if we could roll back Soviet imperialism which, if you remember in 1948 and 1949 was only beginning to dig itself in. The suicide of Mazaryk was only in 1948 and Tito had already shaken it off. It was not like it is today, the wretched empire of the Soviets, it was much more fluid. Where better to start than a country which looked onto the sea and whose population, I was convinced from living with them for the best part of a year, would not be in the least likely to accept Soviet domination.

Some of my friends in the war had moved into the intelligence branch of the government and, of course, I was familiar with leaders of the Conservative opposition, who of course also had their contact with the Labour government. Even the wartime coalition, after all, embraced Labour and Conservatives so they all knew each other quite well. And so by feeding my views in at the higher level of the Conservative party and at a lower level to colleagues of mine who were then working for the secret service, it wasn't too difficult to get these ideas across. An article or two and a letter or two to the newspapers gradually helped to spread the idea. It became very clear to everyone concerned that the only way to stop this war in Greece was to hit back.

I was approached one day by friends of mine in the secret services who asked me to help them to set up the necessary organization to start a counterrevolution in Albania. I was glad to do so and spent the best part of a year helping them to do it. These were friends whom I knew in the secret services in those days who had always kept in touch with me about Albania and other countries which I was supposed to know about. I suppose I was what you call an "informal consultant." I was not a professional. I didn't belong to any of these services. I knew something about the affairs of the country they were concerned with, so from time to time they came to me for advice. Anyway, they were friends and we saw each other.

The first thing they asked me was, "How do we start getting a guerrilla movement going against the communist regime in Albania?" And here there were two problems, the greater problem and the lesser problem. The greater problem was that the Greeks, who were the victims of the civil war, had a claim on southern Albania which they wanted to annex. Clearly, you couldn't expect an Albanian patriot to embark on a rising against their home government if the result was going to be that Albania, which was already small enough, was going to lose a quarter or a fifth of its territory. So there was a political problem to get the Greeks to cry off their annexation policy. As they were in mortal danger themselves, this didn't seem to be impossible.

The other problem was to get the broadest possible support for a guerrilla movement in the shape of a committee that would represent the different trends in Albania. In our country we have enough political parties, but in Albania they have even more. And there were independent tribal leaders in the north, there were royalists in the center and there were republicans in the south, none of whom got on particularly well together. So what I recommended was that we should try to create a representative committee. These were the two jobs to be done, one to form the committee and this depended on the Greeks agreeing to hold back on their claims.

We went on a journey, Americans and British, Hare, McLean and myself and my friend Bob Low from the United States and Colonel Perkins from the United Kingdom. We may have stopped in Rome to discuss some of these things, but our main journey was to Alexandria to try and enlist the backing of King Zog, realizing that the republicans in Albania would be unlikely to accept his official leadership and that the Americans weren't very keen on kings.

I had known Zog for some time in the war when he was a refugee in England. I suppose he was the cleverest man I ever met. If he had lived in the old Ottoman Empire, he would have been certainly Grand Vizier, probably Sultan. He was of the type of Muhammed Ali the Great who conquered Egypt and made himself king of it, he was that kind of man. Soon after he made himself king, because he was a tribal leader who put the crown on his own head, he went on a state visit to Vienna. They took him to the opera for a gala performance. As he walked up the steps, one of his enemies shot at him. In such circumstances some kings lie down, some walk on as though nothing had happened. Zog did neither. He took the gun out of his shoulder holster and shot the man. You deserve to be king if you're capable of doing things like that.

The talk was at his house in Alexandria. He was obviously not pleased that we didn't want him to be the official leader. Equally, he saw the point of doing what we wanted. He made it very much a condition that the Greeks should not press their claim and he was prepared on that basis to give us his blessing. It was a longish talk, about two days.

If Zog had not given his blessing, I think Abas Kupi, the royalist leader, would not have cooperated. I thought he was essential to any combination because in the resistance to the Germans, his contribution had been the most powerful in terms of numbers and of influence in the center of Albania. His was a name to conjure with. He had been really the only Albanian who had successfully resisted the Italian invasion in 1939.

It was important to get the structure of the committee right. We had to appeal to the Albanian people and you don't ask people to rise up in a movement either for money or for glory, important as these are. You have to have a flag which you wave, you have to have a cause. You have to have a cause people can trust. We reckoned in the north there was great confidence in the Kryeziu family, in the center in Abas Kupi and in the south in the old Balli Kombëtar republican party. So the essence of the deal was to try and bring these three together. And we felt that then people in Albania would have some confidence that they would be fighting for people they could trust. They wouldn't be foreign agents.

It didn't take very long to form the committee compared to other talks I had. My talks with Archbishop Makarios lasted five months, my talks with the Sultan of Oman to get the treaty with Oman lasted six weeks. I think we pulled this off within ten days or so, which by Oriental or Balkan standards is pretty quick work.

What does typically Balkan mean? Well, Metternich said, "East of the Lindenstrasse the Orient begins." Certainly there is a point in Europe when you move out of the Western Catholic and Protestant world and into the oriental Byzantine, Orthodox and Islamic world. There is a change. There is a change in the bargaining techniques and negotiations, the customs, the politeness and the cruelty. This is the surface of it, once you know about these things, it's not so difficult to cope with it. All negotiation really is similar, but the manners are different.

Albania was cruel in the sense that it was a country that had never been administered effectively, even under King Zog, certainly not under the Turks, let alone the Italians or Germans. If you have no administration, if you have no prisons—prisons are, I suppose, the most fundamental institutions of civilization—the only way you can punish an offender is by killing him. So any event, great or small, has to be met with death, because what is at stake is not the degree of the crime but the prestige of the victim. So that if somebody offends you and there's no prison, no law, the only way you can punish him is by killing him. Otherwise, what else can you do? Steal some of his sheep in return? Sometimes you get a council of elders to settle for a sum of money, but in that kind of situation death is the only penalty that can be exacted. So the old law of vendetta and blood feud was normal. They weren't cruel in themselves, not sadistic at all. But it was the only way they knew of exacting retribution for a crime.

I had nothing to do with the operations themselves. I was elected to Parliament in February 1950. I thought Ernest Bevin had shown a lot of guts in allowing two Conservative candidates to get on the plan, but once I was elected obviously it would have been embarrassing to have a Member of Parliament who was in on a subversive operation which many in the Labour Party, had they known about it, would have disapproved of. So from that moment on, I lost contact with the operational side. All I did was to help create the committee, help bring them to England where they met a number of people and then they went on to the United States.

The important thing was to convince the Greeks that they had more to gain in helping the Albanian resistance than in pressing their own claim to northern Epirus, since they were in mortal danger. I managed to persuade Field Marshal Papagos that this was the case and therefore he ought to give support to the committee when it was formed. Also, if people who were subsequently introduced into Albania came out to Greece, they had to be properly looked after. And the Greeks had to stop talking about their claim to northern Epirus, until we saw what had happened. This was the only way we could really see of defeating the communist civil war in Greece.

The problem was how to convince Field Marshal Papagos. I had met him, he was a fine and imposing man, some said the natural son of King Constantine. He was extremely busy running a war and running a government. I wasn't sure of the best way to tackle him. Clearly, it wasn't going to be possible to have direct conversation with secretaries and others present. I was told by a Turkish friend of mine that the man who had the most influence with him was an arms dealer called Mr. Bodosaki. I arranged through my Turkish friend for a meeting with Mr. Bodosaki at a taverna by the sea some 20 miles outside of Athens where there was no possibility of a witness. Over two or three hours I explained to Bodosaki what was in our minds and convinced him. He said he would go to the Field Marshal at once and talk to him about it. He said, "I wonder how I'm going to let you know." He asked when I was leaving and I said, "If not tomorrow, then the day after." And he said, 'That's time enough, if it's no, I'll leave one bottle of brandy in your room at the hotel. If it's yes, I'll leave six." I found six.

The Soviet government through the instrumentality of the Albanian and Bulgarian governments, and at an earlier stage the Yugoslav government, were trying to bring down the government of Greece, by backing a communist guerrilla movement which had as its declared aim to overthrow the government in Athens. So there was in effect an East-West conflict going on in Greece. You can't apply the Queensberry rules to one side and not the other. So if they were trying to subvert and overthrow the pro–Western government in Athens, I think we had every right and every justification to try and overthrow the pro–Soviet governments in Tirana or indeed in Sofia if we so wanted to. We tried to do it in Albania and I'm sorry we didn't succeed. If Kim Philby hadn't betrayed the secrets of the operation, maybe we would have not only relieved the pressure on Greece, but even overthrown the government in Albania. Now let it always be remembered, we did relieve the pressure on Greece. As a result of this operation in Albania, the civil war in Greece was called off. The communist forces were withdrawn and have never come back again, except those who have been allowed back as civilians under amnesty. We failed to overthrow the government in Albania and I shall always regret that. But if we did fail, it was mainly because of Kim Philby's betrayal of our plans. The will power went out of London and Washington to roll back the communist tide. I wish it could have been otherwise.

[NB]: If it had succeeded in Albania, could you have tried it elsewhere?

[JA]: Who knows? Who can tell how far these tides will run? A lot depends nowadays on how you see the international conflict. Some people choose to think that the different crises we face are the result of local difficulties. Of course there's no crisis without a local difficulty. Personally, ever since 1943 I've been inclined to see them primarily as a conflict between the two great centers of power—the East and the West. And that every local conflict, however serious its local roots, has to be looked at in that light. Albania was an opportunity for rolling back the tide of Soviet imperialism.

In fact, with Tito's break in Yugoslavia and the Albanian communists' breach with Moscow and Mao Tse Tung's too, the tide has to some extent been rolled back, but not, alas, to the greater happiness of the Albanian people, because the regime there remains an implacable, totalitarian one, but at least the Russians are no longer quite so strong in the Balkans as they threatened to be in 1948.

I got very fond of the Albanians. They are a people of honor rather than honesty. It was embarrassing in Rome because we wanted to keep our talks secret and everyone thought Low was Clark Gable. I suppose it did provide a cover. At the end of the day, they wanted to know how many guns we were going to give them and how much gold. In Alexandria we sat on chests and I remember wondering if they contained the gold from the Bank of Albania. Perhaps we should have roped Zog in a bit more, but some of the republicans didn't like him.

The Albanians had guts and it was a remarkable thing that a Labour foreign secretary, Ernest Bevin, had the guts to give the go-ahead. I'm glad we did it. We took the heat off the Greeks and, if we hadn't been betrayed by Kim Philby, we might have saved the Albanians. General van Fleet confirmed to Robert Low that it had taken the heat off.

Peter Kemp went into German-occupied territory disguised as a woman, but he forgot to take his boots off. It wouldn't have looked so strange today, but it did then.

In every country occupied by the Germans and the Japanese, there was resistance against the occupying forces and there were two wings to the resistance. One was broadly communist and the other traditionalist, pro–Western, generally wishing to restore the status quo: De Gaulle and the communists in France, Tito and Mihailovic in Yugoslavia, Mao Tse Tung and Chiang Kai-shek in China. There was exactly the same thing in Albania.

There was a problem. Which side should we back? I think it is arguable that the communist partisans were the better fighters, for the main reason that they were not defending a vested interest and were quite happy to see enemy reprisals against farms or homes, because they were by definition representing the dispossessed. The nationalist, pro–Western groups tended to represent what had been the vested interests before the Germans came and overran them. Now, which side should we back? While we were losing the war, my own strong recommendation was to support the communists. But after El Alamein and Stalingrad—that is, by the spring of 1943—it seemed pretty clear that we had won the war and what was going to matter was who took power in the occupied countries after the Germans and Japanese withdrew.

This produced a different question in our minds. Wouldn't we rather see the pro–Western elements in power? This certainly was my view where Albania was concerned. I was in Albania at the critical moment when the Germans withdrew. With a very small British and American intervention, we could have saved Albania for the West. In fact we didn't, we pushed it into the communist hands. In Greece we did the opposite, we actually stamped down on the communist resistance movement to bring up General Zervas and the traditionalist movement. There is the equation.

After the Teheran conference in the autumn of 1943, Churchill was on his way home. At a dinner in Cairo, given at Chester Beatty's old house under the pyramids out at Mina, he said, "Oliver Cromwell was a very great man, but he made a great mistake. Obsessed with the power of Spain, he failed to observe the rise of France. Will they say this of me?" What he meant of course was that in fighting the Germans, determined to crush Hitler, he might be letting in the Soviets.

At about the same time I went to a dinner party at the embassy in Cairo to celebrate his birthday. Most of the company were the grandees, commanders-in-chief, ministers of state and so on. But he also invited young resistance chaps like Fitzroy MacLean, George Jellicoe, Monty Woodhouse and myself. Afterwards he took us aside and said, "What do you think about the future of the resistance movement? Who should we be backing?" Then, rather typically, before waiting for our replies, he told us what he thought. And he said he was thinking of backing Tito in Yugoslavia and the king in Greece. Then he asked questions. When he came to me, I said, "Well, there might be some difficulty here, because there is a common border between Greece and Yugoslavia and a mixed population, the Macedonian population. Is it going to be all right, backing the communists on one side and the king on the other?" He said, "You may think it inconsistent of me to back a king in one country and a communist in another, but I still have some influence here and that is my policy." So I was put in my place. I thought about this. I made enquiries and my conclusion was that after the Teheran conference, he knew that British forces were not going to be allowed to invade the Balkans from Italy. The Russians would invade the Balkans. He knew that he couldn't save Yugoslavia, Tito was bound to win, but he might still be able to save Greece. Now, such is the way with great men in politics that Albania was completely overlooked. There is no document that provides any view of what the great powers thought the future of Albania should be. There was no commitment either by the Soviet Union or by the West. Albania was "fair game."

In the years after the war I turned it over in my mind. The first thing I did was to write a book about Albania, about my experiences there, and the verdict of the book was that we could have saved it very easily for the West, instead of letting it go into Soviet hands. (Later as it turned out, they were able to escape from Moscow.) I concluded that it was an evil regime and that we had thrown away a good opportunity of controlling one of the important gateways of the world. Three ways lead to the Middle East; you can go down the Danube valley and through the Bosphorus, you can go through the Adriatic and the Straits of Otranto, you can go down the Mediterranean. The Straits of Otranto are between Italy and Albania, and Albania commands them. So it seemed to me from the geopolitical point of view tragic, firstly, that we did not have Albania in the West, secondly, that the Albanian people, who had fought very gallantly on our side, were being denied a free future.

In 1948 I stopped in Greece on the way back from a holiday in Turkey. I stayed with the ambassador, Sir Reginald Hoare, and saw a number of Greek politicians. I was only there three or four days, but what made an impression on me was the extent of the communist civil war in the north of Greece. I hadn't appreciated it reading newspapers in England, I hadn't realized how near the communists were to bringing down the Greek regime. Then I made some study of guerrilla war, because I'd been involved in it from 1939 to 1945, and it became quite clear to me that the only way to defeat guerrilla movements was to strike at the safe harbors that they often have on the other side of frontiers. Take any example you like. If the guerrillas have a safe harbor to which they can retreat, you'll never beat them. And Albania was the main safe harbor from which the Greek communists operated.

The only strategy is to strike at the safe harbor, either by hot pursuit, which is more normal, or by stirring up a guerrilla movement against the government which provides the safe harbor. This is what I proposed when I came back from that particular visit to Greece. And I wrote an article or two and a letter or two to the papers, lobbied friends in the Foreign Office and the political world. And the argument began to take effect.

Interview conducted December 20, 1983

Vasil Andoni

Vasil Andoni (1901–1994) was Albanian political figure of the World War II period. He was one of the founders and leading figures of the Balli Kombëtar resistance movement. He was born in Elbasan and seems to have studied at Robert College in Constantinople. On his return to Elbasan, he taught at the teacher training college (Shkolla Normale). In 1939 he was teaching at a secondary school in Tirana and in the early 1940s he also taught secondary school in Prishtina. Andoni was closely associated with Midhat bey Frashëri and collaborated with him in 1942 in the founding of Balli Kombëtar, being elected as its general secretary. During the civil war in 1943–1944, he took to the mountains of central and northern Albania with Frashëri, although, soft spoken and pensive by nature, he was never himself a fighter. Andoni, who had opposed the German occupation, fled from Shkodra to Brindisi in southern Italy on a little fishing boat with the other Balli leaders in mid–October 1944 during the communist takeover and, from his little apartment on the outskirts of Rome, he later promoted and collaborated in anticommunist publications such as Albanie libre *and* Flamuri. *He maintained close ties with Mid'hat bey Frashëri and was with him when the latter died in New York in 1949. Andoni served as a leading figure of Balli Kombëtar in exile in the United States right until his death in July 1994. He never returned to Albania.*

The British and Americans contacted our people, Midhat Frashëri and Abas Ermenji, at a time when we had heard that the Yugoslavs and the Greeks were discussing a possible partition of Albania. They told us that they were against this and so we thought that such a committee would be of great use to Albania, to counter this threat. And they also assured us that the committee would receive political and material help for Albania's liberation, to set up a democratic government. These were the two points that convinced us to negotiate with the British and American "sponsors," as they were called.

Balli Kombëtar was represented by Midhat Frashëri and Zef Pali. The Monarchists were represented by Abas Kupi and Nuçi Kota. I think that there were McLean and Amery for the British and Robert Low for the Americans. He was called "Low" but he was very tall.

The main problem in the talks was that the Monarchists wanted the committee to be under King Zog. He would be the king and the committee would be a link between him and the allies. Our position was that the committee must be independent and that the type of government must be decided after Albania's liberation.

In the end this was accepted, although we heard that the king was reluctant to accept it, that he was persuaded by Abas Kupi and by the allies.

We agreed that the expenses of the committee, as well as of its secret military side, would be paid by the sponsors. But Midhat Frashëri insisted that this payment was to be a loan and that it would be repaid to the British and Americans after liberation. So accounts were kept so that exact repayment could be made in the future. Frashëri did not like the idea of being paid outright by foreigners.

There was a consultative committee consisting of 12 members, three each from Balli Kombëtar and the Monarchists and the rest from the other groups. I was one of the Balli Kombëtar members. The military junta consisted of Abas Ermenji, Abas Kupi, Said Kryeziu and Muharrem Bajraktari.

We recruited men for training in Malta from refugee camps in Italy and Greece and they went into Albania two or three times a year over a period of three years, until the summer of 1952. About one-third were killed or captured. The names of the Greek camps were Lavrion and Hadji Kyriakon.

There was a lot of friction with our sponsors. They wanted us to sign orders for men to go on missions into Albania with blank spaces so that they could fill in the names. We refused. We could not give our sponsors a "blank check" to send men into Albania in our name. We felt that we knew more about Albania than the sponsors did and that they might, by mistake, fill in names of Turks or communists or anyone. They kept saying to us, "Don't you trust us?" and we kept replying, "Don't you trust us?"

Company 4000 was formed in June 1950 with 250 men, 100 each from Balli Kombëtar and the Monarchists, 50 from the independents, followers of Said Kryeziu and Muharrem Bajraktari. Our men received some military training, which was necessary because most of them were straight from the mountains and had no military knowledge, and they were used to guard American ammunition dumps.

After a year or so, the frictions became worse. The sponsors thought of our committee as their employees, instead of as an independent body. We felt this was wrong, because we knew more about Albania than they did and we were the guardians of Albania's interest. For instance, they wanted to amalgamate three of our publications—one published by the committee, one by Balli Kombëtar and one by the Monarchists. We wanted to keep them separate.

I spent most of my time interpreting between the executive committee members and John Lee and John Lyall. Michael Burke did a lot to ease the tension in the early months, but after his departure, things got worse. The break came in 1952 and after that no more Balli Kombëtar went into Albania.

The Monarchists carried on sending men in and Hasan Dosti worked with them, but not Balli Kombëtar.

Then our sponsors, especially the Americans, wanted to enlarge the committee so that the majority would be against Balli Kombëtar. And they brought in people who had collaborated with the Italians or even the Germans, members of the Independent National Bloc.

They gave us to understand that they were the paymasters and that from now on we were to work under their orders. We told them that we were not clerks and that we would prefer to fight on our own, without American money. So we broke away, except that Hasan Dosti, who was our leader at the time, agreed to stay with them.

Zenel Shehu was one of the Monarchist's best men. He came over to London with King Zog during the war. And he was one of the last to be parachuted in.

Some of the groups were more secure than others. With some of them you could go to a Rome cafe and find who was going into Albania next week and who had just escaped. Balli Kombëtar was very secure, though. I was given no information about the military side of things and I would not have asked about it, because this was Abas Ermenji's problem.

The point is that in the beginning our sponsors promised us absolutely everything. They were going to help us liberate our country. But then, as things turned out not very well, and as our men kept being caught, it became clear that Albania was being used as an experiment. The

Vasil Andoni (1901–1994), one of the founding members of the Balli Kombëtar movement during the Second World War.

CIA developed this idea of sending exiles into their own country, on the off-chance that they might be able to achieve something, and this ended up with the Bay of Pigs episode. This happened over two or three years and it was a great disappointment for us, because we would never have started the whole thing if we had thought it was just an experiment.

Also we got the impression (after Burgess and McLean fled) that the British and Americans did not trust one another. John Lyall kept asking me, "You saw John Lee yesterday. Why? What did you talk about?" And a few days later Lee would accuse me of talking to Lyall.

Our refusal to cooperate happened when we realized that the whole thing was not as important as it had once been or as we had been told it would be. It was then that Abas Ermenji explained his plan to the sponsors, as a last resort, for an attack on the communists in Albania with substantial forces. He went to England and talked to British intelligence about it. It was not accepted. At that point we told them that we would have nothing more to do with sending men into the country.

Once we had an article in our journal attacking the Greek claims on Albania and the sponsors said, "Why do you write such articles against Greece?" I replied that our job was to see to the interests of Albania. John Lyall also asked us what we would do if we broke with the committee. We had no money. I said that if necessary I would write my newspaper in a refugee camp. I said to him, "Of course, Mr. Lyall, I understand that the whole British parliament and the British people are supporting you in this." And he had to laugh, because we both knew that the parliament and people knew nothing about it.

Before going to Paris and London in 1948, Frashëri paid a visit to the Americans, British, Greek and Turkish embassies in Rome to tell them of his hopes for a free Albania. In the last two instances he saw the ambassadors, in the first two he saw the station chiefs.

Hasan Dosti is still alive and he is an encyclopedia. He lives in Los Angeles. Asim Jakova lives in Boca Raton, Florida. After 1952 he worked for the Greeks and he sent men into Albania like corn into a mill.

Malta was better, from the security point of view. It was cut off from the rest of Europe and very little leaked out. The Munich operation was looser and a lot of gossip about who was going on missions leaked into Rome bars and coffee houses. So, in a sense, there were people doing Philby's job for him.

The committee had a flat in Rome, but we never discussed military matters in the flat. We went out and took a walk to talk about these things. And we never kept any records or minutes of our discussions.

Officially the committee was under the protection of the Free Europe Organisation. John Lee was our treasurer in Rome. He paid out all our funds. I've no idea where he got the money from.

Interview conducted July 10, 1983

James J. Angleton

James Jesus Angleton (1917–1987) was an American intelligence officer. He served during World War II in the counter-intelligence branch of the United States Office of Strategic Services (OSS) in London, where he first met Kim Philby. At the end of the war and thereafter, he was responsible for operations in Italy. From May 1949 he was at the CIA's Office of Special Operations in Washington and worked closely with Philby, of whom he was highly suspicious. Angleton was head of counter-intelligence at the CIA from 1954 to 1975.

Robert Low has condensed the time frame of my career and confused my functions. In fact I did not take over the counter-espionage function until December 1954, so he is wrong to say that the Albanian operation led to the unmasking of Kim Philby.

There were many leaks in the Albanian operation because of the large number of émigrés living in the Western world, particularly in Rome. Émigrés are always a number one target of Soviet intelligence. I have no doubt that the KGB had infiltrated most of the anti-communist Albanian groups in Rome, just as they did the anti-communist Russian groups in Germany. Their success in this field goes back to Dzierzynski and the "Trust." They naturally see anyone who has escaped from occupied territory as a threat and neutralizing these people is their top priority.

Albania is a tribal country and full of rivalries dating back to tribal days. The exiles in Rome had split loyalties and every man was preoccupied with the question of who would prevail if the operation was successful. Also the local Italians have a very good counter-espionage service since Rome was the place of so much Albanian activity, and they were in a good position to put pressure on the exiles who were there with stateless documents which they could only get after being carefully screened by the locals.

The purpose of the operation was noble, but it was fated to fail. The émigré groups turned themselves into paper mills in their efforts to show how efficient and well-informed they were.

At the time I was special assistant to the CIA chief, at a time when there were two chiefs on the American clandestine side. The men in OPC were working in parallel with us and there were differences of view between us.

Telephone conversation conducted April 4, 1984

Sam Barclay

Sam Barclay (1920–2000) was a British sailor and entrepreneur. He had worked in shipping and smuggling in the Aegean. In 1948–1949, with Dino Gregory, built the boat Stormie Seas *that was chartered for the Albanian operation to smuggle the Albanian fighters into Albania.*

During 1944, I was involved in landings in the Aegean from a Levant schooner under the aegis of SOE (Special Operations Executive). It was formed by Adrian Seligman and we were based in Turkey, when she was neutral. Then in 1946, I wanted to get back to the Aegean and I bought an old trading ketch called the *Bessie*. John Leatham and I began carrying cargoes round the Mediterranean. I wanted to paint; he wanted to write. We ended by carrying cargoes in the *Bessie* from Salonika to Piraeus for the British Military Mission. In 1948, we sold the *Bessie* in Piraeus and we thought we had enough money to build a better boat. We started building the *Stormie Seas* during the winter of 1948–49.

While we were doing this, we were approached by the "firm," who knew about our previous work and knew that we were building the boat. We said that we had other plans, but we would think about it if we ran out of money. At this stage they just said that they had a job for us; they didn't give us details. This was early in 1949.

The Greek shipbuilders grossly underestimated the cost of building the *Stormie Seas*, in order to get the contract. When it was half done, they announced that it was going to cost a lot more. We ran out of money. So we told Pat Whinney that we were on. We went down to Malta under sail and MI6 paid for the installation of a very big engine, the cabins and the rest of the boat. We made the boat seaworthy ourselves in Piraeus, with our last pennies, and lost the mast on the way to Malta. We left Piraeus for Malta on February 15, took six weeks to get there and arrived on March 31. The "firm" then flew us to England. I married my wife Eileen and we came back to Malta on July 15. John had gone on ahead. We left Malta finally on October 2. All our operations were over by then. We did three trips to the Albanian coast, to three different places.

The boat was on the slip in Manuel Island, which later became a submarine base. They finished off the cabins and gave us two new masts. The engine had been made for a 52-foot harbor launch, a 90-horsepower Ruston-Hornsby. It took up the boat's entire hold and gave us about eight knots. We weren't armed. The only thing special was the fuel tanks, which contained hiding places. They had built-in header tanks. The engine worked on gravity feed. It had no fuel pump. There was a secret panel in the fore end of the cabin we lived in and behind the panel was a manhole cover about nine inches in diameter. You could get your arm into it. We used it mostly for storing radio equipment. There was a British telegraphist on board called Geoffrey.

There would not have been cabins for all the Albanians on my boat. It would not have been comfortable to take them all from Malta to the Albanian coast. From Otranto to the Albanian coast was only about 50 miles. Eileen did the cooking on board and she was paid by MI6. And there was our dog, called "Lean-to." One reason for taking the wife and the dog was to give the impression that we were no more than a family outing. If you find a yacht anywhere with just half a dozen men on board, it's a bit funny, a bit suspicious. That's why they let her come. We spent a day or two in Otranto, just observing one another, not speaking, and then one afternoon we put out to sea. They went and we followed them to a point about ten or fifteen miles offshore. Then we stopped and transferred the little men on board the *Stormie Seas* by rubber boat, their boat.

All this was observed by the Italians through binoculars from the top of Otranto lighthouse. And they were quite angry. They thought that they were being used for nefarious purposes. We knew then where to aim for, made our way across the straits to a point about half a mile from the Albanian shore, just out of rifle range, put the men into the dinghy and the marines rowed them ashore. We timed it so that we could not be seen from the Albanian shore. We got within sight of it at dusk.

On one of the trips we took the Albanians to Fano or Merlera, islands just north of Corfu. The Greeks knew nothing about it. We were told that only the head of Greek intelligence was in the picture. I can't remember whether we went there for a rendezvous or because of bad weather. Some Greek customs men came out to see us in a boat. We had to stop them coming on board. We offered them cigarettes and a glass of ouzo. Eileen found that she hadn't got any cigarettes. She was fumbling for a packet when a hand appeared up out of the engine room, belonging to someone who wasn't supposed to be there at all, and gave her the cigarettes.

The first landing was onto a steep mountainous coastline. The second was onto a flat sandy beach. There was a third landing. We left Malta for the last time on October 2. We landed Albanians on the way and I think we called in at the Corfu Islands. We reached Piraeus on October 28. There was also a Greek seaman on board all the time. His name was Gregory, but I call him Dino in my book.

John, Gregory and I were all paid £50 a month. They spent quite a lot of money on the boat, but they never paid us a charter fee. They were rather tightfisted. They gave us £500 each at the end and they let us keep the engine, although it wasn't the sort of engine that we wanted. We had to take it out in the end. It took up too much space and we couldn't build any cabins round it. It wasn't what we wanted for chartering. It was a 90-horsepower engine weighing two and a half tons. We replaced it with a 70-horsepower Mercedes engine that weighed half a ton and gave us almost the same speed.

They paid our expenses, but the pay was not good, considering that the boat was at risk. If they'd chartered us on a commercial basis, it would have been a lot more. Still, we weren't doing it for the money and they paid our bills, although they haggled over them, too. We put in for what we spent, whether it was fuel or repairs or food. They would come back and say, "We think this is rather a lot and we're prepared to pay 75 percent." John became furious. He's very English and very upright. He made a row about his word being questioned and then they agreed to pay the full amount. These were clerks in the MI6 office in Athens.

Perkins was half Polish. His mother or father had a factory in Poland making either boots or silk stockings. It had been taken over by the Russians. He hated the Russians and was keen to do them down at every turn. He was intelligent, efficient. Everyone respected him. It's a very funny thing that quite a lot of people who worked for the "firm" got tuberculosis. I often wondered whether the Russians had infected them.

Whinney was succeeded by Christopher Philpots. The CIA chief was Bill Bromell. We weren't meant to know this, but they stuck out like sore thumbs. They had a caique out in Athens that was unlike any other caique on earth. It had a great wheelhouse sticking out of the top.

At the end of 1949, they decided that the *Stormie Seas* wasn't fast enough, so they took us off sea drops and started using the *San Giorgio*, an old SOE boat built to look like a Spanish fishing boat above the water line, but a motor torpedo boat below the water line. During the war she was used to mix with the Spanish fishing fleet during the day and put agents ashore at night. After the war she was used for smuggling by a Maltese until the "firm" got hold of her. She had two Paxman-Ricardo engines and would do 18 knots. They took her on for her speed, but the engines kept breaking down. We had to laugh, because in 1949, the "firm" had been running us on a shoestring, but by 1950 the Americans were in on it and they were paying everybody huge sums of money. We never saw an Albanian patrol boat, but they may have had information that we didn't have, so they decided that they needed a very fast boat.

The owner used to have a little boat called the *Valfrer*. He was an Englishman who used to smuggle from Tangier. He was traveling back to England one time in the Bay of Biscay in October, far too late, and got hove out on his beam ends twice. And when he got to England the customs were waiting for him and they went through him with a fine-tooth comb. Then the "firm" got hold of him and persuaded him to run this boat. And then they gave him the *Henrietta*, which was a converted German E-boat, very fast. Darby Allen sailed with him for a bit, but there was some scandal over his showing favoritism to one of the other marines, so Darby left him and came back to John and me to help us with the chartering. The "firm" let him do a bit of smuggling. They thought it was good cover. There was this E-boat painted green. People wondered what it was doing. They needed a cover.

Our British operation had been run on a shoestring, so it rather rankled when the Americans came in and were prepared to pay £80,000 flying out new engines from Germany for the *Henrietta*. This was in 1950 when Darby Allen was with them.

The second year they had an extraordinary idea. I like to think that it was thought up by Kim Philby. It was to shower Albania with leaflets. They asked us to help them by launching balloons over this mountainous, sparsely populated country, with a few towns and villages here and there. During World War II, the Japanese had sent balloons over the west coast of the United States and by this means they dropped a few bombs on Seattle. Each bomb had a fuse and when the fuse burned out, the bomb fell. This was where the "firm" got the idea from, but they didn't know how the Japanese had done it. For some reason they didn't want to ask the Japanese, so they sent John and me back to England to one of their establishments to work out a system.

They sent us down to some camp near Brighton behind barbed wire, with a lot of wooden huts full of scientists. They were marvelous at working problems out on paper, not so good at the practical application of their theories. The only practical man was an excellent naval engine-room artificer who could make anything with his hands. He was our link between theory and practice. In my view, the whole thing was a joke from beginning to end. At one point Perks had to tick us off about it. He told us to make up our minds, either to take the job on or not, but if we took it on we had to do it properly and stop laughing about it. From then on we did the best we could.

How were we supposed to get the balloon up to the right height? We had to set the fuse before letting go. Then it had to go up and be carried by the wind in the right direction, towards a town 50 miles away, and then the fuse had to burn through and release the load precisely over that town.

We used to sit about 20 miles offshore and wait until we got the signal from London that the wind was right. They also gave us instructions about the fuse setting. Then we had to weigh out the correct amount of pamphlets, bearing in mind the constant pressure. The boys in London presumably imagined thousands of Albanians picking these pamphlets out of the skies, reading them and then preparing themselves for the liberation that was to come by land, sea and air.

Eileen came with us for several trips, then she became pregnant and got off at Trieste and went to her parents who lived in Piraeus. She died recently.

The back-room boys in England worked out the system, but it was John and I and this ERA who made the equipment. They gave us pellets which gave off a gas when mixed with salt water in a converted washing machine with a pipe leading to the nozzle of each balloon. The fuse was made of lighter wick. When the fuse burnt through, the packet of pamphlets, about a pound in weight, fell to the ground. The wick was attached to the balloon. The pamphlets were attached to the wick, with an extra length hanging down below the pamphlets. We lit the bottom end before letting go and the balloon would stay up until the spark reached the connecting piece of wick, whereupon the pamphlets would part company with the balloon, the balloon would go shooting up and the pamphlets floating down. It all depended on the strength and direction of the wind. Still, it must have been very inaccurate and I would imagine that almost all of them fell on the bare mountainsides or into the sea.

We spent Christmas 1949 in Greece. I left Greece for Malta on April 28. Then we went to England for the balloon training and back to Malta on July 10. John arrived in Malta on July 27 and we sailed for Trieste on August 6, getting rid of our first lot of pamphlets on the way. We got to Bari on August 24, then back to Trieste on September 8. We left Trieste on September 17 and got to Malta on September 30. We collected the first lot of leaflets in Malta, the second lot in Trieste. We left Malta on October 11, reached Piraeus on October 15 and put the boat up for sale. My son was born about that time. And that was the end of my association with the "firm." They gave John and me £500 each and let us keep the engine.

It wasn't tremendously generous, but perhaps just as well. If we had done it only for the money, we might later have had second thoughts, whereas under the circumstances we had to convince ourselves that it was a job worth doing. At the time we did think that they were a bit mean, but at the end of it all we had our boat and enough to live on for another year.

There were some that I had great respect for: Whinney, Darby Allen, Philpotts and Perkins. There were others who seemed to be no more than Boy Scouts, in it for fun and games. They were obsessed with the secret side of their work. When we made contact in Malta, we weren't allowed to telephone from our hotel. It had to be from a telephone box, using a code, and then I was asked to meet their man by the sixth milestone out of Valetta on the road to Rabat. I got off the bus, there was no one there for miles around except one person who was looking the other way. Then, it was agreed, he would walk behind me humming a certain song, and I had to make the right reply. They really did it, just like in the films. It was a rule of thumb.

John and I started off in Malta in grand rooms in a big house. Later on, when Eileen and I got married we lived in a hotel. The Maltese did good work on the boat, but they were heavily unionized, far earlier than we were in Britain, and took four men to do one man's job. It took eleven men to strip it. In Greece it had taken three. If one man was late for work, the others refused to start without him. We had to make all the arrangements, going round different firms in Malta and getting quotes. Nothing like that was done for us. In the end it was done as a civilian contract by the naval dockyard.

Bill Brummel, one of the CIA men in Athens, took our boatman Gregory on to his payroll after we left the operation. Brummel was a very nice chap, very keen on boats. He designed and built what they called the work boat. It had diesel engines and did 8 or 9 knots, rather like a trawler but with an extra upper deck. They had a small island in the Gulf of Corinth where, I think, they trained some more of these little men. Gregory manned this boat for the Americans for a number of years. When the Americans pulled out, they gave Gregory the boat.

We had one hair-raising experience during a drop when we tried to put into Sazan Island. There were rumors that the Russians had a submarine base there. As we entered the harbor, it was obvious to us that they had. So we beat a hasty retreat.

Extract from Pictures from Greece, *Athens, September 1958.*

Stormie Seas, *the subject of our cover picture, is a Greek-built "trechandiri" which has become the home of Englishman Sam Barclay, his wife Eileen and six-year-old son James. Sam Barclay, descendant of the founder of Barclays Bank, was inspired to name his boat* Stormie Seas *after a fifteenth-century verse by an anonymous writer that goes: "Rest after toyle, port after stormie seas, death after life, these things do greatlie please."*

An article and further photographs of Sam Barclay's floating home appear in this month's issue of Pictures from Greece, *photo by Vasso Mingos.*

p. 11 Sam's boat is 48 feet long. She makes up to 8 knots in a fair breeze. In a calm, her 75-hp Mercedes Diesel pushes her at 7 knots.

p. 12 Want to roam the world's most romantic sea—the Aegean—in an old-fashioned sailing vessel?

If you can afford the expense, you may do so aboard this two-masted, 43-ton schooner.

You will find it difficult to decide which is the more fascinating: the schooner itself, with its blue and gold paint and billowing, tan-colored sails; or its skipper—lanky, yellow-thatched, 38-year-old, Greek-speaking Englishman Sam Barclay.

Anything to do with Barclays Bank? Why, yes. His great-grandfather founded it.

There, however, Sam's connection with the banking business ends. After setting eyes on the man, you would be the first to admit that the sight of him behind a bank executive's desk would be as incongruous as to see, say, Sir Winston Churchill ballet dancing at Sadlers Wells.

Sam is in his element when he has his hand on the tiller and his bare feet firmly planted on the heaving deck of his schooner.

Had he lived during the reign of the first Elizabeth, he might have developed into another Sir Francis Drake or another Sir Walter Raleigh. In our era of nuclear-powered ships, operating a schooner yacht for private charter seems to be about the only occupation that fits in with his inclinations.

Born and brought up in Norfolk (England), Sam was 20 when he joined the Royal Navy at the start of World War II. "Since then I have never lived ashore," he says, a schoolboyish grin lighting up his weather-beaten face.

War in the Mediterranean was drawing to a close when he volunteered for service in the British-Greek Levant Schooner Flotilla. This was a fleet of small caiques engaged in intelligence operations and commando raids on Axis-occupied Aegean islands. War's end found Greece with most of her caiques sunk. The few that were left were able to command high freights. This gave Sam Barclay the idea of rigging up a trading ketch, Bessie, *and going into the freight business. He did a roaring trade with the islands until conditions returned to normal and wartime losses in shipping were made good. This spelt the end of the freight business for Sam.*

It also looked as if his seafaring life was over. But not for Sam the prosaic lot of the land-lubber! Stormie Seas *was his way of dodging that dismal fate.*

Stormie Seas *was the ship he acquired after selling* Bessie. *Entirely designed by himself, it combined the outward shape of a Greek trehandiri with the underwaterline of a Norwegian redingskoite that made it fit to navigate the high seas.*

The timber that went into the building of its hull was the best to be found in Greece. It came from the island of Samos, the only place in this country where trees are not "bled" for resin.

Its deck and hatches were of the finest teak, salvaged from a wartime wreck in the North African port of Tobruk.

There was nothing fancy about its cabins. They were roomy, comfortable, practical. For the ship was going to be Sam's floating home. Aboard it, he would paint for a living, and roam his beloved sea—the Aegean—for fun.

Things, however, did not turn out quite the way he planned.

At Perama, the Greek ship-building centre where he was having his ship built, there lived a blue-eyed, dark-haired Scottish-Irish girl. Eileen Hay was the daughter of a Shell Company engineer stationed in the neighbourhood. The many exotic places she had been to (she was born in Shanghai and had lived in China, Egypt, the West Indies, South America) gave her girlish charm that aura of romance an adventurous fellow like Sam was bound to fall for. And, too, she played the guitar and sang calypsos beautifully....

"I saw the keel of Sam's ship laid in the shipyard, a stone's throw from our house," Eileen says. "I christened her. By the time she was ready to go in the water, I was ready to marry him."

The arrival of son James started Sam Barclay in the charter business, a more secure means of livelihood than painting.

He has been chartering for the past five years or so. The clients have been many and varied—greying business executives and young honeymooners, society dowagers and groups of students, celebrities like writer John Steinbeck and movie director Elia Kazan.

Charter time lasts from the beginning of April to the end of October. During the winter months, Stormie Seas *is laid up in some harbour or other, with the Barclays aboard. The winter months are far from being an idle time for them.*

Says Eileen: "The more charters we get, the busier we are during the winter. There is so much to do: advertising, getting the ship prepared for the following spring. Sam edges in some painting. I spent last winter teaching my son (now turned 6). That kept me busy!"

Stormie Seas *has sailed as far as Italy, the South of France, Spain and North Africa. But her usual beat is the Aegean.*

To islanders here, she has become a familiar and friendly sight.

Interview conducted April 1, 1983

* * *

I remember our walking past each other on the Otranto quayside, everyone pretending that they didn't know who the other person was.

Otranto lighthouse reaches for 22 miles, so we must have been nearly 20 miles out when we made the transfer and they could just see us through telescopes from the top of the lighthouse. The boat would have taken seven hours to cross from Otranto to the Albanian coast.

I remember mountainous seas as we emerged from the Gulf of Vlora. That's why they didn't send a patrol boat after us. Then we went back to Otranto to land the marines. They made their own way back to Malta by boat.

It was possible to get from Vlora to Otranto traveling southwest against a southeasterly gale, but there was no way of making for Piraeus against such a wind. That's why we stayed a week in Otranto, leaving eventually on October 13. We had an 11-foot wooden dinghy on deck and an 18-foot dory, lent to us by the Marines. We lost the dory before putting into the Gulf and while the soldiers were shouting at us, we pretending to be hoisting out the dinghy. This was after the landing on the sandy beach. In Greece there would have been nothing suspicious about taking refuge in a gulf during a storm, but the Albanian coast was crawling with troops and it was near a submarine base. They fired flares into the air as we fled, presumably as a signal to the island, and that's why we thought we might get a motor-torpedo boat after us.

During the winter of 1949–50 we took the boat up to Istanbul and tried to work ways out of getting men into Bulgaria.

We left Malta with the leaflets on August 6, 1950, and arrived in Trieste on September 8. The right wind didn't blow and we spent 18 days hove-to off the south of Italy. Then the fresh water tank ran dry and our only spare water was in a converted fuel tank. It was stinking by then and I didn't want to run the risk of people getting ill, so I explained the situation on the radio and we were ordered to put into Bari, which we did on August 24 having previously dumped the leaflets and balloons. We didn't want the Italians to find that sort of stuff. It was very bulky.

We left Trieste on September 17 with a new consignment of balloons and pamphlets, released them off Tirana on September 21, called in at Syracuse and reached Malta on September 28. We put sea water and carbide pellets into this cylinder that looked like a washing machine. This created hydrogen gas that came out of a pipe and was filtered through a jam jar containing two inches of water to act as a resistance to control the flow of gas. We filled each balloon from the nozzle, attached the wick and the pamphlets, and then let it sail away toward Albania.

We returned to England from Greece on May 14, 1950, after which they trained us at a very hush-hush camp near Fareham in Hampshire. It seemed to consist of a lot of wooden huts full of weird scientists who never seemed to leave their desks. The scientists worked it all out in their heads, the right gas pressure and the length of wick required, but it took this old naval ERA to actually make something. We kept wondering why they didn't ask the Japanese how they'd done it against the U.S. Maybe it would have been bad for security. We had just two huts for us and the balloons. There were about 20 huts in all containing, say, 100 scientists. I came back to Malta on July 7, John on July 27.

Frank Stallwood, one of Whinney's deputies, came to Malta to help us with the ballooning. We let them go three miles off Tirana, after spending most of the day 12 miles offshore. These high-altitude winds go quite steadily.

Interview conducted November 28, 1983

Zbigniew Bobinski

Zbigniew Bobinski (1921–1995) was a Polish exile pilot recruited for the Albanian operation to fly into Albania and to drop the Albanian fighters in by parachute.

Colonel Roman Rudkowski was parachuted into Warsaw during the Uprising and arrested by the communists. After the war he was allowed to "escape" into West Berlin on condition that he worked for Soviet intelligence, but in fact he worked exclusively for the Americans.

The recruiter for the Polish pilots in the Albanian operation was Flight Lieutenant Ludwik Ciastula. He recruited crews from the Polish Air Force Association. And I think he was manager of the Polish officers' mess in Athens.

I was a pilot in a Polish unit flying out of Wiesbaden in West Germany, flying planes over the Ukraine and the Baltic. I think that the story should be told, because it should be known what we tried to achieve. We were the only people actually fighting the communists at that time. And it was for very little pay, far less than I had received earlier as a commercial pilot.

One of the pilots involved in Albania is Boleslaw Korpowski. He was chairman of one of our clubs here. There was another one whose plane blew up over Cyprus. His name was Bogdan Krahelski. He was liquidated, I think, because he had a girlfriend who was with the other side and there were suspicions about his loyalty.

The Soviets know about me, but I don't think they would take any action against me now, at least not anything public. It was a very long time ago. And also they would not want to advertise the fact of how easily we flew over Soviet territory. We went anywhere we wanted. We could have flown over Red Square if we'd felt like it. And it didn't have to be a sophisticated plane. Any old aircraft could do it, so long as it was not traceable. It is possible if you fly at treetop level with an electronic altimeter, audible as well as visual, to help you stay at the height of about 50 feet. It just does not show up on the radar. That's why the Soviets are so frightened of Cruise missiles.

This was a good system. Only later they developed the U-2 spy plane that flew very high, a Lockheed, and they didn't want to entrust such a sophisticated machine to a Polish pilot, who might perhaps defect to the other side with it. So they used an American pilot, which made it very embarrassing indeed when he was caught.

There was no risk of embarrassment with us. We were stateless and they'd simply have denied that they had any connection with us. That was the deal. They explained it to us frankly and they gave us cyanide pills just in case. And all our clothes and equipment were made in eastern Europe, to make it a little easier for them to disassociate themselves from us. They gave us all Russian watches. We all fully accepted the fact no one would protect us if we were caught.

The crews were chosen through an agreement known as the "Berg affair," an agreement between the CIA and the Polish government in exile. It provided for U.S. funds to be made available to the Polish exile government on condition that they provided these Polish crews. Athens was one of the bases, operating over the Balkans. There was another in Turkey dropping agents into Soviet Armenia. We were at Wiesbaden and occasionally, when we wanted to fly over the Baltic states, we flew out of Bornholm island.

Rudkowski was my commanding officer in 1953–54. He was in London then and we had to send letters from Wiesbaden to London for him to forward to our friends and family. He was a fearless, live-for-today fellow, a great drinker and womanizer.

The planes were unmarked and painted black all over. In Wiesbaden we had Skymasters and for special trips, a De Havilland Beaver, manufactured in Canada. The planes were always bought on the free market from a small airline for cash, to make sure that they could not be traced to the RAF or U.S. Air Force.

The pilots flew at treetop level and flew higher only for a few minutes before the drop. We did not discuss any of the details, though, in the officers' mess, because there were microphones there and men under orders to report our conversations to the Americans.

Our problem was isolated trees or chimneys or churches. This was the pilot's problem. You had to have your eyes peeled the whole time and instant reactions. And the navigators had to be clever, because it would have been very serious if we'd got lost. There are not too many distinguishing features to help the navigator.

In Albania they would have flown along the valleys, if there was a full moon. And each crew worked out its own route. The electronic altimeter would have been a great help. It gave out a "beep beep" as soon as the ground started sloping upwards.

Interview conducted February 16, 1984

MICHAEL BURKE

Michael Burke (1916–1987) was an American military figure, and OSS and CIA intelligence agent. He was born in Enfield, Connecticut, and played football at the University of Pennsylvania. During World War II, he served with the U.S. Navy and joined the OSS, for which he operated in Italy and France. After the war, he was recruited by the CIA and, in 1949 he replaced Robert Low as the American officer in charge of the paramilitary operations for Albania.

[MB]: Leib began to live as if he was chairman of the Pepsi-Cola Company. And it was the standing joke that he even bought himself some European title and had cards printed showing him as "Baron Leib" or "Count Leib." It had a bad effect on the Albanians, because until then they had all been very poor, even destitute. The money went to their heads.

Leib was a friend of Yatsevitch and it was Yatsevitch who brought him in. The CIA in those days was very crudely put together. I remember getting blank looks when I went to Rome and asked what my cover was to be. In the end I created my own cover,

Imperial Films, which consisted entirely of some headed stationery and a post box in New York. It didn't in fact seem as strange as all that, because there were a lot of quasi-film people milling about in Rome and a genuine renaissance of the Italian film. It was nothing like nowadays, where a CIA person gets three years' training before any assignment.

Leib was miscast. He replaced me and I passed all my contacts over to him. He had no previous experience in the secret world. He was straight out of the advertising business. I can only attribute it to the fact that the organization was in its swaddling clothes. Yatsevitch at least had some experience of that part of the world and he has a very keen mind. It was built into his character that he was always going to have problems. He never lasted long in any job and he changed wives in the 1960s. Around that time I hired him for a month or two to get his expertise on the soft-drink business, but he didn't stay with me any longer. And of course, CIA let him go when the Albanian episode ended.

Low and I both lived in Chester Square in the 1960s. In 1949 Low was on leave from Time-Life and when I replaced him he went back there.

The training school was isolated and overlooking a valley. I went there two or three times. It was commanded by a U.S. major, formerly an OSS man, an expert in guerrilla warfare.

We were always looking for good material among the Albanians, but we had no means of judging them. It was up to the Albanian leaders to come up with the right men. Another problem was that most of the best men were tarnished with the Italian brush. So they were crossed out from the start. Most of the men were tough, but not officer material, often illiterate, even though illiteracy does not necessarily mean that a man is unfit to be an officer.

Those who stayed in houses were always caught. Sooner or later they were betrayed. This was not the case in occupied Europe in the war. Gestapo control was nowhere as tight.

I was driven to the school from Heidelberg. It was arranged by the local Heidelberg CIA man. I asked him to find suitable premises and he found the "Schloss" on our behalf, a place about an hour's drive from Heidelberg. The first time was when he took me there to ask if it was OK. We called it the "Schloss" although it was more of a luxury villa.

My reaction to the site was on the basis of my old OSS training in Maryland and Virginia, or my parachute training at Ringway in a nice estate. This house was of the same standard.

Usually, I took the Scandinavian express from Rome to Stockholm. It left Rome at about 10 p.m. It went through the Swiss border at Chiasso, past Munich and Frankfurt to Heidelberg. Sometimes I flew, but I took the train when there was fog about.

I worked out the trainee's program with him, when they got up and when they ate. I recall that he arranged an exercise period every day after lunch. This was to stop them falling asleep after eating. He was the man on the spot, but in terms of hierarchy he was my subordinate.

I acted entirely on the basis of my World War II experience. It was the same old syndrome of preparing for the next war on the basis of the last war. We applied old experience to a new situation and of course it didn't work, either in Poland or in the Ukraine or in Albania (Ringway was the RAF school).

When I was at Ringway in World War II, I did five practice jumps from an aircraft and one from a balloon. I imagine that it was thought impracticable to send these Albanians either to Ringway or to the American parachute school, Fort Benning in Georgia. This is why they had simulated parachute jumps. Still, it wasn't entirely unknown in the war for men to jump without any training.

One of the Poles in the air crew was an experienced World War II dispatcher. He was a dab hand at getting the men's static lines hooked up and getting them out. The only Pole I remember by name was called Rudko. He had commanded a Polish squadron during the war and been involved in drops over Poland. We got all the Poles through Perks.

The first crew consisted of pilot, co-pilot, dispatcher, navigator and Rudko himself. He was not supposed to go, but he went along for the ride. The others had taken the refresher course, which was held at Wiesbaden. He just jumped into the plane and closed the door. He hadn't been on the course. It was very difficult to navigate over Albania: no rivers to speak of, hardly any habitation or lights. The Poles joked when they came back about there being three light bulbs in the whole of Tirana. It was a full moon, a cloudless night. Even so, one hill looked much the same as another. And the danger was that any aircraft over Albania would attract attention and Rudkowski's low-level pass over Tirana must have woken up the sleepiest concierge in the city and put the whole nation on the alert.

The training school was secure. Not even the Albanians knew where it was. There cannot have been many leaks from there. But there would have been leaks from Company 4000 about people leaving for the school. And from the names of the men who left for the school, it was possible to work out where there was going to be a drop, since they were all dropped near their home villages, as decreed by the "old Albanian hands." The normal means of travel in Albania was on foot in groups of four or five. It was dangerous to travel alone or in pairs, while a larger group was seen as a threat.

Yatsevitch was in Washington all the time that I was in Europe. I remember meeting him in Athens with the local CIA chap, McLean. It must have been when he was first given the job. We had dinner and McLean got completely sloshed on ouzo. Drink seems to have been one of the occupational hazards of the secret world.

Hod Fuller had been a U.S. Marine during the war, then he went to Greece with the Marshall Plan as an engineer. He left that and went into the boat charter business, as a cover for his CIA activities as a contract agent.

I left the Albanian operation in February 1951 and I was replaced by Joe Leib. The Albanians gave me a dinner and they all signed the menu. Low briefed me in Washington before I went out. He gave me a thumbnail sketch of the Albanian political scene. And I was physically introduced to the committee by John Hibberdine.

I had dinner with Kim Philby at an Italian restaurant in Soho during my visit to London in December 1949. It was a very sociable and companionable dinner. And certainly we talked about Albania. It's quite terrifying to think about it. He was a sympathetic and witty fellow. His stammer made me feel even more sympathetic towards him. He got drunk, as usual. It was after a daytime meeting in Perks's office in Broadway

Buildings. He was introduced to me there as one of the senior SIS people, a friend and an ally, one of the inner circle, so I was disposed to like him and I accepted his credentials. Obviously, we didn't discuss the operational details of what I was doing, but we certainly discussed the thing in general terms and I would have had no reason to hold back.

There was only one team of Polish pilots, all living in the one house in Athens. Fuller was the man who looked after them.

I remember Rudkowski as a stocky, energetic type with a commanding presence, a man who was very much in charge. One could sense their camaraderie and the rapport between the colonel and the other pilots.

Interview conducted November 12, 1983

* * *

Just before 1949 I was in Hollywood working freelance in the film business. I worked for Warner Brothers for a while. Then I lived in New York doing freelance writing. During the war, I first joined the Coordinator of Information, which was the forerunner of OWI and OSS. This was in early 1942. Then I was commissioned into the Navy and immediately seconded back to OSS, where I remained throughout the war. I was in North Africa and then we had a mission in Italy in the summer of 1943, trying to bring about the surrender of the Italian fleet. We managed to get some scientific people out. Then in 1944 I was parachuted into France in the Vosges region to help the Maquis. I came to England at the end of 1944, after the Battle of the Bulge, when it was clear that the war would not be over by Christmas. There was a great rush then to get agents into Germany. We set up an office in Grosvenor Street to organize the infiltration of agents into Germany and I stayed there until the end of the European war.

I met Frank Lindsay during the war. He had worked in Yugoslavia. Robert Low was the first American attached to this project abroad. He was in and out of Rome a few times. I imagine that Lindsay and the others thought that my experience in France and getting into and out of Italy in 1943 would lend themselves to what was about to be attempted in Albania. I had no knowledge of Albania as such. I just about knew where it was. My first real lessons about Albania were from Julian Amery and Billy McLean.

So I was approached by Jim McCargar in April or May 1949. His bona-fides was established with me through Frank Lindsay, so that I knew that it was a serious proposition. I remember that McCargar's first questions were theoretical. What country did I think might be prized away from the Soviet bloc? My first reaction was to think of Yugoslavia, but it was obvious after a few minutes that Yugoslavia was not what he was talking about. Then it emerged that he was thinking of Albania, a country which hadn't occurred to me, because I had really not thought about it. It was clear that I was to be taken on as a nuts-and-bolts operational character, the person who deals with boats and guns and landing places and that sort of thing. I was certainly not being taken on as a political expert.

The essence of McCargar's proposition was that this was a clinical case. Was it on in principle for the United States and Britain to disrupt a communist regime, unseat a communist dictator? Is it possible? We'd like you to try it. We don't know whether it'll work or whether it won't work, but the governments of both countries have decided that it is worth a try. So we'd like you to be the point man here and see whether this sort of thing can be done in peacetime. And we'd like you to start right away.

I was not a member of the CIA. I was contracted by the U.S. government to take care of this particular mission. I never went near the CIA headquarters and I invented my own cover, which was related to my activity in the film business. I went first to Rome to meet the committee—Dosti, Kupi, Kryeziu, Nuçi Kota, Zef Paoli (?), Vasil Andoni and Koca Goga. Goga was one of Kupi's assistants. They had been got together largely through Amery and McLean. They were the political reference point for everything that we did, a platform, a point of departure, so that we weren't just acting out of the blue. Our aim was to help this group of émigrés, who wanted to get back home and democratize their country.

That was the political reason. The operational reason was for them to produce people who would be the initial agents to be infiltrated into Albania. In the American case they were to be parachuted in; in the British case they were to be landed by boat or put across the Greek border. It was quite simple. They wanted to liberate their country and I was authorized to say on behalf of the American government that we stood behind them.

I was a link between the Albanians and American intelligence. And the reason why I was a civilian contract agent was to give the government the capacity for plausible denial in case anything blew up. The political side was open and indeed publicized. The operational side was secret and always officially denied. All the members of the committee embraced this notion. Each one said that he could find from among his followers men who were suitable and would volunteer for these "pathfinder" missions, initial teams who would be parachuted in to see whether there was any existing resistance movement in the country. If there was, they were to make contact with it. If there was not, they were to generate one.

We started putting people in towards the end of 1950, a year later than the British did. After a short stay in Rome, I came to London and met Perkins, Dick Brooman-White, Amery, McLean and Smiley. I was going to go to Malta to see Smiley's operation, but in the end we decided that it was too risky. I would have had no cover. The only American who was there was John Papajani, a real wild man, absolutely not reliable. He had worked for Wisner and others in the OSS in Cairo during the war. They had a rather grand house outside Cairo and Papajani used to run it for them, fetching girls and generally fixing things. Otherwise, he was of no account. And his number one priority was fixing things for himself. I remember him once coming to me in Rome, before he went to Malta, in a state of great urgency wanting some American dollars. I thought it must be for his family, some matter of life or death. I rushed about and got him the dollars, about $400 or $500, and it turned out that he simply had an opportunity to make some money on an exchange, not a personal problem at all.

During my stay in London, I dined with Philby one evening and we talked about the operation. I liked him very much. And I saw him again in Washington in January 1951, when the CIA wanted me to go to Germany to do something. I went to his house for dinner. But the first time was in London in the summer of 1949. We talked about the operation in general and in my ignorance or innocence I was not guarded with Kim in any way. We did not talk about the nuts and bolts of the operation because he was not involved in that part of the American side of it. I had talks about specifics only with Perks or with Pat Whinney, the MI6 chap in Athens, and others directly involved. Whinney was a charming fellow, a big tall chap with red hair. My impression of Philby is of an amiable, companionable man, someone at the top of his profession.

I had one dinner with Billy and two with Julian, to get the political side of things. And I also spent time with John Hibberdine, who was the MI6 contact man in Rome, well-briefed about Albanian politics. Later, Peter Kemp came out for MI6, a very dashing fellow, author of two quite good books about his war adventures. I was there for about a year with Hibberdine, then Kemp succeeded him.

We met the Albanian committee people often. They always had all kinds of problems. Each one was keen to curry a little favor for himself and his party, and we had to be correct and impartial with all of them. Hibberdine and I met the committee several times, sitting round a table, dealing with administrative matters rather than with politics, documents and pay, and recruiting and urging them on.

I did some running back and forth between Rome and Germany, finding the Schloss and arranging with the United States Army for people to come over and instruct the volunteers, train air force crews for the overflights. I was doing a lot of the preparatory work that the British had already done.

There were labor battalions in the U.S. Army from several east European countries, doing public work like mending roads and planting trees. So we created an Albanian "labor battalion," only instead of community work, its men were receiving military training. In Germany I traveled between Frankfurt, Heidelberg and Munich.

Peter Kemp got ill. He'd been in Poland and went down with TB after being captured by the Russians. In Rome his TB acted up on him and he too had to quit. Right the way through we had a very happy and congenial working relationship with the British. We just shared the available Albanians out between us. We did not exchange information about our targets. They may have done between London and Washington, but I doubt it. I never told Hibberdine or Kemp that on a certain night we were going to drop certain people in a certain place. Nor did I know the night or the place where David Smiley was landing people. There was also the link between Philby and McCargar, though maybe Lindsay saw more of Philby than McCargar did. And in Athens there was "Hod" Fuller, who was Whinney's CIA opposite number. He married a Greek girl and he has a house in Spetsai.

He's rather a remote, taciturn person, a sailor all his life. His grandfather was governor of Massachusetts. He comes from rather a distinguished family, he went to Harvard, became an engineer, but sailing has been his life. He went to Greece originally as part of the Marshall Plan and when he was recalled to America, he refused to go. His Greek wife died just recently.

The Schloss was near Heidelberg in 400 or 500 acres of grounds with woods. The Albanians were trained in World War II guerrilla warfare. There was no political indoctrination. They got all that from the committee. They were equipped with ground-to-air radio sets. In World War II we called them the "Joan Eleanor" sets. We used it at the end of the war, speaking to our agents in Berlin and other German cities from a Mosquito bomber. It used a very narrow channel. They didn't have pedal generators, though I had used them in France in 1945.

Hasan Dosti and Nuçi Kota at the military post in Munich, around 1950.

My job throughout 1949 and early 1950 was administration, getting people to the Schloss, seeing that they were properly transported and properly equipped and reporting to Washington through the Embassy, recruiting, training and dispatching of agents and everything else that surrounds such an operation, safe houses for training, safe houses for dispatching the agents from Greece.

So the Schloss was gradually being stocked with Albanians and American instructors, sent over by the CIA, mostly military chaps, former OSS or men seconded to the CIA from the army, men who knew nothing about Albania.

Koca Goga spoke a kind of English. Said Kryeziu and Kota spoke very good French. Nuçi Kota must still be alive. He was a youngish chap, a very attractive fellow, the most attractive of the lot in human terms. He was at school in France and spoke marvelous French.

We had Albanians from about five political parties and each one contributed people. Kupi was the strongest among them at that time, but the king's men did not predominate.

I went to the Schloss a few times. We had a safe house in Athens where we kept the Polish air crews. And we had another house outside Athens where we kept the Albanian agents who were waiting for air drops. We dropped in six the first time, three teams of two each, in late November 1950. Then for the next three or four nights running the crews flew over the three drop zones again, waiting for radio signals from the ground saying that the chaps were okay on these "Joan-Eleanor" sets. Anyway, the crews did fly over the zones for a few nights after the drop, but they didn't get any response. So we didn't know whether they'd simply taken cover in terror or been captured instantly or what had happened.

I went back to Washington shortly after that, towards the end of 1950. And that was when Dulles and those other chaps asked me if I would go to Germany and take over CIA operations based out of Germany. I went back to Rome briefly to hand over the contact to a chap called Joseph Leib. I passed over all the contacts to him, returned to America and then went out to Germany. So I broke contact with the Albanians a few weeks after we put the first lot of agents in.

Under my administration only one lot were parachuted in. And as far as I know, no contact was ever made with them.

Kim Philby would not have known that those men were being dropped on that night. It's quite possible that, apart from Philby, Hoxha's and Shehu's security forces were so good and so tough and the population so terrorized that our agents were compromised at the first contact. They may have found no one to help them. The local people may have turned them in to save their own hides. I don't know what discussions took place in Washington, but I can't imagine Philby knowing the night and the place where the agents were to be dropped.

The thing could well have been leaking among the Albanians involved. Their sense of security was low, so it could have leaked there. I don't recall any specific leak, but their whole approach to life was haphazard. They had very little sense of the sort of security that one associates with a clandestine operation. They did not have much contact with the outside world in Germany, but they may well have said to their friends before they left Italy, "We're going to be trained as agents and parachuted into Albania." And that had to reach the ears of the communist embassies in home. I would have thought that the Italian communists would have sucked in this information, put it all together and concluded that there was an operation going on, Philby or no Philby, even if they didn't know about times and place. It is a vast oversimplification to say that Philby gave the whole show away. I'm not saying that he didn't tell the Soviets all he knew, but that was just one strand in the whole fabric.

There were between 200 and 300 Albanians in the labor battalion in Germany, in the Munich area somewhere. They were like the Czech or the Polish labor battalions in that they were created quite overtly, only they were not expected to do any labor duties; they were doing military training. Their existence was known. They wore blue uniforms with red flashes saying "Albania." In the Schloss there were about 20 or 25 men.

They were trained for a few months in the Schloss and then flown to Athens to the safe house to wait for good weather or a good moon, a proper flying night. Then they were taken to a remote field where there was an unmarked aircraft, a DC3, painted brown. I saw the first one go, boosted the poor bastards up into the plan, threw their containers in after them, shook hands with them, kissed them goodbye. The crews were ex–RAF Poles, five of them, living in Athens to man the aircraft. They came through MI6, through Perks, who was close to the Poles. He put me in touch with the chief Polish fellow, an older man, who contacted members of his old squadron, lifted them out of factories and farms in England. There was a pilot, a co-pilot, a dispatcher and one other, a communications man.

The first time they flew down the main street of Tirana. They weren't supposed to do that, but you know how crazy the Poles are. They didn't admit it, but it came out over beer and coffee later on. There were no opposition aircraft around in the first trip, so they just larked about, showed off a bit. Otherwise, they flew around the coast, round Corfu, came back and landed in the same place. They then flew the next three or four nights in succession to try and make contact.

The messages were supposed to be uncoded voice and the Albanians had enough English to be able to say, "Am receiving you. Please speak." Anything said from the ground was to be recorded on tape or wire. But we didn't get a peep out of them. And after four or five nights we had to call the flights off. It was getting too trafficky over Albania. And we had intermittent communications flights, again without result, after which they were told to stand by for the next drop. I think they booted some leaflets out of the door, too, while they were dispatching the jumpers.

I remember that there was great tension and great concern at our failure to make contact. We concluded that the situation must be tough and tight, with perhaps a population so hostile that it was going to be much tougher going than we hoped. But I left the operation soon after that first drop, so I do not know whether it was discussed in terms of calling the whole thing off, on the grounds that we were on to a loser.

I am really quite surprised that it went on so long, until 1952 and 1953. The whole idea was that we were doing a clinical test and there had to come a point where, in the light of these failures, we should conclude that the whole thing was not on. Eventually the conclusion had to be that the population was either so hostile to our men or so terrified of the security forces that they just would not welcome them or they might even turn them in to the authorities. At the very best, they might be given a bit of food and told, "Here, take this and go. Get out. Don't contaminate this village." Hod Fuller and I had a similar experience in France, even though there were a lot of friendly people, since there was a very hostile authority in control.

They were quite well equipped and they had money. Each individual had a regular wartime container six feet high with clothing, equipment, food and radio. And they had submachine guns and side arms.

It really took me aback a few minutes ago when you told me that the operation went on to 1952 or 1953. I would not have guessed that, because by the time I left, it was clear that a very big yellow or even red flag had gone up. We put three teams in and didn't get a peep out of a single one of them. They couldn't all have been captured the first night, the moment they landed. It seemed a very ominous initial result, showing that it was going to be a hell of a lot tougher than we thought and maybe too tough entirely.

We might have concluded that it was not possible in 1950 to repeat a World War II circumstance. The whole thing was planned along the lines of World War II. Nothing was different. The only thing that was different was that there was no war and that I, as the organizer of the operation, operated as a civilian contract agent rather than as an officer in the United States Navy. Otherwise everything, the concept and the theory, was exactly the same.

One of the fallacies in the operation's planning was that during the war we could rely on tight security. Communication was either not available or strictly monitored and people were reminded all the time about the need for security and discretion. During the war, every time we looked around we saw Hitler's ear on some poster on the wall and this helped us to keep our mouths closed. None of this applied in 1950.

Joseph Leib worked around the east for a good while. He left the CIA and worked for the Pepsi-Cola Company, then he moved to an advertising agency in New York. The last that I heard was that he moved to California.

The person who knows most about this is Gratian Yatsevitch. He sat at the OPC's east European desk section under Lindsay. He was certainly on top of the Albania thing. My coded signals would have gone to that desk. Lindsay was head of the desk for some time and Gratian worked for him, specifically on the Albanian thing at the Washington end. Gratian told me that he had been directed not to talk about it.

Interview conducted December 27, 1982

Ramazan Cenaj

Ramazan Cenaj (b. 1921) was an Albanian anticommunist fighter from Gostil in the Luma region. In 1944, during World War II, he fought communist partisans in Albania, and escaped to Greece in September 1946. He spent the years 1946–1949 in refugee camps in Greece and 1949–1950 in refugee camps in Italy. After six months of military training by the American army in Bavaria, he parachuted into the Has region of northeastern Albania in November 1950. In May 1951, following six months of struggle and deprivation, he crossed over into Kosovo and surrendered to the Yugoslavs, where he was taken prisoner. In 1954, Cenaj was allowed to leave for Italy and in May 1959, he emigrated to the United States.

We had no special training in Munich, only basic military training. The officers taught us for just one day, after which we had to manage by ourselves. Albanians are supposed to know about guns. The American officer was surprised how quickly we learnt. We worked four hours in the morning and four in the afternoon. But I had joined the company not to guard ammunition, but to fight the communist regime. We were ready waiting to be selected for a mission.

They selected eight groups of four each from the royalists and from Balli Kombëtar, 32 altogether. Everyone wanted to go. We all had a medical examination. No one was refused. Three of the groups, 12 people, refused to go when they were in Greece.

I am not sure where the school was, but a maid told me that it was Berchtesgaden, the same place where Hitler had a house. You could see the town and a lake from the top of the hill. It was a beautiful view. I often see it in my dreams.

There were guards to keep people out. We had plenty of space, three people in a room. It was comfortable. We started exercise at 8 a.m. Then we had training in running, shooting and concealment. We had no parachute training, just jumping from a three-meter height. No one jumped from a plane or balloon.

One night they told us to get ready for a move. We drove to a German airport and took off early in the morning. We had a bumpy ride there, were met by U.S. intelligence and kept in a safe house. Colonel Hill came to see us three days later. There was the Dibra group of four. Toptani led the Tirana group, but his three people refused to go. He insisted on going on his own.

We were dropped into Zarisht forest, a day's march from where we were supposed to land. Everyone knew that parachutists had landed because our stuff fell into the village. There was even toilet paper in it and propaganda. We said we didn't need luxuries. We hid under the leaves in the forest while they were looking for us.

We had just three spare magazines with us. And even those they had wanted to drop with the equipment. We had no food, only vitamin pills and diarrhea pills. The reason we were not caught was that we stayed put for five days, with only water from the streams and vitamin pills. We only moved a mile or so all that time.

We had 18 gold coins each, French Napoleons, and some forged Albanian money. All this time I was with Planeja, Nerguti and Berisha. Friends of ours told us that there were soldiers waiting for us in the place where we were supposed to drop. They told us we should have come earlier, when Hoxha was weaker. We ought to create a "free zone" that would be a rallying point for opposition. And it was crazy to send us in November. The snow started falling two days after we landed. Not only was it too cold, it also gives away a guerrilla fighter's movements, at least when the snow stops.

So we crossed into Yugoslavia and stayed with Nerguti's brother. Our aim was to create a group of 50 and when spring came to attack the border town of Kukës. We planned to attack in the spring. But people were asking, "Where are the British? Where are the Americans?" We expected the British to come first, because we remembered them from the war.

We went with about ten people to try and contact Gjura, hoping that he would have some equipment. Two of us, Zef Shyti and I, surrendered to the Yugoslavs on May 9, 1951. I stayed in Yugoslavia until 1954, when they let me go to Trieste. They gave us forms three months earlier asking us if we wanted to stay in Yugoslavia or leave for the West. The Yugoslavs put me in prison only for one night, because I moved from one town to another without permission. Otherwise, I was not bothered too much.

In 1954, I went to Rome to see my uncle, who was a good friend of Gaqi Goga. In 1957, I had to move into a refugee camp in Brindisi. Somehow I got to Paris in 1958 and the following year I was allowed to go to the USA.

The objective was excellent, but the methods used were bad. We had traitors in the organization. And you cannot liberate a country from the communists by sending in small groups here and there. You have to send a large group, all to one place and establish a stronghold, fight from it and defend it, using Allied air supplies. Also, we could have got guns and ammunition from sympathizers on the inside. But if the Albanian people had known that there was an ANC base somewhere, they would have flocked to join us.

* * *

[I] was born in Gostil in Luma, Albania, in October 1921. In 1944, some months before the communists took power, I was already a guerrilla fighting against them, or hiding from them. I fought and hid in the mountains of Luma and Has from 1944 to August 1946.

In August 1946, I myself and my uncle Asllan Zenel Cenaj, and many others set out on a nineteen-day march through Western Macedonia, Yugoslavia, to take refuge in Greece. The last seven days of this march were a hell of fighting and hunger and thirst. We had practically nothing to eat during those last seven days. We lost twenty-one comrades in fighting during those last seven days. Finally we arrived in Greece on September 13, 1946. I myself, my uncle, and many others, crossed the border with heavy wounds in our bodies.

From 1946 to 1949, I was in refugee camps in Greece. From March 1949 to May 1950, in refugee camps in Italy. From May 1950 to November 1950, I was in a quasi-military company in Munich, Germany.

On November 12, 1950, I was parachuted into Zarisht, Has, Albania. From December 1950, until February 1951, I lived clandestinely in Yugoslavia.

On February 17, 1951, after I was discovered by the Yugoslav police, I escaped fighting and crossed the border into Albania, in order to continue my mission for which I was parachuted into Albania.

From February 1951 to May 1951, I was in Albania trying to gather information for the National Committee for a Free Albania, and to encourage people to be ready for an uprising when the opportune time came! That time never came! My comrades and I fought in about seven or eight battles from February 1951 to May 1951 from the surroundings of Prizren to Luma, Mirdita, Has and Mat.

In May 1951, I surrendered to the Yugoslav authorities in Prizren, because it was impossible to fight any longer in Albania, and because of sickness and lack of food.

In 1954, I went to Italy as a refugee, and in 1958 to France. On May 12, 1959, I emigrated permanently to the United States of America.

When in the autumn of 1949 a National Committee for a Free Albania was formed, of which my uncle, Asllan Zenel Cenaj, was a member, our hopes for freeing Albania became suddenly rosy! We had good reasons to hope and believe, because that Committee was formed under the aegis and the support of America and Great Britain. Who could ask for better support!

In our ingenuity we thought that finally America and Great Britain wouldn't stay any longer spectators of such horrifying oppression and slaughter that were taking place in Albania and in other east European states!

We thought that finally these two great powerful democracies, who had fought a long war in order to put an end to the dictatorial form of fascist and Nazi rule and occupation, were now ready to help the unfortunate nations of Europe to have their own governments through the process of democratic elections!

When I was in the military company in Munich, Germany, I was asked: "Would you go to Albania in the name of the National Committee for a Free Albania, to gather information and possibly fight for the liberation of your country?"

"Certainly," I gladly replied. And certainly and gladly, I myself, Halil Nerguti, Miftar Planeja and Rexh Berisha, on the night of November 12, 1950, were parachuted by mistake or perhaps by design, or pity, into the forest of Zarisht, Has, Albania, instead of Dega, Malësia e Gjakovës (Highland of Gjakova). That mistake was our salvation. The

Albanian military forces were waiting for us to be dropped into Dega! And as one may guess, they must have been disappointed.

The so-called fighting material, which was supposed to be dropped close to us, was dropped in the middle of Zarisht village! Next day the communist forces were all over looking for us. We avoided them by hiding in the forest of Qarri i vogël (Little Oak) first, then in that of Vllahën.

We gave five hundred leks (the basic monetary unit of Albania) to a shepherd to give us news about the whereabouts of communist forces. We learned later that the money was false! Even the beginnings of our mission were showing signs of falsity and mistrust among the population. That money should never have been given to us. We were supposed to convey trust and truth among the people, not falsity!

On November 18, 1950, we moved to Domaj, Has, where we stayed about ten days. From about November 28 until December 8, we stayed in the forest of Cahan, Has.

The material, destined to us, having fallen into the hands of communist forces, made our every move in Albania more dangerous. So we crossed the border and we went to Yugoslavia in the night of December 10, 1950. It was a very cold night, and the snow was about one meter high, because we crossed the border at almost the highest point of Mount Pashtrik, Has.

After we crossed the border we stayed for a while in the forest of Planeja village in order to get in touch with the Albanian refugees in Yugoslavia. By that time, when Yugoslavia was expelled from the Cominform, thousands of Albanians from Albania took refuge in Yugoslavia, where many of them were beaten to death, killed or jailed until they died.

On December 19, 1950, we met in Dobrushta village, Prizren, Yugoslavia, with some of these refugees, friends or relatives of ours, that is with Hysen Nerguti, brother of Halil Nerguti, a member of our parachuted group of four, with Ramadan Voka, now living in West Germany, and with Hysen Muja. We asked them to find for us a place to live in hiding during the winter, since we had no intention to surrender to the Yugoslav police (UDB). In the springtime we intended to return to Albania in order to continue our mission.

The Albanian refugees in Yugoslavia thought that we were important people, since we were sent into Albania by the British and Americans!

On December 27, 1950, the whole group of ours—that is, I, Ramadan Cenaj, Rexh Berisha, Hysen Nerguti, Miftar Planeja—went to the house of Hysen Muja, Prizren, with the intention to spend the winter there.

Sometime during February or January of 1951 we must have been discovered by the Yugoslav police, but they must have kept secret watch on us in order to know what we were doing or intended to do!

On February 17, 1951, we decided to quit Prizren; we were afraid to stay any longer; we decided to go to Albania to continue our mission, this time also with the help of some friends and relatives of ours who had escaped from Albania when Yugoslavia had been expelled from the Cominform.

During the night of February 17, after having been divided into two groups, I myself, Halil Nerguti, Miftar Maloki, Rexh Berisha, Shahin Domi, Zenel Gjuta, Brahim Iljaz Shehi, Ramadan Voka, Ahmet Nika, Zef Shyti, Hysen Voka, Hysen Nerguti, Hysen Muja,

Pjetër Gjikola, Gjin Arapi, Llesh Lufi and Tefik Palushi left Prizren heading for Albania.

We had to fight in order to escape; we fought in many different places: at Trepetnica, a village close to Prizren, at Vlashën, at the Bridge of Vlashën, at the village of Billusha, at the Liqeni i Kuq (Red Lake), Zhur, and close to the Albanian border. All these battles were fought between February 21 and 23. Finally, just before the dawn of February 17, 1951, we crossed the border at Koritnik and entered Albania.

Unfortunately, our suffering and fights were not over. The Albanian military forces had been aware that something was happening close to their border. However, we saw them at a distance and we avoided them.

We reached the house of a friend of ours in Përbreg, Luma, Albania, where we had food, rest, warmth and hospitableness. This friend of ours gave us important information about the location of military forces in Luma.

We learned from our friend in Përbreg that bread was rationed and the economic situation was very bad. We saw with our own eyes people being dressed in rags, and we could clearly see in their faces that they were frightened and terrorized. Many families were in concentration camps, where many were dying, mostly children and old people; and many others were in prisons. A brother of mine, by name Hysni, was in jail.

When we went into Albania, we used to tell people that we have been sent by the National Committee for a Free Albania, and that America and Great Britain are helping us in this fight against communism.

We learned that leaflets dropped by planes were read with high hopes. But the voice of the radio was ineffective. People had no radios.

At the beginning we were well received. Later on, the enthusiasm and the hopes were quickly vanishing. Words were not followed by deeds! No help was being sent by America and Great Britain.

While I was in Luma, in Has, or in other places, I myself, and my comrades tried to spread the net of information through the many friends and relatives of ours. All this net of friends and relatives was of no avail. No one came to our help! No one sent fighting material, food, clothing, money! No one!

People used to mock us: "Where are your English and American friends? Still up in the sky?" We really didn't need any teasing. We ourselves were wondering, are we really material to be dumped out? Material for nothing?

Before 1944, in Luma and Has, there were very few communists. After their victory, they spread the net of claws in every field of life.

Spying on each other became common even among members of one's own family! And teachers were asked to get information through the schoolchildren. The old family ties that had kept Albanian society together were ridiculed and dismantled!

At the time when I was in Albania during the spring of 1951, the shepherds were especially dangerous for the freedom fighters. They were asked and forced to report every movement they could notice or see in the mountains. If they failed to do so, they could pay with concentration camps, jails or even their lives!

Terror, a bullet in the head, hunger, spying, kept and keep the communist government firmly in the seat. The Albanian communist government knew beforehand in what location the freedom fighters are to be dropped. It was easy for the communist forces to surround them, to catch or to kill them.

At the time we were parachuted in, we had no suspicion that we were being betrayed. Who was giving information to the communists that we were to be parachuted in? Terror, killing, beating, jailing, concentration camps, fear of being spied upon even by a member of your own family, kept people their distance from the freedom fighters. Only those who have lived under the communist rule will understand how effective communist terror was. The communists do not use halfhearted means to combat their opponents. Every opponent is an enemy.

The failure of the freedom fighters was playing into the hands of the communist government. People were discouraged to the point that they thought there was no force to dislodge the communist government from Albania. And indeed no real communist government has been overthrown since 1917, except that of Bela Kun in Hungary in 1919.

When I was in Albania in 1951, I was told that the best time to overthrow the communist government was in 1948 when Yugoslavia was expelled from the Cominform. By that time, the communist government of Albania was completely disconcerted.

Besides our group of four, another group was parachuted in—that of Adem Gjura. Pursuant to the orders we had received before being parachuted, I tried to get in touch with Adem, but it was impossible. Adem Gjura, too, was parachuted by mistake into a different location. This mistake was his salvation as it was ours before him. In the group of Adem Gjura were Selim Daci, Salih Dalliu, Xhetan Daci and Iljaz Toptani. When they were parachuted in, as I learned later, Iljaz Toptani lost contact with his comrades. He was betrayed by the person he was staying with, and was wounded in fighting with communist forces, but before surrendering, he burned everything important.

Adem Gjura and his friends were discovered in Martanesh, and fought as best as they could. One of his comrades, Xhetan Daci, was lost, and nobody knew his whereabouts. Selim Daci surrendered, and only Adem and Salih Dalliu were able to escape. Adem then went to his house in Reç, Dibra. He was surrounded by military forces and lost four members of his family and his relatives. After this tragedy, he escaped and crossed the border into Yugoslavia, where he was tortured to the point that he almost went insane. The effect of his being tortured by the Yugoslav police can be seen even today. Adem is now living in Brooklyn, New York.

Sometime during March 1951, my feet were frostbitten, and I was in danger of losing them and dying; fortunately I knew that you should not put your frozen feet in warm water, because the flesh could be lacerated quickly piece by piece. That knowledge saved my feet and my life.

As if it were not enough to have fought so often in so many places from the vicinity of Prizren, Yugoslavia, to Has, Luma and Mirdita, and to have suffered hunger so many times for long days; to have undergone a very cold winter, and to have had frostbite, I got sick with dysentery which sapped my energy to a dangerous point. Despite the dysentery, I had again to fight many times in the forests of Sheba, Mirdita. Our host, a certain Gjok Ndoi, had informed the police where we were. One of our comrades, Kol Tosku, was wounded and next day he was killed fighting. Ndue Gjergji was killed with him. I do not know how many communists were killed. These battles took place in April 1951.

```
I quajturi    SELIM   DACI
i dërguar me misjon te posacem nga Komiteti Kombetar i Shqiperia
e Lire.

    Kerkohet prej cdo shqipetari qe t'a plotesoje detyren
patriotike kundrejt ketij Ushtari te Shqiperis se Lire dyke
i ardhur ne ndihme ne cdo menyre ne rast nevoje per te kryer
misjonin e tij te n lte kombetor: per Shqiperi, per Liri, per
Flamurin Kuq e Zi.
```

                                    Zef PALI

                                    Said KRYEZIU

                                    Gaqo GOGH

Selim Daci's identification paper for his mission in Albania. It reads: "Selim Daci has been sent on a special mission by the National Committee for a Free Albania. All Albanians are asked to fulfil their patriotic duties towards this Soldier of Free Albania by assisting him in any manner according to his needs so that he can fulfil his lofty national mission for Albania, for Freedom and for the Red and Black Flag. Signed: Zef Pali, Said Kryeziu, Gaqo Gogh. National Committee for a Free Albania"

Gjin Arapi and Pjetër Gjikola, although freedom fighters and comrades of ours, had got in touch with communist forces, collaborated with them and received orders to kill me and my comrades! As a consequence of the treachery, the communist forces learned of the whereabouts of Hysen Voka, who by that time was sick, and captured him.

I think there is no deeper discouragement than to be betrayed by your own comrades, with whom you shared suffering, battles, and above all, the joys of a free man fighting for the freedom of others.

As one may see, I didn't always have the same people in my group, due to the losses we suffered in so many different fights; but, most of the time we managed to fill the losses with other freedom fighters who were operating in the mountains independently from the National Committee. In the middle of April 1951, I had these people with me: Pjetër Kadeli, now living in New York, Gjergj Koka, Zef Shyti, Ramadan Voka, now in West Germany, Ahmet Nika, later killed, Llesh Lufi.

I will never forget Zenel Gjuta and Brahim Iljaz Shehi from Shtiqën, Luma, Albania, who, although refugees in Yugoslavia, joined our group of four, to operate in Albania, and gave their lives fighting in Luma, a region that particularly hated the communist regime, on 24 March 1951. Our fatherland and all those people who believe in freedom should remember and revere all those courageous freedom fighters.

After about four long and terrible months in the mountains of Albania, deprived of food, clothing, fighting material, often being sick, it became impossible for me and my comrades to continue fighting any longer in Albania. So I, and some of my friends, thought it would be better to surrender to a non-communist country. The only non-communist country was Greece. Unfortunately, one of my friends, Zef Shyti, fell sick; so our plan was discarded as it was unfeasible for a sick man to travel from Luma to Greece.

We had no other choice but Yugoslavia. In time of necessity one knocks at every door. We surrendered to the Yugoslavs in early May 1951. Halil Nerguti, Miftar Maloki, Rexh Berisha, Ramadan Voka, Ahmet Nika, Hysen Nerguti, Hysen Muja, Tefik Palushi, Ali Muja, Shahin Domi and others had already surrendered.

Rightly or wrongly, we later had the impression that we were parachuted into Albania for propaganda purposes or for reasons beyond our earthly comprehension! One does not parachute people in at the start of winter. One does not dump people and leave them without fighting material. One should keep in touch with one's poor fighters and provide them with food, fighting material, clothing, medicines, money, real money!

But we never questioned the honesty of our visible or invisible superiors! We blindly believed in their words and actions.

Interview conducted August 8, 1983

TERENCE COOLING

Terence Cooling was a British military figure recruited by MI6 in the summer of 1949 for the Albanian operation to train the Albanian fighters in Malta. He accompanied them by boat to the Albanian coast.

Originally we were not taken on to do the drops. Darby Allen and I were recruited to teach the Albanians how to shoot. We were both in the Marines during the war, involved in what is now called the Special Boat Squadron. After I was discharged in early 1949, I got a letter from the Royal Marines Association in Paddington asking me to go to the War Office for an interview. The unit was called the Royal Marine Boat Patrol Detachment and was under Colonel "Bunny" Hasler. They went up the Gironde River near Bordeaux in the war and sunk enemy boats. I was demobbed in May 1949 after serving 13 years.

After the war I worked a bit with people from the "firm" at Fort Monkton near Portsmouth. I had training runs with them, practicing rowing men ashore and landing them on the beach. This was in 1948 and we knew that something was in the wind, but we could have been training for anything. I was with Lieutenant Peter Davies, who later commanded the SBS at Poole. We just landed these men, British people from MI6, at

West Wittering to give them the feel of being landed on a beach. On another occasion we took them out in canoes from Hurstpoint (?). I remember telling Davies that they didn't do it very well and that they were liable to do a bad job if ever they were in the field. This was shortly before I was demobbed. I was 30 years old and I was a sergeant.

When I first met the MI6 people, they told Darby and me that they had a project on and needed some people trained in boat work. They told us that we were going to have to work at an old fort in Malta miles out of the way. They told us that we'd be looked after by young national servicemen from the intelligence corps. They were roped in as the camp staff. To be frank, they were rather conned into the job, because they thought it was going to be glamorous and in fact it was very boring menial work. They had a rotten deal.

They offered me a contract for 12 months in the first instance at a salary of £350 a year all round. It was a bit more than I was getting as a sergeant in the Marines. It seemed reasonable at the time, but then we discovered that the sergeants on cipher work were getting £450 a year. So was Bill Collins, the radio operator who had been with Smiley in Burmah. All the officers and senior people like that lived "ashore," leaving us junior people in barracks in the fort. It was very like something out of *Upstairs Downstairs*.

We flew out to Malta from London towards the end of August. It was the two cipher clerks, Darby Allen, and I on an ordinary commercial flight from Northolt airport. Conditions were pretty rough at the fort. The food was rubbish. There was a little mess room, a sort of sergeant's mess, in one of the fort's buildings for Allen, Ned Kelly, the two cipher clerks and me. The national servicemen lived in another building and the Albanians in a huge barrack room somewhere else. The officers were ashore. So we were four groups.

John Topliss was nicknamed "ToJo." He was a little man with a little moustache and glasses. He was in charge of stores. I only met Ron Little once. That was at Smiley's house. He started inviting everyone to dinner in order of seniority, but when he got down to Darby and me he invited us to lunch. I'm not quite sure what the significance of that distinction was. I liked "Doc" Zaehner. We used to play crib and backgammon together. I could never understand what his job was, but I'm sure he was bloody good at it. He got on very well with the Albanians, too, and they certainly didn't like the big Yankee chap who came over. One of the problems with him was that he spoke an American sort of Albanian and they could hardly understand him. He had been a lieutenant commander in the U.S. Navy. He had commanded a "P-boat" in the Pacific. He was always talking about his "P-boat." It made us laugh. I cannot remember that anyone was in charge of the fort after the training finished for the day and all the officers pushed off to their houses and hotels. It seemed a very loose arrangement.

The basic system was that Smiley was in charge of the whole operation. "Q" Howard was in charge of the fort. And Alastair Grant was assistant to Rollo Young, the MI6 man on the spot. We took the "pixies" out, did a bit of shooting with them, took them swimming, took them for a run to Como, the island between Malta and Gozo. We had dummy runs and dummy landings. It got them used to climbing in and out of boats. They were men from valleys and I don't think any of them had ever seen a boat.

If I am landing you from a boat, then I'll be the one to jump in the water and I'll carry you ashore, to make sure that you land dry shod. I can even keep my boots on if I want to, because I'm not going anywhere. My job was going to be to piggyback them ashore, to make sure they didn't start on their first night's march going squelch, squelch.

Rollo Young told me that the Italians and Greeks had tried landings in Albania a bit earlier and their parties had been shot up on the beaches. So there was not going to be time for the men to take their boots and socks off before wading ashore. We had to move as quickly as possible. While I was landing them, the other boat with Darby was going to lie a bit offshore to give us cover in case anything went wrong,

When we were training them, we were supposed to operate through one of the Albanians who spoke a bit of English. Usually though, I told Darby to do something, he did it and then they followed his example. It was quicker that way and easier. They were friendly enough. You could skylark about with them. The only problem was that we couldn't understand a word they were saying.

I didn't think that they were the right sort of men for a job like that. They weren't the commando type. I was told though that they were not going to have to fight. They would just make their way home, merge in with their local community and prepare the way for larger groups. I remember worrying about them going into the field, but then thinking to myself that they were all displaced persons, they had no country, no work, nothing much to lose. Still, I thought, they should have had someone with them, an officer or a leader of some sort, someone to keep them together. I was told that they would elect their own leader, that a leader would naturally emerge quite soon after they landed on the beaches.

It was Rollo Young who asked us to row the "pixies" ashore and he put us in touch with Leatham and Barclay. We were a very good team. They were excellent seamen. We used to embark them on an MFV in a little rocky bay just below Ghain Tafiyor Bay near the fort. They just climbed from the rocks of this little bay into dinghies and we rowed them out to the MFV. The MFV was commanded by a sub-lieutenant, with a stoker petty officer to look after the engine and four other men. Darby and I went there the first time with the nine "pixies."

Rollo Young allowed me to take photos, but he wouldn't let me have them developed ashore. He sent them back to London, where they kept the negatives just let me have a few prints without any Albanians in them.

The transfer took place at sea. We just came alongside the *Stormie Seas* and got on board, got straight in and off we went; Darby, John, Sam and I shared watches.

We had two boats to do the run in. I took the first boat with the men, five the first time and four the second time. Darby came second with the gear. I remember there were a lot of tins of butter. It took us a long time to get to the land. We seemed to take all night over it. They must have stopped more than a mile off shore. Eventually, we got back and asked Sam to come in a bit closer, which they did. On the way back the second time we could see the boat from a long way off. There was Mediterranean lightning flashing on the rigging.

We pulled steadily, but we would only be doing three knots. So the first time it took a good hour there and back. We had to be strong and fit and know how to row a boat, slowly and steadily. We made our way in and at first all we could see was a steep cliff and we couldn't imagine where we'd be able to set them down. It was only when we got close that we spotted an inlet. As we went up it, there was a great boulder overhanging us. I remember thinking that if there was a guard up there we'd have stood no chance. It got very narrow and then opened up a bit onto a little sandy beach. I rowed the boat onto the beach and piggybacked the men ashore. Then Darby came alongside and we both passed the gear across. We said something like, "See you in a minute." Then we rowed back to get the other four.

It took us half an hour to get back to the *Stormie Seas*. We told Sam that he was a long way off and he said OK, he'd come a bit further in. We were rowing towards land the second time when the "pixies" started pointing to the top of the cliff. They were very excited, they thought they could see a light there. Of course, I was rowing with my back to the shore and by the time I turned round it had gone, if it was ever there. Anyway, we carried on until we had all nine of them on the beach with their gear. We shook hands and said goodbye.

We pulled away and five minutes from shore I realized that with all the fuss of getting the men ashore, I'd left my submachine gun leaning against a rock. So I said to Darby, "I've got to go back and get it." I rowed back and, to my surprise, the nine men were still there, just standing and waiting, not quite knowing what to do. I grabbed my submachine gun and motioned to the men to get moving, to get inland.

On the way back Darby and I were transferred to the MFV again and we were taken back to Malta. The second drop took place a few days later. Rollo Young got a bollocking from his MI6 bosses. They said he shouldn't have been there. A man of his rank was not supposed to go behind enemy lines. He knew quite a lot and they would have screwed it out of him. The normal rule is that MI6 men of that type don't go into the field.

We were sent a letter, Darby and I, telling us to come to St. James's Park station, to wait outside until we were contacted. A little man, who later turned out to be a major, came up to me and said, "Lofty Cooling?" I said yes and we went straight across the road into a cafe.

We sat down at a table with the two cipher clerks and Jessica Aldiss. They gave us instructions about how to get to Malta, how to get kitted out in Pioneer Corps uniform, and they gave the four of us ten pounds each.

Then it turned out that they had forgotten something and the major said, "I'll nip back to the office and get it." But Jessica was smart. She said, "It'll take you a long time." The major then realized what he'd said and carried on, "Ah, yes, well, I'll take a taxi." In fact, of course the "office" was just next door.

The second operation was better organized. We'd only just about got clear of the north of Malta when Sam and John were alongside. The MFV skipper was a bit upset about our being too close to Malta. We might have been spotted. Anyway, we got ourselves and the gear and the "pixies" into the *Stormie Seas* and that was it.

The landing was a lot smoother, too. It was onto a beach with some woods nearby and we were in and out in less than an hour. Our only problem was that the "pixies" were seasick going across. And so was Ned Kelly, the radio operator. He was a nice young chap. He looked like a ballet dancer. You can see him in the picture, not looking very happy, where we were drying all our gear out on the handrails. Everything got wet because the ship was full of water. It was a hell of a storm.

The timing of the landings was influenced by the moon. Zaehner had all the charts and he worked it out. We wanted as little moon as possible. And if there was a moon that night, we wanted to finish the drop before it rose. In fact it wasn't too bad because the moon rose in the southeast, the other side of the landing beach. If the moon had risen in the west over the sea, it would have been easy to spot us from the land.

After the last landing, we had to put into the Gulf south of Vlora. I remember the island hanging over the entrance to the Gulf like a great sugar loaf. There were only Sam, John, Gregory, Eileen, Darby, Ned Kelly and I on board. So we were "clean" really, though if they'd boarded us, I daresay they'd have found plenty to rouse their suspicions. Kelly had been so ill that he hadn't sent out any radio messages. He was behind schedule. So as soon as we got inside the Gulf and the boat stopped rolling, he felt better and started sending messages. That's what we were doing down below when the shooting started. I was down in the cockpit with Kelly. He was getting ready to send his Morse signals, to let them know in Corfu that we had landed the men safely. All I knew about it was a lot of yelling on deck with John shouting in Greek, giving the Albanian guards a story. They saw two of the Albanians lying down on the shore and Darby said, "They've got a light machine-gun." Gregory suddenly dived into the cockpit, ducked down and grabbed the tiller. Sam dashed for the controls. The engine roared to life. John cut the anchor rope with a knife. The boat began to surge forward and we heard a put-put-put of machine-gun bullets flying overhead. No one was hit. The only casualty was Kelly who was half dead with seasickness.

The wind died down a bit. Kelly started feeling better again and he said he felt hungry, so I said, "Why don't you have an egg?" Sam kept a bucketful of hard-boiled eggs just in case anyone was hungry during a busy time. Kelly grabbed an egg, only he took it not from the bucket but from the store of raw eggs, so when he cracked it on his knee, the whole thing fell apart and trickled all over his shorts. And that was enough to set him puking again. Kelly had replaced Rollo Young, who did the radio work on the first trip.

The "pixies" looked very strange after they trickled back to Malta through Greece. As soon as they got into Albania they started growing moustaches. And when they got to Greece they all had their heads shaved. They were a bit subdued and to tell you the truth, so were we. We all felt we'd put so much effort into it and got no result. After that we saw even less of them than before. They hid themselves away. After the day's training they just went and stayed in their barrack room. We'd hear them singing, but we never saw them. No one seemed to know what to do with them. Rollo Young even told me that they were thinking of sticking them on one of the forts in the Solent.

We came back to London at the end of 1949 and they paid us off, even though we had half our contract left to run. We came home on a troop ship to Liverpool. We had a number to ring and it was arranged for us to meet Jessica Aldiss and Rollo Young in a dive bar near Victoria station. They told us basically that they had no more use for us. We reminded them that we were under contract for a year but they said they knew nothing about that. Of course there was nothing in writing. Eventually they agreed to give us a "bonus." It was £97—why £97 I don't know—all in £1 notes. It wasn't what we'd agreed, but I didn't complain. I went back to Devon where I was living at that time.

Then suddenly around May or June 1950 I got a letter out of the blue saying that they'd like to keep me on the strength and pay me a retainer. They enclosed a check for £20. I took it, even though I knew it meant that I was liable to be called up for duty. And I reckoned they would call me up, because those boys don't send you checks for £20 without having something in mind. They weren't just going to keep me on the "on call" list till I was 90.

Interview conducted August 25, 1984

Ramazan Dalipi

Ramazan Dalipi was an Albanian anticommunist fighter from Macedonia. After World War II, he was in a refugee camp in Greece and later, from March 1949, in southern Italy. In July 1950, he was sent to Bavaria by the American army for guard duties and later for military training, and was parachuted into eastern Albania, between Luma and Dibra, in October 1951. He only survived a few days in Albania, before escaping to Macedonia in order to get back to his home in Kërçova. From there, he crossed over into Greece and in March 1952 was sent back to Bavaria by the Americans, where he served for five years (1952–1957) in Company 4000.

I was with Hysen Salku's group which went into Albania on October 15, 1951. We were parachuted between Luma and Dibra: Hajrulla Tërpeza, Hysen Bajrami, Hysen Salku, Ramazan Dalipi, Hakik Abdullah. Three of us were from Kosovo, Salku from Albania and I was from Macedonia. Both Salku's legs were broken when he landed. We then tried to collect our equipment, but some we could not because it was hanging from the trees. Then during the early morning of October 16, around 6 a.m., we were attacked in the hills. We had not moved more than 500 yards from where we landed, because Salku could not walk, they just carried him a little way. Salku and Bajrami were killed. A bullet went through my clothes. I don't know how big the enemy force was, but there were machine guns and mortars. They must have been waiting for us. They were in action against us so quickly.

The three of us escaped and it took us four days to cross the border and three days to get to my home in Kërçova, Macedonia. We got some bread there and then made for Greece, three or four days away. We crossed into Greece on October 31. We had to leave, because we did not know the country, we were all from Yugoslavia. Only Salku was from Albania.

We were interviewed by the Greeks and then turned over to the Americans, who took us to a house near Athens. In March 1952 we were taken to Munich, where we spent five years in Company 4000. We left the company in 1957. We did no more training in this five-year period.

In March 1949 I came to Italy from Greece, to Santa Fara, hoping to emigrate to

Canada or Australia. There was no U.S. immigration quota then. But Italy took us only for a year, on the understanding that we would find somewhere else to go, then they asked us to go back to Greece. So we contacted the NAC and registered with them. And then the committee sent us to Germany. No one told us about any expedition to Albania, although I heard rumors about it in Santa Fara. We were just told it was a labor battalion.

We got to Germany on July 12, 1950, by ordinary train from Bari to Munich. They put us to work guarding depots. We were sent to the training school in August 1951. I was told it was at Garmisch, near the Austrian border. There was a big library and there were twenty of us there. Two of the instructors spoke Albanian. One of the instructors gave me a knife and I asked me to attack him. But I didn't even try. I knew he'd take it away from me. Albanians aren't used to knives. We use guns. They gave us vitamin pills and we were trained for two months. It was not enough. The training did not cover enough aspects. We asked for parachute training, but the Americans refused, they said one of us might break a leg. I said, "I'd rather break a leg here than in Albania." Anyway, we got no parachute training, only jumping from a 10-foot height onto a sawdust-covered floor. And we were advised not to land on our heels. It was completely wrong, this training.

Interview conducted August 1, 1983

Sali Daliu

Sali Daliu was an Albanian anticommunist fighter. He escaped from Albania and was in a refugee camp in Greece in 1946. He was recruited for the Albanian mission, given military training in Bavaria in the spring of 1949, and was parachuted into the Dibra region of eastern Albania in late 1950. After many problems, he crossed over to Yugoslavia with Adem Gjura.

At the training school they taught us how to get close into the enemy, how to parachute, how to land, how to fire the machine guns, both American and German. Conditions were good. There was a friendly relationship between instructor and trainee. They didn't shout at us, they explained things to us. What counted for me was to have the chance of doing something for my country with my friends, for instance with Adem Gjura, whom I had met in 1946 in a refugee camp in Greece; I respected him very much as a soldier, a patriot.

We arrived in Greece in two groups, one from the north of Albania, the other from the south. The group from the south refused to go. They were afraid. They stayed in Athens and I have no idea what happened to them. Their leader's name was Sadiq.

We stayed in a big house in or near Athens for longer than a week. I remember a long corridor with rooms on either side of it where we slept three to a room. We never went out of the house. We spent our time together waiting and talking about what was going to happen.

Company 4000 in Bavaria, around 1952.

One evening they took nine of us to an airport in a closed truck. The aircraft had no number on it and it was painted white all over. We got on board around ten or eleven o'clock and flew off towards Albania. I remember asking Gaqi Goga before we left whether this was a true mission of patriotism. He assured us that it was and we felt much stronger as a result.

I had no idea that the crew were Polish. Our orders were not to talk to anyone about our mission and that applied to the crew as well. We just knew that they were friends.

Our orders were to parachute at a place called Kaptinë Martaneshi. It means the plain of Martanesh. British and American agents parachuted there during the war. But we couldn't land there this time because it was blocked by the communists. So we turned round and went back to Greece to check if anything had gone wrong. Then we stayed six more days in the same place and set off again. Again we found that the plain of Martanesh was blocked.

They asked us whether we wanted to jump or to go back to Greece again. We decided to jump in another place. We found a place called Moet (?) Allamanit, a wooded and hilly area in Dibra, about 60–70 kilometers from Martanesh.

When we jumped, the air pressure threw us upwards. I remember looking down and watching the aircraft make a circle below us. Halil Nerguti jumped in a place nearer Martanesh where he had friends and family.

I was with Adem Gjura, Selim Daci, Xhetan Daci and Iliaz Toptani. We tried to find one another, but after an hour or so there were only four of us. Toptani seemed to have disappeared. We found each other using passwords and signals in the dark. But it seems that we had been spotted already by the communists.

We stayed together in the forest, the four of us, until the afternoon of the next day. We spent the morning eating some of our rations and trying to work out what to do. At a point in the early afternoon we felt that we were surrounded.

We never found any of our equipment. It was meant to have been thrown out of the plane with us, but it must have been dropped in a different place. I suppose they did not know where to throw the equipment out, since we jumped in a spot that had not been arranged beforehand. We had a machine gun each, ammunition, grenades, some food and water and a few aspirins each.

We saw some civilians coming towards us and some soldiers following them. They crawled up close to us, then they stood up and someone shouted, "Surrender, we've got you surrounded," We quickly decided that we would not surrender, that we would make a break for it and that anyone who got away would meet up with the others on a certain hill a few kilometers distant. Then we stood up and walked towards the men as if we were surrendering. Suddenly we made a dash for it. Two ran to the left and two to the right. After that moment we never saw Selim Daci or Xhetan Daci again, Adem Gjura and I ran together. We had no idea whether the two Dacis had surrendered or whether they had been killed.

Gjura was not well. I think that the change in pressure when he parachuted caused him to have a severe headache. And when we ran away he was wounded in the leg, too. And when we ran, we really didn't know where we were. We marched this way and that way looking for landmarks. We moved about for two or three weeks hoping to find allies and somehow to continue our mission. We marched during the night only and found a corner to hide in during the day.

Gjura was walking with difficulty because of his wound. He had to stop and rest every now and again. But he was determined to carry on and get through somehow. When we found an isolated house, we went in and asked for bread and salt. We didn't demand anything. We asked politely. And we only asked for bread and salt. And we paid for that. Every time we gave a gold Napoleon. I had 50 gold Napoleons. I think that Adem Gjura had more, since he was the group leader.

We told the people in the houses that we were communist partisans, but they didn't believe us. Usually they said, "No, you're not partisans, you're the men that the partisans are looking for. Leave us as quickly as possible and don't come back."

After a week on the run we got to the outskirts of Elbasan and then we realized where we were. It was there that we met a man who was very kind to us and looked after us for two weeks. After that we decided that we had to escape into Yugoslavia and we made off towards the frontier, stopping eventually in a house not far from it. The owner of the house wanted to give us away to the communists, so we told him that we were going to stay for a week to reassure him, and in fact we left that evening. We found a local man and gave him 28 gold Napoleons to take us across the frontier.

The Yugoslavs put us in prison for three months in Skopje and then sent us to Kosovo.

Interview conducted in Brussels April 26, 1984

RODNEY DENNYS

Rodney Onslow Dennys (1911–1993) was a British intelligence officer. He was of a Devon family, worked for the Foreign Office from 1940 and was in the intelligence corps from 1941 to 1947. After World War II, he was a senior SIS officer in Turkey and Paris (1948) and was subsequently involved in the Albanian operation. He shared a room with Kim Philby for six months.

We are more squeamish nowadays than people were in the Middle Ages. I believe that subversion and encouragement to rebel are extensions of diplomacy and therefore quite legitimate courses of action for a government, if carried out with the aim of protecting the population.

I was stationed in the Canal Zone from January 1948 to 1951. Then I was posted to Istanbul, succeeding at one remove Kim Philby. I was told about the Albanian operation only in very general terms. I knew none of the details. But I suspect that it fell down through poor intelligence and poor planning. I wonder, for instance, how old the intelligence was and whether it was based on fact or wishful thinking, provided mainly by émigrés who always assume that they would be welcomed back home as their country's rulers. Émigrés have few people to talk to and you cannot trust them not to gossip.

Kim would not have heard much about the operation while in Istanbul, but when he came back to London on his way to Washington he would have been filled in about it in some detail, especially since CIA were involved. The Albanian operation was something that he needed to know.

The operation smacked of World War II. It was the dying twitches of SOE. It was a case where, momentarily, SOE came back into its own, since it involved agents in the field and it involved the Balkans, an area where they had more expertise than any intelligence outfit in the world.

It was like Bonnie Prince Charlie coming home to raise the clans. In fact what happened was that some of the clans rose and others didn't, so that Charlie was defeated at the Battle of Culloden. If, on the other hand, the French had put their own troops ashore with their prince, then maybe they would have achieved their objective. But they didn't want to take that risk. It goes to show that, if you're going to interfere in the internal affairs of another country, you ought not to do it in a halfhearted way.

The marriage between SIS and SOE, though a shotgun marriage, went quite smoothly. Everyone in the secret world knew that all services were going to be cutback drastically after the war, so there were not too many people who elected to stay on.

Parachute drops were not really suitable in the Albanian case. Aircraft make too much noise. In wartime there are plenty of aircraft all over the place. The only question then is whether it's one of ours or one of theirs. But in peacetime a plane flying over a deserted area at night sticks out a mile. Small boats made much more sense. They make no noise and they don't show up on radar.

Interview conducted June 30, 1983

LAWRENCE DE NEUFVILLE

Lawrence de Neufville (ca. 1913–1998) was an American intelligence officer from Hartford, Connecticut. As a CIA agent, he worked for the United States Office of Policy Coordination (OPC) under John McCloy, the military governor of the American zone of occupied Germany after World War II. He designed the labor battalions, under the cover of which the Albanian refugees went to Germany for military training.

I worked as special adviser to John McCloy in Frankfurt. He was the United States high commissioner in Germany and I was OPC's "ambassador" to him. Ben Shute was McCloy's chief of intelligence, my boss, and my job was basically to protect McCloy from diplomatic embarrassment. Alan Gerhart was McCloy's chef de cabinet and Al Lightner was his State Department adviser, only he didn't want to know anything about anything. Roland Dulin was the CIA man at army headquarters in Heidelberg. I remember that he used his passport as a notebook and had problems because of that.

I was the one who invented the idea of the labor battalion and I cleared it through Gerhart. The Albanian battalion was the only one about which there was anything mysterious. It was designed to disguise the trainees and one of the conditions laid down by McCloy was that once they left Germany they would never be allowed back. He was afraid that they might come back to Germany and talk about what they had done in the field. This would have been very embarrassing.

There was an occasion when this condition was broken. A team of Albanians under the command of Alex Alexandrov, a Russian, flew off to Greece from Rhein-Main airport (Frankfurt), but when they got to Athens, Burke wasn't able to get them admitted. The right Greek liaison officer was not there to meet them, or something like that. Anyway, they had to fly right back to Germany and this was a breach of McCloy's conditions. And it was very embarrassing to me. I complained about it to OPC in Washington and Yatsevitch came over to apologize to McCloy personally. It was my job to protect McCloy from that sort of problem.

Interview conducted June 11, 1984

JANI DILO

Jani Dilo (b. ca. 1911) was an Albanian anticommunist fighter. He had studied law, and spoke French and Italian. He escaped from communist Albania at the end of World War II. He was recruited for the Albanian operation and worked for it as an interpreter in Corfu and Malta. He later settled in New York.

I first met Smiley and Billy McLean in July 1943 near Korça. Later we had a meeting with Hoxha there and all the communist leaders. Hoxha was in my class at school. We were in school eight years together. I am from Shepër near Gjirokastra. McLean was in Shepër and he met my father there. My father was an Albanian teacher. Mehmet Shehu and Koçi Xoxe were at the meeting with Hoxha. McLean was there and two other Albanians, one of whom is dead and the other in an Albanian prison. He was a judge called Kapshtica (?). I left Albania with the leader of the party of Midhat Frashëri on November 25, 1944.

After that I stayed in a camp for displaced persons near Brindisi. We had about 100 Albanians in a camp at Santa Maria di Luca (?), Balli Kombëtar and Zogists. We stayed about two months there. There was a moment when they had it in mind to give Midhat Frashëri and Ali Këlcyra back to Hoxha as war criminals. Then I went to study in Turin at law school. In two years I finished law school. I stayed there until Midhat Frashëri went to see his sister in Istanbul, made contact with British and American intelligence, then came to see me in Turin and told me the story.

Frashëri told me that we had to "create an Albanian army." He was the son of Abdyl Frashëri, who was the father of Albanian nationalism. He was the man who created in 1878 the big national meeting against the Serbs in Prizren, a small town in Serbia. This was in June 1949. In July I went to Malta. But it was against my better judgment; it was just to please Frashëri, because I respected him as the leader of all Albania. I was skeptical all along.

The British gave me a document with a false name and flew me from Rome to Malta. I was very surprised with the setup there. They treated the men very well. There were 22 or 26 men. I had a room in the fort and so did the American John Papajani. He lives in Seattle now. He left Albania when he was three years old, but he still speaks Albanian well. He was a state senator and now he is retired.

I was giving instruction for self-defense and intelligence. I spoke only French and Italian. The British gave us very good conditions, treated us like friends, which means a lot to an Albanian. British officers talked to the boys, went for walks with them. It was like a family. I was teaching in a classroom with a blackboard, two or three hours a day, telling them where to go, whom to meet, what to say, because I know Albania. I didn't do any radio or weapon training. That was done by the British people and Papajani.

The Albanians came to Malta on June 1, two or three people. There were about 22 by the time I got to Malta at the end of July. The first party left for Albania in the early days of October. I know that because Midhat Frashëri died here in New York on October 3. They knew that before the boys went. But they didn't tell them. They kept it secret so as not to depress them. I was told about Frashëri's death only after the boys had gone.

The head of British intelligence in Malta was the brother of a senior minister in the Labour government, perhaps minister of aviation. All the people in Malta in 1949 were Balli Kombëtar. Ermenji was a history teacher in the Korça lycee. He came to Malta towards the end. Two groups of eight people each were sent in the first landing, eight to Vlora and eight to a spot further north.

I was the first one to make contact with the boys in Albania, after about ten days. They came on the air from the Berat mountains and Korça, saying that the authorities knew everything about them, that three of them had been killed. They were so scared. The villagers were saying to them, "Why are you doing these things? Everyone knows that you are here." All the villagers would do was to give them a little food and ask them to leave Albania. "We are in danger and you are in danger," they told them.

I thought that it must be because we Albanians are so divided. Information must have leaked from our side. I could not imagine that any member of British intelligence was giving them away.

Abas Ermenji is from Tomorica, a district of Berat, near Skrapar. I talked about it to Papajani at the time. I said, "There is something wrong. Is it with us or with you?" This is why I refused to take part in the operation later on, in Germany and other places. It was suicide. I helped bring the ones who escaped back to Malta through Athens. Recently two of them, Gaba and Butka, committed suicide in the United States, in New York and Detroit. Three or four of the first group were killed during the fighting. None was taken prisoner. They would have killed themselves rather than be taken prisoner. Two of those killed were cousins called Lepenica.

On December 31, 1949, I left for Rome and the following July 7 I came to the United States. My brother had been here for a year already. Before that, I spent a little time in Malta interrogating the survivors and preparing a report for Smiley. I met them on the airplane from Athens and spoke to them in Malta. I spent January 1950 in Rome, then went to Turin before I left for the United States. All I did in 1950 was to write a report for the central committee of Balli Kombëtar and for the Free Albania Committee.

They had 50 gold sovereigns each with them. Most of it they gave back to the British. They just spent a little money, to get a guide, for instance.

Hasan Dosti was a weak man. His tragedy was that during the war a bomber killed his wife, his brother and his two sons. This was when we left Tirana with Abas Kupi in September 1944. He was never intelligent, but after this happened he became stupid. He was Balli Kombëtar. Frashëri was 69 when he died. He was a friend of Edith Durham, whose son came to visit the displaced persons (DP) camps after the war. Churchill sent a telegram not to Frashëri, but to Mehmet Konitza.

Interview conducted May 23, 1981

* * *

I soon got the impression that there was something wrong with the operation, quite apart from the Philby business. These were simple Albanian people, without any money or education, suddenly finding themselves involved in something important. So they were talking about it in all the cafes and there was no one to keep discipline over them. Hoxha had good intelligence in Italy and all the information was getting to him.

Hoxha was very weak in 1949. The Greeks were pressing their claim for northern Epirus and the Bajraktari clan still had a lot of power in the north. Hoxha survived because of Shehu's strength. But we were even weaker than he was. It was an illusion to take 30 or 40 people and imagine that with those few people Albania was going to be liberated.

I was very impressed by the way the British officers and sergeants worked with our boys, all day and all night, teaching them about radios and maps, right from the beginning. No one knew anything about it before. I had meals at Smiley's house and we were like a family in Malta. Papajani was very witty. Papajani was there as an interpreter, representing the American side, a wonderful man to spend an evening with.

I met Princess Elizabeth at a polo match with Smiley and Ihsan Toptani. We talked only about the polo and we spoke French, since I spoke no English at that time. Prince Philip was playing in the match. Toptani's English was not very good at that time. Hare had to either spend time improving it or else he gave it to me to put into French. Toptani's Albanian was also not very good, since he had spent most of his education in Vienna. Also our young men were from the south of the country and he was from Tirana. He married the daughter of Mehdi Frashëri, but they divorced.

I transmitted the orders to our men in Albania and Toptani had to translate their replies. But we did not get much out of them. People were frightened to talk to them. They said to them, "Leave Albania. You are in danger, we are in danger and our families are in danger." Security was so tight that the boys were moving only at night and hiding up during the day. So what could they find out?

I was in a British colonel's uniform in Malta. Only I could not speak English. So I was given documents showing that I was a Canadian colonel who spoke French only.

Hare was very nice to us and it was a beautiful villa. I lived like a pasha. We ate and joked together. Hare spoke French and a bit of Italian. I was in Corfu from October 5 to November 10.

The boys left Malta for Albania on September 21. I arrived there with Papajani on August 31. Smiley met us at the airport and introduced us. We had separate rooms at the fort and stayed three months together. When Ermenji came, they put him in with Papajani. Papajani didn't like it. He said that Ermenji and I were from the same part of Albania and we ought to be together. I said that I was less important than them, so I ought to be on my own. Ermenji spent his month in Malta talking about history and the Napoleonic period. He was a teacher of history rather than a political leader.

On December 31, I left Malta and stayed a short time with Dosti. I wrote a three-page report on what happened. Then I left for America.

Interview conducted August 31, 1983

ABAS ERMENJI

Abas or Abaz Ermenji (1913–2003) was an Albanian political figure and resistance fighter of the World War II period. He was born in Skrapar and educated in Berat, Shkodra and Paris, where he studied history at the Sorbonne in 1934–1938. He returned to Albania in 1938 and taught secondary school in Korça. In November 1939, he was arrested by the Italians in Greece when he was attempting to gather a fighting force of Albanian exiles, and was held in captivity on the island of Ventotene until 1941. On his second return to Albania he became a leading figure of the Balli Kombëtar resistance movement and helped liberate Berat of Italian influence. During the war, he was in close contact with Julian Amery. When the communist partisans took power in Albania, the extremely anticommunist Ermenji fled to Greece (1946–1947), initially to Salonika and then to Piraeus. Billy McLean, Julian Amery and Alan Hare recruited him there for the Albanian operation and assisted him in getting him to Italy, where he quickly selected candidates from the refugee camps in the Naples area. Because of his vociferous stance against Midhat bey Frashëri and against the royalists, the British removed him to Trieste in order to avoid dissension among the Albanian fighters. In Paris in August 1954, Abas Ermenji and Vasil Andoni founded the anticommunist National Democratic Committee for a Free Albania (Shqypnija e lire) that included numerous Balli Kombëtar figures in exile. Ermenji returned to Albania in 1991 when Balli Kombëtar was restored and led the party throughout the 1990s, though it never regained much popularity.

During the war I fought with Balli Kombëtar in south and central Albania. When the communists took over, I went underground with a small group of bodyguards and crossed into Greece at the end of 1945. First I was imprisoned by the Greeks in Salonika and I believe that they might have eliminated me, because they knew of my firm stance on the question of Albania's southern frontiers. In April 1946 I was moved to Piraeus and kept as a prisoner of war.

Later, I was allowed to live in a small flat in Piraeus and other Albanians helped me to live. It was there that I was approached by Julian Amery and others in early 1949 and asked to help form the Albanian National Committee.

Amery and McLean said that there was a danger that Yugoslavia and Greece might make an agreement and march into Albania, since Tito was no longer Stalin's ally and Albania was geographically isolated from the Soviet bloc. The Greeks did not want to allow me to leave the country and the British had to intercede with the prime minister to get permission for me to leave. The prime minister agreed, but secretly, so as not to lose credit with the supporters of "northern Epirus." I told Amery and McLean

Abas Ermenji.

that I accepted their proposal, but I wanted to consult Midhat Frashëri who was in Istanbul at that time. Frashëri was president of Balli Kombëtar and would have to take the final decision. I was issued with a passport in a false name and let through the control at Athens airport.

My problem in Rome was that I was living with false documents and members of the Independenza could have had me arrested. There were many of them in Rome and they had great influence with the Italians. They had helped the Italian fascists during the war. Their leaders were Ernest Koliqi and Ismail Vërlaci.

The Americans spoke to Midhat Frashëri in Istanbul and persuaded him to allow royalists into the committee.

The American plan was to have Frashëri as the committee's president and Abas Kupi as commander of the armed forces. We thought that it was bizarre to have a president who was not also commander-in-chief. Personally, I thought Abas Kupi a capable commander, but far too restricted by his royalist convictions. During the war he was always very careful. He did not expose himself. I liked him, I tell you frankly. He was very amiable and wanted to be good friends. He obeyed the orders of Toptani.

Frashëri and I had angry talks with the Americans about who was to be commander-in-chief. Several times we had to get up and leave the room. In the end we came up with the idea of a junta consisting of Abas Kupi, Said Kryeziu and myself. It was only after this agreement that the Italians agreed to regularize my position and issue me with a refugee passport.

My guess is that half of the fighters trained by the British and infiltrated into Albania returned safely, whereas almost all the American-trained fighters were killed or captured. There were no leaks on the Albanian side but the operation was given away by Philby. My main complaint is that we were deceived by the British and Americans. They promised to provide us with the means to liberate our country. In actual fact, they only trained a handful of people. And they promised to gain the cooperation of Greece and Yugoslavia.

I found most of our people in camps near Naples, others from Greece. They knew that I understood the situation in the country. They trusted me and they volunteered to fight because I persuaded them. Almost all of them accepted. They wanted to liberate their country and their families.

My idea was to gather substantial forces and parachute them into Albania. This was the only plan that could have succeeded. The groups that were sent were too small. If they had followed my plan, all the people would have risen against the communists. This was the message that our groups brought back: "Send substantial forces, five or ten thousand, then the entire people will rise in revolt."

I went to Malta for a month in July/August, firstly to give them instructions, as to what to do and whom to contact, secondly because they would never have gone if I hadn't asked them to. However, I believed then and I believe now that no communist country could ever be overthrown by methods of small-scale subversion. In fact, the British and Americans were treating Albania like a guinea pig. If it had succeeded, they would have tried another country and another people. As for the suggestion that the operation helped to crush the communist rebellion in Greece, all I can say is that our aim was to liberate Albania, not Greece.

The operation continued with Balli Kombëtar men throughout 1950, but in 1951, I refused to help anymore. From then on it continued mainly with royalists. Then in December 1953, they tried to reconstruct the committee and include former fascists who had worked with the Italians. We refused to go along with that. But by then we had been on bad terms with the British and Americans for two years already.

In 1954 Zog agreed to have ten or twelve men from his Royal Guard parachuted into the Mati area. Zog had no scruples about sacrificing the lives of his close supporters. These men were all captured by the communists because Philby had informed them. Messages were sent on their behalf saying that they were well received by the population. This encouraged the Americans to send even more. The communists then executed not only the Albanians who had been parachuted into the country but also all those with whom they had made contact, about 400 people in the Mati area. They did this only at the end of the affair, after the Americans finally understood that their men had been captured.

Interview conducted in Paris April 15, 1983

* * *

Bajraktari was a member of the consultative committee, not the junta. He played no serious role. During the war he asked for £40 million in order to form a big pro–Allied army in the Balkans. He wanted to liberate Albania with gold.

The people we chose in 1949 had already taken part in the fight against the fascists and the communists. They already knew how to fight. They were brave, like most Albanians, and experienced in battle. I chose them too for their intelligence, their ability to make contact with the people, to prepare the way for liberation. I wanted men who were capable and well-known in the place where they were to operate, good at forging links and collecting information. These were the 30 who went to Malta.

They knew it would be very dangerous, but they were ready to make any sacrifice. Our people had made contact with high-ranking officers in the Albanian army and they were ready to abandon the regime. At that time no one in Albania thought that the regime was going to continue. Only the incomprehensible weakness of the British and Americans prevented it from collapsing.

Our sponsors deceived us. They had no intention of intervening seriously. Their most serious failure was in not persuading Tito to accept our plan, in allowing him to set up his own committee under Taref, a Slav and a pro-communist. Taref's committee was the Yugoslav answer to our committee. The Yugoslavs would only accept the overthrow of Hoxha if it was replaced by a pro–Tito regime. They would not allow Albania to become democratic.

So when the British and Americans began sending in their guerrillas, the Yugoslavs did the same and so did the Greeks. There was no coordination. The Italians too sent in a team led by Alush Lleshanaku, who was a supporter of Ismail Vërlaci, the son of the man who was Albania's prime minister under the Italian occupation. They were the richest family in Albania. Vërlaci was succeeded as prime minister by Mustafa Kruja, who was more intelligent. The Lleshanaku group was liquidated.

We had hundreds of émigré Albanians who were ready to go into Albania and fight, maybe even thousands. When I went to the camps near Naples to choose the men, there was discontent about why I had chosen only those 30 and not others. Everybody wanted to go. We could have got thousands of Albanians—and others too, Bulgarians, Croatians, a force big enough to free the country.

The method chosen by the British and Americans could never have worked. It was no good sending in four or five people to look for local leaders to start a revolution. All such people had already been destroyed by the communists. We should have sent thousands in and created areas of opposition to the regime.

We could only recruit the numbers that the sponsors demanded. The British told us they wanted 30 for Malta. The Americans told us they wanted a company of 200 in Germany. So we had no opportunity to put more men into the fight. I didn't go to Naples myself. I sent someone and gave him the names. And they were under orders not to breathe a word about it to anyone else, not even to their own brothers.

All the émigré Albanians were enthusiastic in those days. The British and Americans should have taken what I told them seriously.

The men went to Malta in July and August. I didn't go there myself until September. I had problems with the Italians over my visa. My impression in Malta was that the British instructors were good and that my men were full of enthusiasm. I was there one month and I left after the first group was sent in, after Frashëri's death.

Smiley was very pleasant. The British did not accept certain of my conditions, however. I wanted the guerrillas to report to me in the first instance, then to the British. I said that Albanians should give their first loyalty to other Albanians. And they would be more frank with us. Our interests might not always be the same as British interests, let alone Greek or Yugoslav interests. The matter was solved only when a senior British officer, a brigadier, intervened and then I allowed the men to go.

I was glad because a few months later, this brigadier invited me to dinner in Rome on his way to the Middle East. He told me that he had told his colleagues in London, "When you work with the representative of other peoples, do not assume that their interests are always the same as British interests."

The British training was very good, more serious than the American training. And British security was better. This was because Malta was an island and because the Americans put their trust in the Zogists, who were a group without order, discipline or sophistication. Also, the British made better arrangements for the delivery of men into Albania. I saw the first embarkation in October 1949 and I was impressed by it. There was never an accident with the delivery by the British of soldiers into Albania.

September 1949 was the time of great hope. I began by staying with Colonel Smiley and his family at their home in Malta. Then after a few days I moved to the fort. Jani Dilo was the man who dealt mainly with the trainees. I briefed each group leader. Then I returned to Rome, where I lived in Corso Trieste. I went back to Malta a year later and already had my doubts. I tried not to raise any false hopes with the men. By the middle of 1951 I was sure that it was not going to work. I came to London that summer and met members of the British and American intelligence services. I told them that either we should act seriously and liberate Albania with substantial numbers of men or we should call the operation off in the interest of saving men's lives. They heard me out and begged me to go to Malta once more. So I went there in September 1951. I would not give my authority for the dispatch of any more groups into the country. I think they did one more group without me, with the help of Ihsan Toptani.

Michael Burke was very intelligent and understanding, but after him Joe Leib was a disaster. And the secretary of the executive committee, who was also secretary of the Zogist movement, was an idiot, almost more idiotic than Leib. I went to the training school in Germany once. It was a big house, isolated, with a park. Mangelly was a man of about 30, with a wife and son. His parents had come to America from Albania. And I went to Hohenbrunn once to calm the people down over the incident of Zog's tomb in the snow. It was a stupidity that was threatening to become a battle between the two parties.

Everything that Leib and Goga decided became known to the communist embassy in Rome. Goga talked about it in cafes. The communists had agents among the Zogists, in particular a certain Rapo Binieri. It was not only the Albanian embassy, but the Soviet and Yugoslav embassies also. And then there was Philby on the British side. Goga knew all these details in advance, the dates and places of the landings, and he was gossiping about them to Binieri and others. He was very well paid by Leib and he spent every evening in the Casino delle Rose with his mistress. He dressed in very good taste and went everywhere by taxi. He lived in a very nice apartment in Rome. I hardly saw Leib more than two or three times. I saw at once that he was a useless type. When he wanted to see me, I usually sent Andoni or Zef Pali, and they made an excuse why I couldn't be there.

Ernest Koliqi and Vërlaci were the main pro-fascists who came into the committee, with Xhafer Deva, who was minister of the interior under the Germans and a Gestapo agent. Hasan Dosti was a miserable type. He made intrigues with the Zogists, and the Americans knew that Dosti would do everything that they asked him to do. Dosti was a feeble type who could never make an impression on people who were stronger than him. It wasn't a question of money with him, although perhaps it was with others. We had nothing against his having been a minister under the fascists, under Mustafa Kruja. This was at a time when the Italians were in favor of colonizing Albania with the Arbëresh, who were people of Albanian origin who had emigrated to Italy. Dosti found a pretext to become minister of justice in the nominated government in order to oppose this. He sacrificed himself for a good cause. He had Frashëri's approval for this.

McLean and Amery were in Rome during the summer of 1949, but they did not take part in the discussions that formed the committee. I was contacted by McLean and Amery in Athens in May 1949. I was the only BK leader there at that time. I was living in a flat, but the Greeks were keeping me as a hostage. We talked about Yugoslavia's expulsion from the Cominform and they suggested to me that Albania had become a country without defense, that it had become a vacuum between Yugoslavia and Greece. We all thought it likely that Greece and Yugoslavia were going to take military action against Albania. However, they said, the American and British authorities were against this. They suggested to me that it was wrong to leave a vacuum there. This was why an Albanian action was necessary, to protect Albania's interests, to curtail Greek and Yugoslav ambitions. The idea of liberating Albania from the communists went hand in hand with this. Albania was to become a country capable of offering resistance to her two neighbors, of course as a member of the Western camp. Amery and McLean told me that I was the only person who could take such an initiative and make it good. They knew my popularity among the Albanian youth.

They did not tell me that at the same time the Americans were making contact with Midhat Frashëri in Istanbul and that of course certain other allied personalities had spoken to Zog in Cairo. I accepted in principle, but I told them that I could not take the main role because we were a political party and the party's president was Frashëri. At that stage there was no mention of the royalists taking part, nor was there with Frashëri in Istanbul. The first mention of them was in Rome, at the end of May or beginning of June.

I accepted the participation of the royalists not because they meant anything inside Albania, but because of the outside world, which knew Albania only as Zog's kingdom. We could not convince the outside world that Zog was no longer anything in Albania.

The British and Americans took me to Trieste. But later they realized that Frashëri would not enter into any agreement without me. Then they came to Trieste and spoke to me threateningly. If I continued my opposition, they said, they would abandon the fate of Albania and hand it over to the Greeks and Yugoslavs. They took me to Trieste partly because it was an international city and they wanted to protect me from the Italians, who were out to arrest me any day, partly to put me under pressure to agree to what they wanted. They thought it would be easier to manipulate the others if I was away from Rome. But the others would not come to a decision without me. When the British carried on threatening, I said that if necessary I would knock at the door of the first Soviet embassy I could find in order to save Albania. The Soviets are intelligent, I told them, and they know what our party represents.

It ended happily though, even in laughter. I telephoned Frashëri in Rome and advised him to agree to the proposal of a junta, of which I was to be a member. Then, after the agreement, I was asked to come and see the Italian governor of Trieste. He received me very well, gave me proper documents with a residence permit, after which I was taken by car to Udine and then by American military aircraft to Rome. This was in early August, about three weeks before the proclamation of the Free Albania Committee in Paris on August 26.

I wanted our sponsors to give us the means to train a small and well-equipped army, also to land them in Albania and supply them by air. This would allow us to establish centers of resistance and then raise the population against the communist government. The people would have sided with us at once and units of the Albanian army would also have joined us. This was our information. At that time no one thought that the Albanian regime was going to survive. It was certainly the most propitious moment to try and overturn it.

An Albanian army colonel in Gjirokastra told one of our agents that he and many others were prepared to move, provided that we sent a substantial force and parachuted in the necessary equipment. So there were some positive indications as a result of the first landings from Malta. All this information came from the British-trained groups. We got virtually nothing from the American-trained groups, who were almost all wiped out.

We also found out that there was a Soviet submarine base at Ishëm, north of Durrës, as well as the main base on Sazan Island. These results were not discouraging, but what was discouraging was the attitude of the British and Americans, their lack of will to undertake an operation in the grand style. It was a pot that could not be brought to the boil on a small flame. It was not possible in Albanian conditions to assemble groups of people and create five-man or six-man cells. The controls were too tight.

Also, the British and Americans hesitated too long. This allowed other countries, especially Yugoslavia and Greece, to prepare and send in their own agents. And all this confused the Albanian people. They could understand and accept an operation mounted by Albanians under British or American sponsorship, but who were these agents of Greece and Yugoslavia, the two countries that wanted to destroy us? So after these first attempts we told our sponsors that liberation was a practical possibility, but only with serious forces.

The Americans used less sophisticated means than the British. And they had to deal with the royalists. And there were leaks on the royalist side. And there was a strong police force inside the country and a terrorized population. This is why it all failed.

The main carnage was in 1954. After the trial of Zenel Shehu and Matjani, the communists killed about 400 people in the Mati region. First of all, the families of those condemned in the trial were shot. Then there were the people whom Zenel and the others were supposed to contact. Zenel gave the communists all their names under torture. Then when these people were arrested, they implicated other people, also under torture, often people who were in no way involved. They would do anything to stop the torture. Such bloodshed would never have occurred if our party had been involved, but 400 Albanians, more or less, was something that Zog didn't care about.

Interview conducted in Paris July 23, 1983

QUEEN GERALDINE OF ALBANIA

Geraldine Apponyi (1915–2002), later to be Queen of Albania, was born in Budapest as a Hungarian-American countess. King Zog, who was in search of a bride, invited her to Tirana where she arrived shortly after Christmas in 1937. She accepted the king's proposal on New Year's Day 1938 and was married to him on 27 April 1938. A year later, on 5 April 1939, Geraldine gave birth to a son called Leka. It was, however, in that very week that Italian forces under Mussolini invaded Albania. The royal family was forced to flee abroad, never to return. After spending the war years in England, they lived in Egypt from 1946 to 1955 where King Zog made some attempts to organize anti-communist resistance, including the Albanian operation. After the death of her husband in Paris in April 1961, Queen Geraldine moved to Madrid (October 1962) and later to Bryanston, South Africa, where she lived in exile with her son and his family. She returned to Albania on 28 June 2002 to spend the final months of her life in the country where she had once reigned.

The king spoke Turkish, Arabic, Persian and German very well. His French became quite good, but he never learnt English properly, even though he lived for some years

Queen Geraldine (1915–2002) and King Zog (1895–1961), surrounded by two of King Zog's sisters, at Chateau de la Maye in Versailles (France) on 10 August 1939.

in England during the war, near Henley. He never got me involved in politics, but in 1949 he asked me to sit in at this meeting with British and American representatives, to interpret for him. There was one Englishman (Julian or Billy), two Americans and Philby. I remember that he wore striped trousers.

They started very undiplomatically. He said that they wanted to establish Albania as a democratic country. He invited the king to suspend his royal prerogatives and to hand over the leadership of the country to the Free Albania Committee. When I translated this, he turned to me and said, "Ask them to leave immediately. Tell them that it was I who made Albania and that when I left it was with the authority of the Albanian parliament to defend the country until the end of my life. I cannot pass on this debt to any other person other than my heir." They were very upset and they left, but before leaving they asked the king to think things over and agreed to come and see him again in a day or two.

It was very unfortunate that Midhat Frashëri died, because the idea was that Frashëri would hold the committee together and report to the king regularly. On this basis the king would support it.

Some months later, a group of Americans came to see the king and asked him to find some of his men to go into Albania. They were not sure of the men they had there already. It was over this episode that Philby broke everything up. And it was not only the men themselves that died, but it was their families, too. We heard excerpts from the trial on Albanian radio. They said to the king, "You give us some of your men as volunteers. We will then be able to believe everything that they report to us. And they can take into Albania a word of hope from you." We had about 15 officers with us in Alexandria and Captain Zenel was the head. Five or six of them volunteered. Only the Americans didn't give any money, so the king gave them a bag of gold each.

Before leaving Alexandria, Zenel gave me his personal belongings to take care of and, if necessary, pass on to his son. So after he had gone, we devised this code word. We would ask him on the radio where he had left his things. If he replied, "With the lady of the house" or "with the mother," it would mean that everything was all right. If he made any other reply, it would mean that he was captured.

They went in once, got out and reported to us. Then they went in again. After a few days an American intelligence officer came to see us. He told us that there was bad news. They were getting messages in Morse from Zenel, he said, saying that he had broken his right hand and so he was transmitting with the left hand. We asked the American why he hadn't put our question. But it was too late. Other Albanians, Adem Hoda (?) and others, had gone in at the request of these Morse messages. The next we heard from Zenel was his voice on Albanian radio saying, "At last I have told everything that your torture made me tell." Then his voice was cut.

The Americans made all these arrangements, but Philby was pulling the strings. He produced a revulsion in me. My husband had an eye for people and he told me that Philby was never to be allowed into his house again.

Interview conducted March 12, 1983

* * *

I remember the Americans contacting my husband in Egypt and saying that something had gone wrong with the Shehu/Sufa mission. They wanted to see him urgently. They said that the radio operator was not identifiable. His "fist" was not what it ought to have been. And he was explaining this by the fact that he was transmitting with his left hand, because his right arm was broken.

The Americans said that apart from this, the radio signals were fine and the code phrases were being answered correctly. But these phrases were known to about 30 people. They would only have had to torture one man or have a spy in their midst and they could find out the code phrases.

Then I remembered that I had some

Queen Geraldine (1915–2002) and Prince Leka (1939–2011) in London in December 1940.

valuables belonging to Zenel Shehu. The king had given him and Sufa a bag of gold before they went on the mission. Shehu had left it with me, together with some other bits of jewelry that the king had given him. Only the king and I knew about this. So I said to Colonel Yatsevitch, "Ask Zenel where he left his valuables." If everything was all right, he would then answer, "With the lady of the house," or "With my mother" or some such expression.

So the Americans put my question to him and the answer was, "Stop asking us stupid questions. Leave us in peace. They're in Greece with all my other things." And the Americans accepted it. They didn't take me seriously. They preferred to rely on the code phrases, which were known to several people, rather than on something that was known only to the king and me.

The king said to Colonel Yatsevitch, "Didn't you go and look for his valuables in Greece?" Yatsevitch said he had, but they hadn't found them. They found all the valuables belonging to the other group members, but not Zenel's. He was the only one who had left his things with me.

After the first meeting with Philby in 1949, the king would not have him in the room again. He hated him at first sight and so did I. It was a woman's intuition. Philby was there for the first meeting, but not for the second.

Interview conducted July 24, 1983

BARDHYL GERVESHI

Bardhyl Gervishi (b. ca. 1930) was an Albanian anticommunist fighter. He was from the Gjirokastra region, escaped to Greece with Haki Gaba at the end of 1947 and was interned at the Hadji Kyriakon camp near Athens, from where he was transferred to Bari and then to the Cinecittà refugee camp in Rome. He trained in Malta and was smuggled into Albania in the autumn of 1949. He managed to get out of the country alive and later settled in England.

[BG]: I was born in 1930 at Gjirokastra. How did I get involved with the resistance? The fact is that everybody was involved in politics. It was taught at school and everybody was involved—your friends and teachers, at high school and at college. Then you joined the party, in my case the Balli Kombëtar.

When the war ended, I was fifteen and at that age you realize what politics really is. My friends and I joined Balli Kombëtar in Albania. We stayed for a while but the communists were stronger than we were. At first we believed there was going to be democracy similar to that in the West. But once they took over, there was a different story altogether.

Hoxha had said there would be elections. He was expecting all the other parties to surrender and then he would have no opposition.

I had no connection with the British during the war. I only came across the British in Greece later. We all escaped from the technical college in Gjirokastra, then joined the Balli Kombëtar. The communists were better organized and stronger because they promised things they weren't going to give in the end, bribing the people.

I left Albania for Greece about Christmas of 1948. There were eight of us who went by foot into Greece. We had to wait for six months to cross the border because the Greek communists were escaping from the British and the Greek nationalists and coming to the border. So we had to wait about five months until they came to the border close to us, because if we had gone before we would have been mixed in with them and the Greek authorities wouldn't know who was who. So we waited until the communists came into Albania and we crossed into Greece.

Although there were some easy crossing places, these were all guarded, so you had to go to some remote area. By day it would have taken two or three days, but we had to go at night and it took five or six days. And it was forest and all uphill, with no proper equipment. All you had were polythene sheets, to collect water. I walked for two days without shoes or food.

All eight of us crossed the border and reported to the Greek authorities. They weren't suspicious of us. A lot of Albanians crossed the border. In southern Albania there were a lot who spoke Greek and as soon as we arrived we knew all the intellectual people like teachers, doctors and so on who had been in Albania. They had been in contact and knew the whole story. They could check up on us without any problem.

Then we went to the camp. The next day after, the British came because they wanted information. There was quite a young person from the British embassy who had us in an office and tried to get as much information as possible. The Greeks allowed this. The Greek government was being propped up by the British. They were as demoralized as everyone else after the war, and the officers were very poor, not intelligent because most intellectual people were left-wingers.

From the camp I went to Piraeus, from there to Italy and then Malta. I stayed in Italy at a Balli Kombëtar camp at Bari, run by the British and possibly Americans for refugees, then at Cinecittà near Rome and then to Malta.

[NB]: Can you remember how you were recruited?

[BG]: They didn't ask for volunteers. They knew who was well organized and devoted to that party. We were party organizers in Albania so they knew who to pick out. Frashëri was in Bari, as well as Abas Ermenji and Ihsan Toptani.

They said we had to do something to get our country back and liberate it. When your life is devoted to your country, you are prepared to do anything for it. We weren't getting any money for it. The first time they gave us fifteen pounds sterling in gold. I never kept any of it. I remember Dr. Zaehner saying to me, "Keep part of it." But I told him, "No, I'm not here for money, I'm here for the freedom of the country."

It was Toptani, Jani Dilo and Ermenji who explained the whole operation to us at Bari. They told us it was dangerous, that we would be landed in Albania by plane or by boat. They wouldn't tell us how because people talk. It can slip out when you are talking to friends or girlfriends.

Thirty-eight were chosen for Malta, and then there came another twelve. In the camp at Bari there were about 120 or 130. They chose the most active party men, young men, of course.

We flew from Bari to Malta in a British airplane. All 38 together. I did not speak any English, only Greek and Italian. We were taken in a truck to Fort Bin Jema. Life was very good there, they couldn't have done more. All the facilities we needed. We didn't even do any cleaning, the young British soldiers did that. We just got up in the morning at eight o'clock and did training and lectures on how it was to be organized and so on.

[NB]: So you were being trained as a guerrilla leader?

[BG]: Partly, yes, but at the same time we were being trained politically, how to organize the resistance, the cell system. Each man was to recruit five others. Each of those would recruit five more. And so on. No one was to know who was at the top. We were taught how to organize the underground. I knew two or three officers there who were part of my family. The idea was to build a system of cells.

We were instructed by Dilo and Sino, in British uniforms, and we had weapons training on the same principle as the SAS, poison in your pocket in case you were caught. In fact, I still have it. Also, radio operating with a pedal generator, no batteries, and how to organize against the communists for the freedom of the country, political lectures. When you've been involved in politics since the age of 15, you never get away from it.

We were trained exactly like the SAS. When we were in Greece, we jumped from a big mound with a rope, swinging 20 feet above the ground, and then we threw the grenades over.

The training in Malta lasted nearly three months in 1949. Then we were landed in Albania, a group of 24 in a boat. Then we split up. One group with Bido Kuka had to go in one direction, we had to go in another, and a third group was to go to Elbasan. There were three groups of eight. They dropped us on a beach near Vlora. In my eight there were Ago Dauti, Haki Gaba, myself, two other chaps who are dead, Baki Hyseni who killed himself in America, and two others who died in Australia. None of our group were ever captured in Albania.

Actually, our group did better than the others. When we reached Gjirokastra, we made contact with Toptani in Corfu over the radio.

Our boats went ashore. There were two men waiting, both English, and a woman, very friendly, probably from intelligence. It was a fishing boat and the woman was there so that if they were caught, they could say they were a family who'd got lost. We got ashore, shook hands and then went our way. We had maps to follow. Each group went to his own country. All eight of us were from Gjirokastra.

We went across the mountains. We had some dried food with us, enough for four days to get us to where we were going, and 15 gold sovereigns. We wore ordinary rough clothes and had a British Sten gun, a pistol and one grenade each. We only traveled at night. In the day we just laid low. No movement at all in the daylight, so you had to work out how long it would take from place to place so that you would arrive before light. It took us four nights and we had no problems getting to Gjirokastra. When we got there, we went up into the mountain and contacted a shepherd who we knew from before, one of our party. We contacted him and he gave us food. We told them we had come to liberate the country. We made some good contacts and stayed together in the hills for two and half months.

Then we thought we had enough information. We were in contact with Toptani in Corfu. We used Morse and a special code. Each letter or group of letters corresponded with a given phrase. We received information as well as giving messages. Then we broke contact because the radio broke down. Then two of us decided to go to Greece.

We met about 60 different Albanians in different places, always armed. Sometimes if we were going to the village we would leave the automatic rifle and just take the pistol. Ago Dauti and I went to Greece when we couldn't fix the radio. It took us two days. We went to get another radio.

The Greeks wanted information from us. But we didn't tell them the truth. They asked who we worked for and we said the Americans. We had been told right from the beginning not to say who we worked for. We had a short note what to say. When a Greek intelligence officer came to us and told us that the code we had was British intelligence, so he knew who we were. The Americans had got suspicious and thought we were spies. We had given no names of the people we were dealing with like Papajani and Dilo.

When the Greek fellow found out we were involved with the British, he contacted somebody and this young British man came to see us in the north and we exchanged passwords. We said in Albanian, "The sun has gone down," and he said, "That's it." But he didn't speak Albanian, we had an interpreter. Toptani said that no one spoke Albanian.

We explained what we wanted to the British. But they didn't want us to go straight back. They gave us more training in Greece, based in Kifissia in Athens, a house the British consul used. Then they asked us if we wanted to go back by plane or overland. We said by land. We were in Athens for about a month and ten days. It was February–March of 1950.

Haki Gaba was with me when I left Albania at the end of August 1947 when I was 17. He lives in Milwaukee. We went through the mountains, collecting snow in an army ground sheet and then melting it for water during the day into a helmet or an old tin. In the evening, we would creep into a farmhouse and steal some food, trying not to show that we had been there, otherwise they might have reported us. Or we would steal a goat or a sheep, but always from a different valley, never from the one near our base or our cave. We stayed in Janina. We were interrogated by the Greeks, then the British took us to DP camps near Bari. At that time, Greece was more or less run by the British. There were British officers in every garrison. We were taken down to Athens, about 400 of us, and we were flown to the camp in Bari, then to Cinecittà near Rome.

There were thousands of people in barrack huts near Bari from all countries in central and eastern Europe. There were Czech areas, Yugoslav areas and Albanian areas. We found other Albanians there who had escaped across to Italy by boat. Altogether there were more than a thousand Albanians.

People were always leaving the camps in quotas for Canada, Australia or the United States. So when we left for Malta, it was nothing unusual. As far as the rest were concerned, we had emigrated. The recruiters were Ihsan Toptani, Vasil Andoni and Abas Ermenji. The men were selected individually, each one recommending another. First there were 20 sent to Cinecittà by train and we found royalists there. Then another 18 went. Then we flew to Malta, 20 Balli Kombëtar and 18 royalists.

The fort was all there and ready for us. There was nothing to complain about. We were the first Albanians to arrive. We never knew whether people's ranks or names were genuine. Zaehner used to wear either a major's uniform or a captain's uniform. In fact he wasn't an officer at all. Grant was in charge of physical training. He took us for runs in the countryside, by night and by day. We used to spend evenings in Slima and Rabat, having a drink and meeting girls. We never said that we were Albanians. We were always Greek or Italian, depending on what language we spoke. Albania didn't exist outside the fort. I spoke Greek, so I said I was Greek. We used to walk into Rabat or get a lift in a truck, arranging to meet at 10:30 or 11 o'clock for the ride back.

We practiced paddling rubber boats and we were taken across to Gozo in a fishing boat for more physical training, running with our arms and equipment. We had hardly any personal belongings and no civilian clothes. We didn't need any, because we knew we were going into Albania and we didn't know if we'd be coming back.

There were twelve of us in the first group to go into Albania. Haki Gaba was the group leader. There was Dervish Sulo and Bido Kuka and his brother. They caught Nezir Tomorri. Hysen Ramis was also caught. He had a big patch on his face.

On the boat that took us over, there was an Englishman and an Englishwoman, a cat and a dog. This was the make it seem that they were a family on holiday, in case the Albanians stopped us. There was another big tough guy called Colin, about 30 years old, who paddled our rubber boat ashore. I remember him telling us not to open fire from the boat, even if we were fired at, because our shots would give away our position in the dark. There was a motor in the rubber boat, too, in case we had to make a fast getaway, but we never used it. So the boat that took us to Albania contained 12 Albanians, two Englishmen, an Englishwoman, a dog and a cat. Colin was a very well trained man, like an SAS type.

We knew what the landing spot would look like, because we had aerial photographs in Malta, very good photographs. You could see every detail of the landing spot, you could see little stones. But after the landing we were on our own. They didn't tell us where to go, other than to find our way to our own area, where we knew people. The group had been chosen so that each member knew a certain area of the country.

We made contact with shepherds. Two of us would approach a shepherd while the other two covered them with their guns. We called each other by false names.

We landed on the Albanian coast in the evening. It was dark and we had worked out a route from there to a forest before daybreak. We spent each day in the forest, either sleeping or on watch. We had to be careful of people coming into the forest to gather wood, or farmers wandering in with their goats. We did not contact anyone until we were well into Albania. We traveled only about 12 kilometers a night, because it was mountainous terrain and we had to zigzag, avoiding the villages because of the dogs. We kept clear of places where there was sheep or goat dung, because it meant that the shepherds would probably return to that spot in the morning. Before every dawn we had to find a cave or hiding place where there was no sign of human beings. The forest was the best place, otherwise a cave or a place covered with big stones. And we had to work out where the sun would rise, so that we would have some warmth in the morning. It was too cold in the mountains to spend the whole day in the shade. We were not cold when we got down into the valley, because it was warmer and we were on the move, but it could get uncomfortably cold doing nothing high up in the mountains.

We were on the move for eleven days until we got to Gjirokastra. Of course, we didn't go into the town. We sent our first radio message from there on the twelfth or thirteenth day. It was only about 50 miles in a straight line to the receiving station in Corfu. The reception should have been good, but there was something wrong with the generator. It hadn't been properly oiled or something; it was a bit stiff. The man had to work very hard on the pedals to generate enough electricity. Toptani and Sino were in Corfu with Alan Hare.

We contacted Haki Gaba's brother and cousin. Haki's message to his brother was to organize, to make a cell, to prepare to overthrow the communist regime. Our plan was to create roots there, then to clear out and leave the radio with them. That was our intention, but Haki's cousin made a mistake. He contacted someone whom he trusted, but it turned out that this person was a commissar. He picked the wrong person.

Haki, Ago and I were in Albania for about a month. I knew the area and the various routes into Greece. We kept a lookout for the patrols and eventually made our way into Greece through a different route from the one I had taken in 1947. I knew the area quite well because I used to drive around near the border with my parents when I was young. Haki knew the area even better, because he had family there. Nothing went wrong. We just walked over the border.

Our only difficult moment in Albania was when some shepherds came up to us in our hiding place during the day. They just walked right up to us. There was no point in running away. They might have reported this to the authorities. It was better to stay there and talk to them. We covered our guns with some clothes and told them that we were surveyors, mapping the mountain region and making temperature readings. We thought about killing them, but decided that this would create a blood feud and we would have all their families after us, so we just talked to them and started joking with them. We kept very calm and asked them for a cigarette. One of them gave Haki some tobacco to roll one.

When we got into Greece, we asked for a particular Greek officer by name, a man who knew what we were doing. I don't know whether it was his real name or a code name. The Greeks interrogated us, but they never asked anything about Albania, just stupid things like "How many Albanians would like to be united with Greece?" I wasn't interested in anything like that. An Albanian is an Albanian and that's it, but the Greeks had their own purpose. They took us to a private house in Janina where there was a British officer known as "Johnnie." He was a nice guy, he looked after us, we had a rest and then we flew to Athens and stayed three days in Kifissia. A Greek colonel arrived and asked us the same silly questions.

Then we flew to Malta and had a full debriefing, just before Christmas. By then, they had some more recruits, mainly royalists. We had nothing against them. They too wanted a free Albania and if they won at the ballot box, good luck to them. We didn't want to fight over something unnecessary.

The same four of us went back into Albania overland from Greece in May 1950. First they wanted to drop us by parachute, but we had heard about the ones sent in by the Americans a bit earlier. They were all caught. A plane flying over Albania during the night was very conspicuous. It would have alarmed the local authorities. So we said no, we'd rather walk. It was the safest way.

They didn't execute any of the ones they caught from the American drop. This was to discourage people from committing suicide. More of our people would have killed themselves with the lethal pills that we had if we had known that those captured would be executed. They wanted to torture our boys, get every scrap of information out of them and then keep them for more interrogation later. It makes sense to execute innocent people, but not those who really fought against them.

I still have the lethal pill they gave me, though it's probably no good anymore. In Albania I kept mine under a bracelet on my wrist.

The second time, we walked across the border and contacted Haki's brother. He told us that the communists had caught his cousin Hysen, tortured him and taken the radio that we left with him. He also told them some of our code words. They executed him later. Betas Gaba was frightened that he would be given away, too, so he came out with us and he lives in the United States. We stayed in Albania for just over a month, then came out and were taken back to Malta. They decided then not to send us into Albania anymore and asked us where we wanted to go. We said to England, all four of us, because we still wanted to fight and we didn't want to go thousands of miles away from Europe. Zaehner offered to get me to Australia, put me into school, but I didn't want to leave the other three.

I went into Albania for the first time in September 1949, stayed a month, went across the border to get a better radio and came back into Albania. In May 1950 we went in a third time.

The Americans said to some of us, "Don't worry, if they catch you, just surrender and we'll come and get you." It makes me angry to think about it. All we wanted to do was to free our country. We were, if you like, using the British and Americans for this purpose. The Americans just sent in big planes to fly across Albania, and dropped their men as close as possible to the right place, making a lot of noise, without any organization. Of course they were caught. And they were given too much equipment to carry. Betas Gaba told us, on the information of the fellow that his cousin contacted, that this was how the American-trained men were caught. Some of them didn't know the area where they were dropped. They had maps, but maps are no good in such country.

Smiley did everything he could for us, but it was impossible. The communists were too well organized. By 1949 they had a strong grip on the country. Haki's brother told me that he tried recruiting about 15 people. They all refused. They didn't want to get involved. And one person that his cousin Hysen tried to recruit turned out to be a communist and reported him.

Interview conducted June 4, 1982

Adem Gjura

Adem Gjura, also known as Adem Gjuraj, was Albanian anticommunist fighter. He was a military officer in Albania and served in the royal gendarmerie in the late 1930s and 1940s. During World War II, he was a noted anticommunist fighter in Albania and escaped to Greece in August 1946. Gjura was initially interned at the Hadji Kyriakon refugee camp near Athens and in March 1949, he was transferred to the Santa Fara camp near Bari in southern Italy. He was recruited for the Albanian mission in June 1950. Gjura was given military training in Bavaria and parachuted into the Dibra region of eastern Albania in November 1950. He survived his stay and later crossed over into Yugoslavia.

I was in charge of a group of 16, but in the end only nine of them parachuted. Nerguti was second in command of the Kukës group. We were separated almost as soon as we landed, because of the fighting. We landed at about two o'clock at night at Bulqiza, instead of Martanesh, and we waited until five or six o'clock. Ilia Toptani was separated from us at the start, I don't know why, and he was captured two days later in the house of Sima Hoxha.

We spent the first two days looking for Toptani and then trying to make the radios work. This was after we were attacked around ten o'clock on the first morning. One of us, Cetam Daci, was killed and Selim Daci was captured. Daci ran away after being wounded, because we had an agreement to kill any one of us who was wounded. He ran away and was captured because he thought one of us was going to kill him.

I was wounded, too, in the left leg and I ran away with Sali Daliu. I learnt later that in 800 houses in Martanesh, where we were supposed to land, there were Sigurimi officers waiting for us. Even in the Bulqiza region, 40 kilometers away, there were members of the security police in the village of Dushaj where we actually landed. Also, the main security group in Martanesh were immediately informed of our arrival. We were warned about this by a woman we met early that morning.

Demer Manukaj (who now lives in Brussels) was at home in Albania then and he remembers being approached by the police two days before the landing and asked to help them catch Adem Gjura. They knew me well, because I spent 1944–46 in the hills fighting the communists in the Kukës and Mirdita regions. There were five or six groups in the hills at that time and we fought until we decided to cross into Greece via Yugoslavia in September 1946.

After I was wounded in 1950, I tried to get to my home village, where my people were. It is a ten-hour walk, but it took eight days for us to get there, passing the security forces all the time. We had German machine guns with us. And we had a very good special uniform, camouflaged and designed to protect us from rain and cold.

Another reason why I know that they were expecting me is that, before I landed, they arrested about 40 members of my family: nephews, cousins and brothers. All but ten were either killed or died in prison. They wanted to catch me particularly.

I treated my wound with salt, sugar and water. It was very difficult to walk and painful. I could never keep up with Sali Daliu. We had no medicine, not even tobacco, which we usually put on wounds. So the sugar was an anesthetic and the salt a disinfectant. I was six weeks in Albania with this wound. Then it was treated in Yugoslavia.

It was very cold, but our clothes were excellent and protected us. After six weeks Sali Daliu and I crossed into Yugoslavia. We hid for ten days before surrendering to the security police, under false names, and I managed to inform Xhemal Laci by letter, again writing with false names and in code, asking him not to send any more men. I wrote, "Don't send any more packages to this address, because they get lost on the way."

Then I was four months in prison in Skopje in a small room with no windows. Then I wrote again to Gaqi Goga in Rome asking him not to send any more men. After that I lived two years in Kosovo and 15 years in Serbia, in Shabac, living on a refugee's allowance. The Yugoslavs kept asking me, "Why don't the Americans send you money?" They called me a spy for Enver Hoxha and I said, "I could understand your calling me an American spy, but not a Hoxha spy." Still, the worst thing they could call you was a British spy. They thought that the British were more dangerous.

I have always been sure that we were betrayed. I do not say that we would definitely have succeeded, but we ought to have been able to start a revolutionary movement in Albania, if we hadn't been sold out before we started.

It is true that there was loose talk in coffee houses in Rome where Tirana could have got some information. But only Philby could have given them details, times and places.

I kept asking the Yugoslavs to let me go. And I tried escaping. Eventually I got asthma. In Greece we were looked after by the International Rescue Organisation. They helped me get from Greece to Italy, to Santa Fara, half an hour from Bari. They were giving us training for various jobs.

They came to me in March 1949 and Gaqi Goga asked me to collect my friends and take them to Germany. I recruited 25 men myself and they all went to Munich by train. The Americans took us to a camp at Dachau and we spent two months working there and training. Then we were taken to the training school a six hours' drive away, near Garmisch, south of Frankfurt, called Berchtesgaden. It was high up in the hills, reached by a spiral road, a very big and beautiful house. It had three stories and tunnels in the basement. Once I was told that I was sleeping in Hitler's bedroom. There were 16 Albanians there. Most of the things we knew already, but we did learn something about parachuting, topography, map reading and first aid. Most Albanians know already how to handle guns. There was a firing range with moving targets. I was a well-known guerrilla fighter and that was why Goga chose me as group leader.

I do not agree with the way it was done, but if I got another chance, regardless of the number of members of my family that were killed, I would do the same again, because I cannot tolerate Albania remaining under the slavery of the communists.

Briefly, this is my biography. In 1932 I attended an army officers' course for six months. After one month the government demobilized 170 men. They kept some senior men, for financial reasons and pension rights, although they did recognize seven months obligatory service.

On January 1, 1933, I registered at and attended for a short time the school for non-commissioned officers (or aspiring officers) of the Royal Gendarmerie in Durrës. After selecting about 30 of us who had enough schooling (qualifying education not specified), we were sent to Shkodra to keep the peace (or as peace officers). We had theoretical lectures daily and practical training under the school's commission whose members were Colonel Gjaklin Martin (he must mean E.C. Dekenzy Martin—a British officer), First Captain; Skender Çami, commander of Shkodra; Captain Arif Konica;

Captain Shaqir Alushi, commander of Koplik; Captain Kamer Proda, commander of Lezha; Captain Qemal Balili, commander of Puka; First Lieutenant Qazim Hajdari, an aide to the commander of Shkodra.

After eighteen months I graduated successfully and was seventh in my class. Along with me another hundred or so qualified as sub-officers, but the entitlement was considerably delayed for budgetary reasons.

On April 7, 1939, under the command of Captain Shukri Baftiari and Sergeant Major Isuf Jashari with 14 gendarmes from Kukës, we arrived in Kruja. After meeting with Captain Shukri we traveled to Preza. There we met Major Murat Basha who told us that he had been ordered to pull back as King Zog had left Albania. From that day on, with my men I continued to fight the occupying forces, until 16 November 1940.

Then, illegally, I went to Greece with 40 other soldiers and civilians from Korça, knowing that we would meet the forces of King Zog. This is what I and five others were told, but things turned out otherwise. On June 25 we were arrested by the Germans and taken to Albania where prison and death sentences were awaiting us all. Here are the names of the other five with whom I was condemned to death three times: Sergeant Mustafa Imeri, from Puka; Adem Gjura, from Dibra; Idriz Sadiki, from Tropoja; Qerim Verediki, from Selenica, near Korça; Gaqo Sotiri, as well as others from Dardha near Korça who were condemned once only.

On January 17 we were freed and lost all rights under the fascist regime. Immediately after leaving prison, I joined the guerrilla movement. More than five times I fought bloody battles against the Italians and Germans and I have friends with whom I fought who can testify to this.

To begin with in Albania, I had political relations with Muharrem Bajraktari, formerly commander of the Gendarmarie, and with Cen Elezi (who were both northeast Albanian chieftains) and later with Abas Kupi until his death. In 1944 after an appeal by the then Regent of Albania, Mr. Mehdi Frashëri, I presented myself in Tirana. After it became obligatory to serve in the Gendarmerie, I was given my early command and posted at the Kala e Dodës (Doda's castle) as commander of the second zone of Gendarmerie of that region.

After four months I was promoted to full lieutenant. On August 1 of that year, under special orders, I was made vice-commander of the Gendarmerie of the region of Bicaj, as you will see from the testimony of the subprefect of Bicaj, Mr. Nezir Spahija. On September 7 we were attacked by the Fifth Partisan Brigade under the command of Col. Shefqet Peci. After a short but bloody fight, we were defeated, leaving many dead, among them Captain Ziber Lita, Lieutenant Kadri Lita and reserve Captain Ali Velija, all from the region of Kala e Dodës.

I fled into the mountains with my cousin Shaban Gjura and others. I participated in all the meetings of the anti-government forces, in particular the meeting of Bresht Toroshi which took place from the end of June until July 18, 1945. In this meeting I represented the guerrilla forces of the region of Dibra and their chieftains, some of whom are still in exile in the West—for example Mehdi Ndreu and Qazim Lusha, with whom I have been corresponding. Others like Dalli Reçi, chieftain of Reçi, and Sali Shehi, also from Reç, are either dead or still alive in Albania. In all these meetings, 95 percent were political opponents. I, as the representative, spoke only for the establishment of the

Abas Kupi (left center, wearing raincoat) with the men of Company 4000, around 1952.

kingdom (monarchy). As the communists took power, I and my friends remained in flight in the mountains, fighting almost daily with the communist forces.

In 1946 I had a meeting with Muharrem Bajraktari and discussed our situation and decided to flee to Greece (via Yugoslavian Macedonia). On August 18, with 56 others, we fled to Macedonia. On the way, we were attacked by the Yugoslav army and lost 27 friends, among them Mirteza Haxhi Agaj from Puka and Nebi Seda from my original group from Arrni i Lumës. We also had a large number of wounded.

On arrival in Greece, in the camp Haxhi Ciriakos near Athens, we immediately formed the Monarchist Movement. The members of the founding committee were Ihsen Tërpeza, Sejdi Bajo, Adem Gjura, Miftar Spahija, Ihsen Salki, and Fiqri Dine was elected chairman. I was in charge of the youth movement, Ihsen Salki correspondent and Miftar Spahija was elected general secretary. The day-to-day running of the chairman's office was done by Ihsen Tërpeza and Sejdi Bajo. Membership exceeded a thousand. The correspondence was kept going with difficulty, and sometimes we had to sell our bread rations.

On March 29, 1949, with the help of the IRO we arrived in the Santa Fara camp near Bari. In June 1950, we were selected by an American army unit in West Germany. In command of the Albanian unit was Xhemal Laci, and second in command was Adem Gjura, with orders from Abaz Kupi and Gaqi Goga.

After a two-month course, Xhemal Laci told me that for political reasons the second in command should be someone from southern Albania. I always put aside my personal interests in favor of those of king and country and I would have objected to the post going to Neki Kushova who had changed sides more than once. Xhemal Laci came under the influence of Major Çaush Alia who was the Balli Kombëtar representative and turned his back on his friends. While I was with the unit, I tried to prevent his falling entirely into the hands of Major Alia.

On October 17, I was ordered on a military mission without being told where. When we arrived, we were taken to a *kula* on a beautiful mountain where we found five civilians who were introduced as Colonel Smith, Major Wells, Major Emil, Captain Joseph and some called Giovanni. The Colonel told us, "You are on your way to Albania and your commander is Adem Gjura and who disobeys him, disobeys the Americans." There were no problems or misunderstandings during our short instructional course.

We were divided into four groups. In charge of the Dibra group was Adem Gjura, second in command Selim Daci, and Sali Daliu and Gjetan Daci were members. In the end seven were withdrawn. They were a group from Vlora with Sadik Rama in charge and Daver Agaj as second. Also withdrawn with them was the Kruja group with Qazim Hoxha in charge and Iliaz Toptani as second and he later joined our group and I was pleased to have him.

While we were in the aircraft and about to parachute over Martanesh, I changed the plan so that we dropped into Bulqiza near Dibra. I knew that in Martanesh we were expected by the communist forces. Someone had given us away. Even there we were expected. At 2 p.m. on November 12, we had a battle with the communist forces where I lost three comrades and I was wounded in the left arm and leg. We withdrew and a friend and I started for my region, Reç.

The communists went to my house and executed my cousin, Rexhep Gjura, 23 years old, and my uncle, Imer Leka, 40 years old. In a short time they had arrested more than a hundred of my relatives of whom some died at home and some in camps. My family was interned in Berat. Two children died there and a young man died later at home of TB. Another two children of my cousin Shaban Gjura died in camps.

In spite of all the misery that my people and I have suffered, the sacrifice was worthwhile for king and country. I was very hurt when it was said that I had been sent by foreigners. I went to Albania under orders from our committee and Abas Kupi and carried out by Xhemal Laci. Because of our sacrifice Abas Kupi was promoted to general and Xhemal Laci to colonel and the latter without even fighting, while we are still treated as if we were serving a foreign power and not our king and country.

I don't want to say anything further as it reminds me only of misery and the period afterwards spent in Yugoslavia. The whole thing was very tragic. I just want to explain that I fled later to Yugoslavia only to tell the committee that the communists in Albania knew of our existence in advance and to prevent others from following the same fate. Nobody listened to me and subsequent groups were sent out and died uselessly.

One day Xhemal Laci and the committee will answer for all this. My actions for king and country are well known. I only wanted to live to inform others of our fate. My life is not worth anything anymore, as I did not succeed in my mission for freedom and country. I draw the attention of Your Majesty to the people that still surround you, as facts speak for themselves.

Interview conducted July 31, 1983

GAQI GOGA

Gaqi Goga was an Albanian royalist leader and exile figure. He was an Olympic athlete and became minister of sports under King Zog. He escaped from Albania by boat with Abas Kupi and was in Italy at the end of World War II, before joining Zog in Egypt in 1945 and serving as his private secretary. In this connection, he had dealings with British and American envoys sent to the king to negotiate about the Albanian operation. He was later in Rome where he assisted in finding Albanian refugees for military training for the operation. Goga later worked for a news agency in New York where he changed his name to George Gogh.

I first met Philby at Billy McLean's wedding in Rome in 1949. He was introduced to me as a car dealer. He was a very pleasant person, so nice, so witty, in spite of his heavy drinking. Abas Kupi and I were introduced to him by Billy McLean. On another occasion I saw him with John Hibberdine in the bar of the Flora Hotel near the Borghese Gardens in Rome. He was with a group of Albanians whom I remembered from the past, all of them involved in Albanian history. I asked myself, what does this car dealer have to do with Albania? This was after the committee was created.

I think that Philby was posted to Washington, partly because of the Albanian operation, partly because of the Ukraine. These were to be the two bases for an attack on the Soviet empire. There were still American and British agents in the Ukraine at that time. It was also the time of the Korean War, when the Americans were starting to think seriously. At least, that is what we imagined at the time.

Tito was in trouble too at this time. He was in a shaky position and afraid of the Russians. So it was the ideal moment to launch the Albanian operation.

Before 1949 I was private secretary to King Zog, living with all the family in Alexandria at 13 rue Laurens, Ramleh, Alexandria. It was a private villa belonging to Gougy Bey, rented from him. Zog's statement about the committee was given by Minister of Court Martini to the U.S. chargé d'affaires. The king came to Port Said from London in 1946. (His eldest sister Adile stayed in London.) I came to Egypt in 1945 from Italy. He first of all lived in the Hotel Manor House near the Pyramids. He asked me to find him a house. There were five sisters with him: Nafije, Senije, Myzejen, Maxhide, Ruhije. They had a Swiss maid called Clare Graf. There was Tati Kosova, nephew of the king, and Hysen Doshishti, another nephew. Tati was the son of Ceno Kryeziu. Kemal Messare came later as Royal Chamberlain. The colonel of the Royal Guard was Hysen Selmani. The captains were Zenel Shehu, Halil Sufa, Ali Gurabardhi, Muharem Gjoka, Qazim Preni, Bajram Neli. Leka had a Swiss governess, Elizabeth Aegerter, who was also Queen Geraldine's personal assistant. The driver was Ali Temali. That was the king's entire entourage in Egypt, all in the one house in Alexandria.

The king worked from 9 a.m. until 3 or 4 at night, all the time planning for the liberation of Albania. It was hard work, though we did play games after dinner, bridge and poker. The king did not sleep easily, so Minister Martini and I were condemned to staying up with him. We played for symbolic money only, 10 Egyptian pounds that the king put into the middle of the table every evening, but at least once a week King Farouk would visit us and then we played for real money.

King Victor Emmanuel of Italy was also in Alexandria and I was one of those who helped to make peace between him and King Zog. There was also King Simeon of Bulgaria and his wife Queen Joanna. So there was quite a circle of royal exiles in Egypt. King Zog's position was that he had a mandate. The government and the parliament had both confirmed his position as king before he left the country in 1939 and this was the legal position.

At the first meeting, the king and queen were present with Bob Low and another American called Robin. They came to see the king's reaction to the idea of Frashëri's presidency and afterwards, Minister of Court Sotir Martini was asked to make a statement about this and about the King's rights. During the talk, King Zog did a little biographical sketch of Frashëri, described his career, how he had given Frashëri the concession to sell his books to the ministry of education and helped him to make money. He said that he had no objection to Frashëri, but he wanted fighters on the committee as well. (He meant Abas Kupi.)

He stated, too, that after liberation there would be a referendum on the monarchy and free elections supervised by the United Nations. This statement was sent with Martini to Cairo and given to the American chargé d'affaires. The chargé d'affaires' wife and daughter had previously been introduced by me to Queen Geraldine.

The second meeting was a few days later. I was merely to confirm the above agreement. Afterwards Bob Low invited Kupi and me to dinner in Rome at which Kupi asked us to enlarge the committee. But Low preferred to keep it as it was and wanted the king to recognize it publicly, which he never did. Low had a very difficult job obtaining agreement on the committee and the junta. It is not easy to get Albanians to agree to anything. It's the same with all Balkan people and with the Arabs. We do not like to make compromises. It was the same problem as we had between the different parties when we were in Albania, only a bit worse.

I held several posts in Rome—secretary of the executive committee, secretary of the junta, director of press and propaganda, director of *Shqipëria* and still private secretary to King Zog. I was a great admirer of the king. He was very skillful and very intelligent.

The Malta operations were not done under the committee or the junta. The recruiting for them was done before either came into existence. And I am still not sure on what basis this was done. I think that it was part of the sponsors' plan to divide Albania into spheres of influence—the Balli in the south, the king in the north, the Kosovars in Kosovo. The British had their main interest in southern Albania, because of their predominant position in Greece. The Malta guerrillas did Balli propaganda in Albania and this was reported to me by Hamit Matjani from his camp in Greece. We had a disagreement about it in Rome. The Malta operations were all right from the military point of view, but not from the political. The junta only started discussing operations after their return from France, Britain and the United States. Malta was freelance activity by Ermenji and the British.

The British were qualified about the country. They had experience. The Americans knew nothing about it. But later it changed and the Americans began to play the game seriously. And they had the money. Money plays a very important role in Balkan politics.

The junta met in my 12-room apartment in Piazza Santiago di Cile, Rome. It was a special room with one table and six chairs, regularly inspected to keep it secure. The executive committee also met there sometimes. Leib lived ten minutes away in the Frascati district in a very nice villa. The Balli people criticized him for his high living and for all the money he spent, but they were only too glad to get their share of the money that was going. Anyway, it would have made a bad impression on Albanians to have attempted the thing on the cheap.

I went to the training school in Germany three times and, even though it sounds crazy, I still don't know where it was. It was halfway up a hill surrounded by trees with a beautiful view overlooking a valley. I always arrived there at night, after long detours, with other members of the committee or junta. I remember having dinner there and then spending the next day watching karate and knife training.

I remember Major Emil. He was the most powerful personality and he spoke Albanian. He was strong like a weight lifter. There was another officer close to him with a glass eye, not in such good physical shape. He was round faced, like a Slav, and Burke told me that he was a Pole.

I am sure that the training was expert, that the officers were competent, but the period was too short and the trainees were physically and mentally not up to the task. There were no officers among them, no leadership potential, and they were physically not strong enough. I know what I'm talking about. I was a decathlon champion with 5900 points and I was good at 100-meter hurdles, tennis, skiing and gymnastics. I know that you need more than five or six weeks to get a man into shape. And he has to have a good physique at the outset. He has to have a lung capacity of over 6000 cubic centimeters, so that he can run properly. He needs a 16-inch neck, not a 12-inch neck like a chicken or a 34-inch chest. It is true that most Albanians are short, except the Albanians from the north, but I don't understand how they chose these people. They had no shoulders, no arms. They couldn't run. Their lungs were not good enough and they had no education. They were brave, but not up to the job.

We had about 500 Albanian officers in exile, but most of them had first of all served King Zog, then King Victor Emmanuel of Italy, then the German regency. So there was not great trust in them, because they had collaborated with the enemy. The view was that we needed people who were clean in this respect. So that is why they weren't sent.

The men who went were probably capable of living and working in areas where they were born, where they had friends and cousins, but they were not up to living in the open in unfriendly territory, carrying out tasks of a political nature. At the outset I proposed sending better qualified people. I suggested sending someone from the executive committee. They needed a famous name, I said, someone with a reputation, someone to guide them. But they said, "No, it's only a start, we don't need to send out political leaders yet."

The first team that went in November 1950 was the best that we had. And they did achieve something. By that I mean that they achieved two or three out of ten rather than zero.

The Matjani operation was our last hope. It was studied and analyzed in every detail. It was so well done, much better than the other expeditions. And it had a military purpose. Matjani had developed contacts with the Albanian army during his previous operations. Shehu and Sufa planned to use these contacts and organize a rebellion of Albanian officers.

As for the others, not all were volunteers. The party obliged them to go. It was capable of taking measures against them, even liquidating them. And each party was keen on recruiting members. The Albanian exiles were poor, uneducated, living in camps, with little hope of finding jobs. The parties were able to offer them something, dignity as well as decent pay, using American money.

In Athens in November 1950, the men did not want to go. Michael Burke said to me, "George, I don't want to see a failure." He had his doubts, too, and he sent me to talk to Ramazan Cenaj. Cenaj said he did not want to go with a team composed like it was, without leadership. I told him that he had given his word, he had signed a promise. And the aircraft was waiting to take off. Eventually he agreed to go, but he warned me that others in the future might well refuse. I was there with Said Kryeziu and Zef Pali. They wanted someone qualified and well known, with good local connections, and I agreed with them, but I had no power inside the junta. There were former Albanian officers who could have gone.

I feel sure now, having read the books that appeared in the past ten or fifteen years, that Philby gave the Soviet Union information about this mission. It is true that Albanians, especially in groups of four or five, tend to talk too loudly. They are not very quiet in their conversation. But I cannot see how any Albanian in Rome or anywhere else could have known about the dates or drop zones of the missions. Only the Americans—and perhaps Philby—would have had such information.

The training school was isolated. No Albanians left it to go for a drink in bars. They were not allowed to write letters from it. And they themselves did not know dates and places until the very last minute. Such detailed information cannot have come from Albanian sources.

I think it probable, however, that general information about the missions did reach the communists from our people. Men were writing letters from the Labour Battalion in Munich, complaining about the men who had been chosen, sometimes even giving their names, asking why so-and-so was going on a mission and not so-and-so. Tirana might well have obtained this information from their agents in Rome.

Yatsevitch came into the Albanian picture at the same time as Joe Leib. He was mainly in Greece, some of the time in Italy, but Leib was the one that I saw most of all. He lived with his wife Mildred, who was in poor health, and he had a very good salary, a good standard of living. The Balli people criticized him for this, but his view was that you have to spend money in order to succeed, especially in the Balkans. I was his close friend.

I heard that three destroyers and two submarines were sent from the island in the Gulf of Corinth to Sazan Island. But all they did was to release hundreds of buoys, all with Free Albania flags flying from them.

Matjani went in and out of Albania six times. He was known as "Tiger" and everyone was afraid of him, but once the trap was laid for him through Zenel Shehu, he was lost. The question now is, were he and Shehu betrayed by Philby? My information is that after 1951 Philby was in Turkey and it was to Turkey that King Zog sent word first of all to find the two emissaries that he needed. One of them was called Rexhep Radomira. The king asked them to do it and they refused, so when the Americans asked him to try again, he replied that the only two men he could send were from his own Royal Guard.

"They are ready to give their lives for me," he said.

But why did these two people in Turkey refuse to go on the mission? I think that Philby was also in Turkey at this time and there could be a link here, although I do not know whether he was in a position to know about the Shehu/Sufa operation.

Hamit Matjani had prepared a number of officers before leaving Albania for Greece the last time. He had a plan ready and the two Royal Guards were to reinforce this plan. All three of them were to encourage Albanian officers to rebel, Shehu in Dibra and Sufa among the king's men in Mati. The British had always wanted to do something in Mati with Bilal Kola, ever since 1946.

Interview conducted August 9, 1983

Dino Gregory

Captain Dino Gregory was a British sailor and entrepreneur. He had worked in the Aegean and in 1948–1949, with Sam Barclay, and built the boat Stormie Seas *that was chartered for the Albanian operation to smuggle the Albanian fighters into Albania.*

I helped crew the *Bessie* from Athens to Volos and Salonika in the winter of 1947–48, running cargo for the Greek government troops. We sold the *Bessie* in August 1948. I was with Sam and John building the *Stormie Seas* in the winter of 1948–49. She was launched in January 1949, rigged in early February. Then we sailed for Malta on February 15, arriving March 31.

I worked with Sam and John on the building. We rented a corner of a yard and built it with an adze and a Jacob saw. I stayed in Malta on my own while John and Sam were in England. (John was best man at Sam's wedding.) I used to meet the crew from a ship called the *Cougar*, belonging to the Goulandris family, playing bazooki music and danced with the crew from Andros Island, while the *Stormie Seas* was on the slip on Manuel Island, Malta. I saw them fit compartments concealed by Sam's drawings hanging on the wall. At the time I was too delicate to ask what they were for, but I learnt later that they were for arms.

I remember Lofty, a very amusing fellow. I don't know what rank he was. They never wore a uniform. The first time, we left Malta by ourselves and took the "pixies" on board on the high seas. They came up to us in an old, round fishing vessel. Two or three of them spoke Greek. They showed me the new watches they'd all been issued with and their money. They were enthusiastic about the watches. A few were calm, but most were rather tense and nervous.

We were struck by lightning at the south of the Adriatic and it was then that we put into one of the islands off Corfu, to put right the damage to the radio caused by the lightning. A Greek harbor patrol came up to us and we had to make an excuse to persuade them to go away. I think it was Merlera Island, also known as Erikoussa.

We waited half a mile offshore, with the engines idling or maybe just drifting, waiting for the dory to come back. I remembered that we seemed to be making a terrible lot of noise. Darby and Lofty took their boots off, rolled up their trousers, beached the boat and waited while the "little men" went ashore.

A sirocco, a high wind from the southeast, got up soon after we had landed the men. We were driven to the north and we lost a dory. We had to run for it in the wrong direction and then reach for it into the enemy harbor, into the Gulf of Vlora. It really was a case of "any port in a storm." It is amazing that we weren't spotted, because there was a Russian submarine base on Sazan Island. I remember seeing the lights of Vlora. We anchored and hoped to wait until the storm abated.

At dawn we were riding at anchor and we saw some soldiers taking up positions on the shore opposite to where we were. They were pointing their rifles at us and gesticulating to us to come ashore and explain ourselves. When they saw that we weren't going to do that, they opened fire. It seems that they made no attempt to communicate with the garrison on Sazan Island. Either they had no radios, or else they wanted to keep all the glory of capturing us for themselves. And they made no effort to put a boat out.

The only way in which they would have caught us, in fact, was if we had surrendered. But as soon as they opened fire, we slipped the anchor and ran back to sea as fast as we could, leaving the anchor behind. The weather had calmed down a little. So we extricated ourselves from the Gulf of Vlora, slightly peppered and minus one anchor, but otherwise intact. All this was after our second landing, at the end of our voyage, after which we returned to Piraeus.

That was the end of my work for the British with Sam and John, but it was through them that I was taken on by the Americans. Frank Vernoudakis was a very good friend of Hod Fuller as well as of John and Sam. He introduced me to people from the American embassy and then I was made captain of the *Surcouf*, which belonged to the embassy. Vernoudakis knew that the Americans wanted crew. Vernoudakis was the one who arranged our pay at that time. He was an ichthyologist from Constantinople working with the Americans.

Frank would have known about our runs to Salonika, but not about the Albanian business. He would have known that I was used to move them or sail round the Mediterranean. Vernoudakis was my link with Hod Fuller.

I took members of the U.S. embassy on pleasure trips to the islands and then I started using my own boat, the *Poseidon*, supplying the American island in the Halcyon Sea. The island was called Panaghia, but the islands were also called Kalanissia, the "beautiful" islands, because they had water and safe haven.

Panaghia is the main island, with the monastery and the church. They are on the southeast side. The west of the island is barren. There was only one monk and one priest. Fishermen used to call in occasionally and a family used to stay for a few days once a year to harvest what the priest had sown. It was only about a mile in circumference.

The *Poseidon*, the boat that did all this work, was in the name of me and my brother Nikos. We built it in 1951–52 and it was ready at the end of 1952, at Perma, where we also built the *Stormie Seas*. We often stayed on the west side of the canal and went back through it once a week to Piraeus. We went up the Adriatic, but never beyond Corfu. The authorities had become suspicious and it was much harder to make sea landings.

Interview conducted October 8, 1983

SIR REGINALD HIBBERT

Sir Reginald Alfred Hibbert (1922–2002) was a British military officer and historian. Born in Hertfordshire, he was educated at Queen Elizabeth College in Barnet and at Worcester College, Oxford, where he completed a degree in history in 1946. During World War II, he served as a British liaison officer at the Stables Mission of the Special Operations Executive (SOE) in northern Albania. He was parachuted into the country in December 1943 to help maintain contacts with Albanian resistance fighters. After the war, he joined the Foreign Service and held appointments in Bucharest, Vienna, Guatemala, Ankara, Brussels, Ulan Bator (1964–1969), Singapore (1969) and Bonn. He ended his diplomatic career as British ambassador to France (1979–1982) and retired in Wales. Hibbert's insider view of the Albanian civil war during German occupation in 1943–1944 is given in his book Albania's National Liberation Struggle: The Bitter Victory, *London 1991, the first objective history of the period.*

I joined the Albanian mission in December 1943. We were being chased around the highlands in the north. The Germans had launched a winter offensive to shatter both the partisan groups and the nationalist groups in that area.

I was dropped into the borders of Kosovo and marched south. I was dropped on the border, moved into Yugoslavia and then moved out again. At that time, Dibra was Albanian. It is now part of Yugoslavia. It is part of the territory the Germans gave the Albanians when they occupied Yugoslavia.

We were on the mountain heights between Kosovo in the north and Peshkopia and Dibra in the eastern center, with Montenegro behind us and the mountains going westward to the sea in front of us. The Germans had carried out an important offensive and shattered all the groups, partisans included. The north was then virtually without effective opposition to the Germans for the winter. This was not the same in the south, because during the winter Albania is more or less divided in two by the river Shkumbini, with no communication between north and south across the Drin valley.

In the south the partisans kept going in spite of the German offensive, although they were reduced to rags and tatters. Mehmet Shehu kept the First Brigade, the "vengeance" brigade, going in terrible conditions through the winter. They were chased by the Germans and they survived, but they were a tiny group by then.

We stayed in the mountains in the north. I was a very junior member of the mission. There was a man called Richard Riddle, who was my chief, and Tony Simcox was his number two. And there was a Pole, Michael Lis. He's still alive, in Paris. There was Neill and Hands up in the north, and Kemp who came through. By the time I got in, Peter Kemp was in a very disillusioned state of mind. He had been with the partisans, but his particular group had been shattered.

Following this German offensive that winter, all the British missions attached themselves to whatever surviving resistance they could find, most of it in hiding and covert. The British missions were chased around the mountains, partly by the Germans, partly (one has to say it) by avaricious Albanians who thought they could get gold and goodness knows what out of us, partly by sincere nationalist Albanians, and partly by remnants of the partisans. Little partisan *chetas* survived in small numbers, a group of ten in a district.

During the winter we all moved around the place, making contacts, talking to people, trying to feel out the ground, trying to encourage resistance, trying to find out who would

Sir Reginald Hibbert (1922–2002), British historian and member of the Special Operations Executive in northern Albania during the Second World War.

be effective. And some missions became more heavily committed to the partisans. It depended entirely on the political circumstances. But the whole thing was ineffective in terms of resistance to the Germans, except that their existence there made the Germans feel very uneasy. This was the reason for the drives that the Germans conducted into the villages through the mountains to try to chase us.

The man that we had most dealings with in our mission was Muharrem Bajraktari, the chief of the Luma area. He was an engaging personality, spoke a bit of French, knew a bit about the outside world. What he was saying was, "Give me a million gold sovereigns and I will give you Albania." He was quite serious about this. If you reckon that there are a million Albanians, it was one gold sovereign per head and in a sense cheap at the price. He wasn't stupid and he knew, as the other chieftains knew, that the real trouble was that their authority was slowly being totally undermined by German violence.

The Germans, in their sweeps for partisans, spread destruction and ruin wherever they went. When you destroy a village, and you chase the people out and you burn their houses; in winter, in Albania, these people really do become a proletariat. They have nothing left, except their children. And what did they do? Flee from the village into the hills. And who was there to receive them, but the ragged partisans? If they stayed behind, they were slaughtered.

In effect that winter the Germans were the recruiting officers of the partisans, because they didn't succeed in crushing and destroying the partisans totally in the south. They did succeed in destroying a good many villages and dwellings and arms with the result that these people, although not believing in communism, had nothing left and only one way out.

The chieftains would say, "You must realise that the people do not want a chief who will lead them to destruction. What they want is a chief who will protect them. Therefore we, the chieftains, cannot just launch our people blindly against the Germans, because if we do, we destroy them and ourselves. What we should do is recruit people, keep the place steady and hold everything ready for the day when you, the allies, invade the Balkans. We shall then deliver Albania on your side." A perfectly reasonable proposition actually. Of course, our demand was something different. We wanted them to do something now, to distract the Germans and enable us to invade Europe more easily.

One has to say that the only people in Albania then who were sufficiently ruthless and whose politics fitted in with the idea of immediate action were the communist partisans.

Everyone saw Albania as something secondary in importance to Yugoslavia. We used to have the greatest difficulty finding out what were the real links between the Albanian and Yugoslav partisans. That the liaison existed is undoubted and that the senior partners were the Yugoslavs is also undoubted. I'm not saying they controlled the Albanians, but the Albanians were in a predicament where they needed any help they could get and the only communists around who could help from outside were the Yugoslavs, with the Russians helping largely through the Yugoslavs.

In the spring of 1944, Billy McLean, David Smiley and Julian Amery, who had been the first people into Albania (or at least Smiley and McLean) had done the first recce, were dropped back into Albania with the idea of encouraging the Zogists. They came into the north more or less with a brief to support the Zogists and of course they were a powerful team for supporting them. The real truth is that by that time, the Zogists were a very localized group, concentrated mainly in the Tirana area. McLean, Smiley and Amery came with a brief, I would say, to prove that Albania could be made Zogist.

But by the time they started operating, the future fate of Albania had really been decided by what had happened in the winter in the south. The survival of the partisan force, however shattered it was, its mere survival combined with the destruction wrought by the Germans and the consequent recruitment for the partisans, made it possible for the partisans suddenly to multiply as soon as the good weather came in April. The First ("Vengeance") Brigade was down to something like 400 men at one stage in the south. But as soon as the good weather came, in a matter of weeks, even days, to everybody's astonishment, the brigade became a division. Suddenly the partisans in the south turned out to have an army at their disposal, a small army, but nevertheless an army.

Hoxha at this time was in the south with the British mission. Colonel Palmer was with him and Victor Smith. They remained with Hoxha. So as the partisans grew, Palmer became the liaison officer in Albania with the most potential military force. I was still in the north. The partisans, having a clear political aim of their own, did not want to get too bloodied fighting against the Germans. They were fighting the Germans only insofar as was necessary to establish their credentials. They turned north with the clear political aim of precipitating what they had already precipitated in the south. In April or May they crossed the Shkumbini and came north. And the man who came north was Mehmet Shehu, the man who had kept the partisans together in the south during the winter, with what was then called the First Partisan Division.

By the end of the winter, our mission had become very disillusioned by the nationalists around us. We had been chased around the mountains and they had done nothing. The partisans were reforming in the north at that stage and we were partly with the nationalists and partly with the partisans. McLean and Smiley were fully committed to the Zogists, and the other missions about were committed to one side or another.

Shehu arrived in the Dibra area and immediately sent out a contact to us, because we were the mission in the area, but at the same time delivered an assault on the Germans at Dibra, a well-judged assault, but I think a political assault. What he was doing was precipitating precisely the polarization that suited the partisans. They fought the Germans, thus forcing an Albanian-German confrontation in which the Germans started burning villages and destroying the Albanian economy, as a result of which the Albanians started joining the partisans.

Our mission immediately received instructions to help the partisans, including Mehmet Shehu. Our standing instructions were that we were to support any Albanian force which was thought to be taking action against the Germans.

The battle of Dibra then took place and it was quite a serious business. The partisans were badly mauled, but then so were the Germans. After this mauling, Mehmet Shehu and his First Division were compelled to retreat into Macedonia, that is to say, into Yugoslavia. We retreated with them, because there was no future for us otherwise. And once this battle had taken place, the nationalists immediately started helping the Germans. The Germans were after the partisans and also after us.

We became the mission working with Mehmet Shehu. Hoxha was still in the south. We then teamed up with Shehu and his division and it was quite an experience, and went up into the mountains of Macedonia in the direction of Chechevu (?) and we pleaded with Bari for supplies for Mehmet Shehu's division. Of course, other missions were pleading for help for the Zogists and other groups. This was Bari's dilemma. After a few days in Macedonia, we got British air drops from the Balkan Air Force for Shehu: ammunition, weapons, clothing and footwear, things they needed. It was not all that much in quantity, but the effect on morale was terrific.

The drops came from airports outside Bari, controlled by the Balkan Air Force, which was a unit of the Royal Air Force dedicated entirely to flying sorties and missions over the Balkans. There was a commander and American planes attached to it. It had ties with SOE. It was dedicated to supporting Tito mainly, also Greece and Albania. Mehmet Shehu was then able to say, "The allies are with me." That was what he wanted.

Shehu led his division back—and us with it—to resume the battle of Dibra. This time he succeeded and we got the Balkan Air Force fighters in with rockets against the German barrack areas, and this time the battle of Dibra was won, in June or July 1944. In no time at all. The partisans had not one division up there but three. A tremendous multiplication took place, a recruitment of people who simply went over to the victors. We helped them with air drops.

We established ourselves on this plateau which occupies an important geographical position at the center of the north of Albania, in a key position in relation to Tirana, the river Shkumbini and Peshkopia. We became the supply base for these partisan divisions, existing ones and those in the process of formation. Then the partisans, having established their credentials in fighting the Germans, turned to wipe out the nationalists and Zogists. They struck northwards pursuing the Zogists in about July or August.

By now, the partisans were also going hammer and tongs for Balli Kombëtar chieftains. There was a man called Hali Ladiair (?) who had been one of the great men and caused infinite difficulty throughout the winter in our area. The partisans went for him straight away and overnight all the people who had previously sworn that they were his faithful servants became partisans. And that was the end of him.

What was serious was that they started chasing the Zogists, who had a degree of organization and had had shown a degree of resistance to the Germans. There was Smiley, McLean and Amery saying, "For God's sake stop the partisans." And here we were saying, "You can't stop them, they have become a natural force and we are not talking morality here; we are simply saying what is happening."

Riddle sent me out into the Zogist area with our own guides. The whole thing was chaotic at the time. I was to try to find McLean, Smiley and Amery to bring them back to our mission, so that there would not be a direct clash between the partisans and them. It was a foolhardy thought. It could not possibly work, and they would not have come even if I had found them. I did not find them. I could not get away from the partisans.

We had had a conference in the spring of 1944. McLean had summoned us all to a conference. We had all discussed partisans, nationalists, Muharremites, Zogists and so on. It was about a week before the partisans crossed the Shkumbini and so our discussions had been in vain, because it was the partisans crossing the Shkumbini that decided the situation.

By this time what had become obvious to us in liaison with Mehmet Shehu was that there was some link between him and the Yugoslavs. We met the odd Yugoslav, we even met the odd Russian, but it was difficult to find out what they were doing. We then transferred to the Third Division under a man called Bedri Taku (?). We organized supplies through the Air Force for them, helped them, and took part in skirmishes on the outskirts of Tirana. They actually fought in the outskirts, carrying out raids; they did it rather well. It was effective and pinned down a number of Germans.

By that time the partisans had fanned through the north, recruiting their followers, until the north was effectively under partisan control, with pockets of resistance from nationalists here and there. During those months it was a civil war with one side also fighting the Germans. By this time the Germans were beginning to use the roads for traffic out of Greece. And the partisans were camping along the road on both sides, picking off a convoy here and a convoy there.

From the point of view of our mission, the interest had gone out of it. We had become disillusioned with the whole thing. There was a frightful confusion about who was on whose side. It became rather distasteful, the quarreling among British missions. If you look up the signals, you would find each mission passionately pleading for what it saw as its cause, for its own Albanian group. The one thing all the missions were agreed on was the total incompetence of the people at Bari who, poor devils, had to send us contradictory instructions.

By October '44 the partisans had really won. They were crushing the nationalists and it was not a very tasteful situation. After all, we were not there to preside over a revolution as well as a war against the Germans. They did not need our help any more and they were becoming nasty towards us because they said we were not supporting them enough. So Richard Riddle said, "Well, let's get out." Again, we could not get much clarity from Bari and communications were very difficult. So we marched south.

Richard Riddle, Michael Lis and I set off with mules and Italian people to help us. By this time we were part of the establishment among the partisans. We said goodbye to them and said, "Look, we are evacuating ourselves." Mehmet Shehu gave us letters for Enver Hoxha. There was an extraordinary mixture of thoroughgoing partisans mixing with local people who were almost all Balli Kombëtar. It was the days of the united front, but it soon ended, and not happily for some. We marched for about a week or ten days and finally came to where Enver Hoxha was. We were received by Hoxha. We met Victor Smith and Brigadier Palmer. We contacted other British missions as we went and there was a great camaraderie amongst us. We discussed with Hoxha what the position was and he thanked us for what we had done for the partisans.

We marched further south and finally came to the coast opposite Santa Quaranta, opposite Corfu. And it just happened that Italy was carrying out a raid on the coast, as we got there. We made contact with the SAS and hitched a ride back to Italy in their support craft and turned up totally unexpectedly in Bari to the SOE staff. This was October or November 1944. Julian Amery and others were evacuated about this time. We had our anxiety about their welfare and what the partisans would do to them if they got them. This was why I was sent out to help, but they got away by their own means.

At that time the Yugoslav influence began to emerge pretty clearly. When you went talking to Hoxha at his headquarters you could feel it. It was perfectly understandable because Yugoslavia was the nearest place. Then as the Albania communist party came to the fore, the sheer force of events put them to some extent under the Yugoslav thumb. There was no reason why any Albanian would want to be permanently under the Yugoslav thumb, but this was where they were getting help from. The link between Albania and Yugoslavia was very close and we were in a disadvantageous position in that the transition from a Mihailovic pattern to a Tito pattern had been carried much further in Yugoslavia than it had been carried in Albania. This was because of the slower maturing of the war in Albania. So the Albanians were much more resentful of us than Tito was. And of course Tito had his own ambitions over Albania and did not particularly want the British around.

One thing that worked against Britain and caused the break with Albania was that the Albanians never really earned their spurs in battle the way Tito did. The revolution in Albania was not carried through in wartime as it was in Yugoslavia. The Yugoslavs had their own designs for Albania and did not want the British around there, although they did not mind having them around in Yugoslavia.

Then what happened was the Yugoslavs overbid their hand, as communists do, in the postwar years and actually went for control of Albania. There was a man called Koçi Xoxe who was really the number one pro–Yugoslav in the Albanian leadership.

Very soon after the war there was a crisis and Xoxe was eliminated just at the moment when the Yugoslavs were aiming to carry out their coup to make Albania part of Yugoslavia under a single communist leadership. Enver Hoxha resisted it and got rid of Xoxe. Hoxha's policy after the war was to oppose in a very bloody way any movement that would bring Albania into play as a pawn either for or against Yugoslavia.

If the war had stopped and the allies had won their victory with Mihailovic powerful and at large in Yugoslavia, we would have had exactly the same anti–British emotions as in Albania.

The plain fact is that the partisans asserted themselves, they recruited people. Had Britain decided to send all the drops to the Zogists and not to the partisans, the Zogists would still not have won. The partisans would have won, but later and with greater difficulty and greater bloodshed.

During the war the main idea was to cause damage to the Germans. Julian Amery used to give us little lectures about how we were contributing to communism, but there was never anything about that in our instructions. The decisive factor was the sheer brutality and violence of the Germans. It was this that communized Albania. The communists were there but they would never have achieved anything if the Germans had not gone through the country with such brutality. The Bulgarian auxiliaries were particularly frightful. They would slaughter everybody down to the last child. This altered the social structure of Albania, because the chiefs could not protect the people against the killing. And so they lost their authority and their followers. The communists came along and harvested both.

I would not have thought that the personal views of SOE officers had much difference. Bari did what they had to do. If we as a mission were with a partisan force that was fighting the Germans in Dibra, we qualified for assistance. The same applied to any other group. And whatever Amery, McLean and Smiley may say now, the fact is that the partisans did almost all the fighting. I remember a famous telegram from McLean. Bari sent us a copy in the field by radio. "At last the Zogists are moving. They have launched an attack on a bridge. They have blown up the bridge. Smiley, Amery and I took part in it." It was marked, "Please show this personally to the Secretary of State for India." Julian Amery sustained a wound in the course of it, a bullet grazed his chin. And the Secretary of State for India was his father.

McLean was putting on the best face he could, but he really had to scrape the barrel to produce evidence of actual Zogist resistance. And this was at a time when the Germans in Dibra were being invaded by the partisans. And after that battle I personally looked after 30 partisan wounded, with absolutely no medicines, men lying there that one could do nothing for, mangled and with broken limbs. And here was McLean at the same moment talking about this terrific engagement in the north—the blowing up of a bridge.

Towards the end of 1944, the partisans were operating against the Germans on a far greater scale than the Zogists. By midsummer 1944 the partisans were in the field, taking action with forces, which simply outnumbered and outclassed anything the nationalists could put in the field, except the government, but they were already hand-in-glove with the Germans.

I was totally unmoved by Amery's outburst in his book at the way Bari treated

Abas Kupi. We could all have played that game. Every mission had people to whom they were under some sort of personal obligation for their work together and the protection they had enjoyed. It gave no one any special claim for a particular candidate. I really think one should not be too moved by that sort of thing. Everybody's personal emotions were terribly tied up with the people you had been working with there. It can't be otherwise when you are living so close to people in such circumstances.

Abas Kupi had done something, but he had not been effective. He could have been effective if the partisans had not come north, if they had been crushed by the Germans in the winter, if we had given him enough money and brought arms in. As the Germans collapsed, Abas Kupi would have been effective. But nothing overcomes the fact that the partisans were not crushed. Mehmet Shehu was the hero really. He was a terrific commander and he kept them together.

My comment on the postwar period is that it was a pity, the way things went. It was a pity that the revolution was less advanced than it was in Yugoslavia. The long-term British and western European interest in Albania is precisely for Albania and Yugoslavia to work together. The best chance of achieving that would have been for Albania to enter the postwar world with satisfactory relationships with Western powers. That would have meant Britain and America, because we were the people who were there.

It is a tremendous tragedy that the Corfu Channel incident occurred, because it was used as a tremendous stick to beat Albania with. Albania regarded it as something the British were using to crush them. The crisis between Albania and Yugoslavia was at breaking point and Albania simply turned against us. At the moment when Xoxe was eliminated, it would have been a very good thing if Albania had had links with the West. That might have saved it from all the terrible things that followed.

Peter Kemp is an old warrior. He was on the Franco side in the Spanish Civil War. In Albania he was pretty tough, especially after his disillusionment with the partisans. He was a tough anti-partisan man.

It was historically wrong to think that one could overthrow Hoxha, because the people Britain and the United States were using for this had lost their merit. There was no chance that anybody would re-establish things against Hoxha. The only thing to do at that stage was to try and find some way of staying in the picture, so that eventually, when it suited Albania, proper relations could be resumed.

John Hibberdine died a little while ago. We dropped into Albania together. He later joined up with Kemp, or maybe he joined with Neill. He stayed up in the north and was involved to some extent in contacts with Gani Kryeziu, who was one of the Kosovo chieftains. We developed a good liaison with the Albanian chiefs in Kosovo, which did not suit the Yugoslavs after the war. I think Gani Kryeziu was worth more than Abas Kupi. Hibberdine came through our camp in the summer of 1944, when his activity in the north had been totally shattered by the communists moving north and Gani Kryeziu fled. The nationalist side turned out to be historically the wrong side. Hibberdine came through our mission and we handed him to someone else for evacuation. I think that he then went to Southeast Asia for SOE and after the war he was recruited by MI6. After the war Kemp became a thoroughgoing anti-communist on any basis whatever. He wrote a book called *No Colour or Crest* or something. I am sure that people like me are an anathema to people like Kemp, simply because we worked with the partisans.

Elliot Watrous was the section staff officer in Bari. There was a Major or Colonel Leach in charge of the Albanian section in Bari. Elliot Watrous then succeeded him as head of section. For the whole of the postwar period he was in Bush House, in BBC overseas services, doing something in connection with the Balkans. He is now retired and lives somewhere in Surrey or the Thames valley. He was a really disillusioned man when he left. He would have seen all our telegrams that went in. Like all of us, he was dealing with a situation he simply was not trained for. After all, who is trained to be a civil war expert? What was not really explained when one went in was that this was really about the future of these people's lives.

It was not in our power to choose whether it would be Hoxha's Albania or anyone else's. If the Germans had crushed Mehmet Shehu and his remaining troops in the winter of 1943–44, we would not have had Hoxha's Albania. This was nothing to do with us. They then asserted themselves in the spring through conditions which had grown in Albania not in any way due to Britain's making, not under our control and at the time not understood by us. There was no way in which Britain could have said, "Stop, we are going to make you a Zogist Albania." Even if we had spent £5 million on arming Zog and Bajraktari and Gani Kryeziu, we would only have had an Albania consumed with civil war after the German withdrawal. And that civil war would have been decided by Tito.

Unless you predicate the possibility of our defying Tito and continuing to maintain Mihailovic, the very thought of our altering the issue in Albania is absurd as Tito had the forces. No amount of effort from us in Albania could have stopped Tito having it his way. He would have swept through with Mehmet Shehu and Enver Hoxha as his faithful allies. Things would have been different, but we would not have seen the Zogists in Albania. To think that we had a choice is vain. And then a few years later we were again robbed of choice by the Corfu Channel incident. I don't criticize the British government for what they did then, but I think it a pity that in more recent times we have not tried to overcome it.

The Albanian authorities now, as then, are bloody fools. They are very difficult. In Paris the Albanian ambassador presented his credentials on the same day as me. So by protocol we were always seated next to each other at public functions, although we had no official relations. I used to say to him, "Why is your government so silly, always insisting that it has to have the gold and all that before we establish diplomatic relations? The sensible thing is to establish diplomatic relations and then talk about these problems. You would get much further that way. Albania would have a footing in the Western world, which would be additional to the relations you have with France and Italy, and, if I may say so, more valuable, because of the legacy of those wartime days and our links with America and so on." This chap would listen quite amiably. Then at the next function he would say, "I have been thinking about what you said and the position is that it is up to Britain to make the first step." And I would say he was just being foolish. It is just a continuation of this rather shabby tragedy that has gone on since the war. But it is really important because of the damage that Albania can do Yugoslavia. Albania can be the detonator of Yugoslavia.

The BLOs had only a marginal influence on the course of events. Only a landing in Albania by substantial Allied forces could have compelled events to take a different turn.

The outcome of the war in Albania was disappointing to all the BLOs, whichever side they had supported. The disappointment of those with the nationalists was the simple disappointment of defeat. That of the BLOs with the partisans was more complex. In one sense they had the satisfaction of being on the winning side, but, in another, they felt the victory turning sour even as it happened. Relations with the partisan leaders were never wholly smooth and became more uneven as Enver Hoxha and his colleagues scented victory and power. The long dispute over Kupi was ended too late for there to be a chance of relations with Enver Hoxha's government starting on a footing of confidence or even respect. Enver Hoxha's charm proved invariably to be a short-term tactical weapon: his strategic moves tended always to be unfriendly and damaging. Those who worked with the partisans were left in the end with a feeling of having been used. The victory was not theirs; the achievement was flawed; the war against the Germans had shifted away from Albania; Albania had never been quite an ally and now became increasingly alien.

The men who served as BLOs were marked by Albania in the sense that all of them carried away strong feelings about the events in which they had taken part. Albania's relative insignificance and its self-imposed isolation from the rest of Europe have provided no normal channels for the expression of those feelings, such as have existed for those who worked with the resistance forces in other countries. The strong feelings have persisted nonetheless for over forty years; and to this day the former BLOs divide into those who were with the partisans and those who were with the nationalists, and they keep their old differences alive.

I experienced these feelings twice in a very direct way in the course of my career in the Diplomatic Service. In 1951, I was told by the then head of the Security Department at the Foreign Office that information had been laid against me by someone who had known me in Albania to the effect that I had been a communist at that time and had acknowledged that this was so. I was duly interrogated. The case was dropped. I worked out in the course of the interrogation that the informant must have been the Hon. Rowland Winn, and when I put this to the interrogator he tacitly confirmed it. As my diary has shown, I was in contact with Winn for three days in late September 1944, at the very end of my stay with the Stables mission, Winn had broken his leg when he dropped to us on September 19 and he and I argued fiercely whenever I came near him about the rights and wrongs of supporting the partisans or nationalists. He, with all the zeal of the newly arrived, told us we were wrong to support the partisans. I, with ten months of Albania behind me, said that the partisans were the only ones worth supporting. I expect I added that had I been an Albanian, I would have been a partisan. I would have been conscious, in saying this, that by September 1944 the word was becoming synonymous with communist. Winn evidently marked me down as a dangerous man. In 1951 he had returned from a hard experience with his regiment in Korea and was apparently full of a crusading spirit against communism and those whom he chose to suspect of being its servants. Winn and I used to encounter each other from time to time at events in London, including oddly enough at one or two regimental reunions after his old regiment, the 8th Hussars, had been merged with mine, the 4th

Hussars, to form the Queen's Royal Irish Hussars. We exchanged courtesies but never discussed Albania or his allegations against me. I did not raise the matter as my knowledge of his initiative was strictly privileged, and I assumed that he did not raise it because he did not know that I knew.

Many years later, at the beginning of 1980 when I was ambassador at Paris, I was warned by the Foreign and Commonwealth Office that Rowland Winn (by now Lord St. Oswald) had once more been laying information against me, this time to influential acquaintances in France, including Count Michel Poniatowski, a very close collaborator of the president of the Republic, M. Giscard d'Estaing. He had, it seemed, told them of his contact with me during the war and of my alleged communist sympathies. The FCO told me that they were taking steps to remind him of the careful investigation of his allegations which had been made in 1951, which had found them to be groundless, and to persuade him to desist from giving them further currency. It may be thought extraordinary that a brief and insignificant encounter in the Albanian mountains in the autumn of 1944 should continue to have a reverberation nearly forty years later. To someone who served in Albania, it is not so surprising. Those who took part in the events of those days still feel strongly about them, and those who believed in conspiracy theories then seem still to believe in them today. Most would not push their passion or fanaticism to the extreme of delation or of trying to discredit their own country's ambassador, but many trace whatever they regard as evil in the modern world to an origin in their own Albanian experience. Such was the vividness of that experience and such its long-lasting effect on those who endured it.

In reality, the process which we witnessed in Albania in 1943 and 1944 was, like most historical processes, a very complex one for which the blame and/or credit were widely spread. The BLOs were small figures on a very large scene. Enver Hoxha himself was not a large figure at that time. It was the events which were large. At close hand and within a very short space of time, we saw the fate of a nation turn on chance encounters, narrow margins, narrowly missed opportunities and extraordinary turns of luck. The events were momentous for Albania and can now be seen to have been important for Albania's neighbors. The British officers who took part in them can perhaps be excused for assuming that some of the responsibility for them lay with themselves and for continuing to regard that responsibility seriously. It is difficult not to take seriously something which has been lived so intensely. But the fact remains that it was and is the Albanians themselves who determined the fate of their country under the harsh pressures imposed on them not by Britain but by the German war. And eventually it will be the Albanians who will have to deliver a verdict on the outcome.

Interview conducted January 25, 1983

GEORGE JELLICOE

George Jellicoe (1918–2007) was a British political figure and diplomat. He was the youngest child of Admiral Sir John Jellicoe. He spent his youth in New

Zealand where his father was governor-general. During World War II, he served with British forces in the Middle East and Greece, being among the first Allied soldiers to enter German-occupied Athens. After the war, he joined the Foreign Service and was seconded to Washington in March 1948 where he was secretary to Donald MacLean and Kim Philby. He left the Foreign Service in 1958 as the consequence of an extra-marital affair. Lord Jellicoe was the longest serving member of the House of Lords (68 years), from 1939 to 2007.

I went to Washington in March 1948. It was my first foreign posting in the Foreign Office. I was the FO representative in a four-man committee running the Albanian operation. Bob Joyce was in the Policy Planning Staff of the State Department, under George Kennan. I've never been in SIS. I was the FO representative in the committee because I was the Balkan specialist in the embassy.

I remember meetings in Frank Wisner's office, but I have a much clearer memory of bilateral meetings with Kim Philby in the embassy. We looked at the telegrams together and discussed the operation generally. But it was very much under his control operationally. He did it all very professionally. How on earth he had the time to do two jobs I just don't know.

I liked Kim very much—and Aileen. I remember him coming to Patsy's and my house in Waterside Drive quite often. I found him very convivial—the same word that he uses about me—and very intelligent.

Burgess had the office next door to me in the Washington embassy. He usually arrived late and the worse for wear. He was dirty and his fingernails were ghastly. I did not share any admiration for Burgess. And before that, Donald MacLean was my boss in the Chancery there. Dennis Allen was Head of Chancery and MacLean his deputy. I knew them both quite well. My meetings with Kim were always in his office and I put any steer on the decision that I thought necessary from the diplomatic point of view.

I remember Bevin giving the OK to start the operation at a meeting in New York when the thing was put to him by Gladwyn Jebb. I remember being quizzed by Gladwyn about it on the way from Washington to New York.

When I was in London in June/July 1951 on my way to Brussels, I received a letter from the Permanent Undersecretary at the FO, Derek Hoyar-Miller, advising me that Philby was under suspicion and that I ought to avoid contact with him. I was outraged. It was the McCarthy period and this seemed to me an appalling example of the paranoia of those days. Still, it was an order and I obeyed it. I got it as Head of Chancery in Brussels. I suppose that it was a round robin to all those who had worked with him.

I recall the complete openness of our relationship with the Americans. We had total rapport. It was a hangover from the Grand Alliance.

Interview conducted June 15, 1984

Robert Joyce

Robert Joyce was an American diplomatic figure. As a career diplomat, he worked for the United States Office of Strategic Services (OSS) during World War II and, in the following years, was active for the State Department as a liaison officer with the CIA. In this connection, he had dealings with the Albanian operation.

[RJ]: I was a member of the Policy Planning Staff at the Department of State. The director was a man called Paul Nitze. He was a Democrat and when the Republicans came in he was put out to pasture. My job was liaison with the CIA. I worked first for George Kennard when he was director and then Paul Nitze for four years. I had to give a green light, a yellow light or a red light to the CIA. That's how I got mixed up in the Albanian field operation. I represented the Department of State. Your man who represented the Foreign Office was George Jellicoe and the man who represented your intelligence service was Kim Philby.

I was never in the CIA. When the war was over I reverted to my old career being a member of the career diplomatic service. The last intelligence service I was with was the OSS which was put out of business in late 1945.

We were called in during the last part when all the technical discussions were over. This was done on the level of CIA and your chaps. Then the diplomatic officers were supposed to give political advice on whether, from a political point of view, this should be undertaken at all. I was not privy to the technical discussions, and this applies to George Jellicoe, too. We were in at the end. We heard what they had to say and, after consulting our superiors, I in the State Department and George with the British Embassy and Foreign Office, we said okay, go ahead. We gave a green light to it.

During this period, in London, I had dinner with my oldest English friend Tony Rumbold and he had Donald MacLean there. So I saw quite a lot of Donald MacLean and he was chief of chancery at your embassy in Washington. I never saw any of these chaps socially. I was a foreign service officer on the Policy Planning Staff and all of these operations I was much removed from. I was just called in when they had done all their groundwork and presented the operations. I never saw Philby in Washington at all, just once when the final okay was given for the Albanian operation.

This was the first time since the end of the war that the West was taking a bite at the Soviet empire. The thing was terribly tightly held. Frank Wisner had a very good nose, he was a brilliant fellow, a first-class lawyer. He had a whiff of suspicion and he tracked it down in his own mind. Who possibly could have given this thing away? He thought it was Kim Philby. He said this to me, for one. I don't think he talked to anyone in the CIA about his suspicions because he had no proof. Philby covered his tracks so completely. He didn't want to take it up with the British because they would say, "What evidence have you got?" It wasn't a logical suspicion; he just had a feeling.

You counted up the people who were privy to the thing. In the CIA there were no more than half a dozen. With your chaps maybe about the same. He went down the line, all these people could have given it away. The only person he could narrow it down to, with a sense of smell, was Kim Philby.

[NB]: I suppose there were written reports about the Albanian proposal?

[RJ]: No, it was all by word of mouth and terribly tightly held. No one talked about these things. I'm certain I didn't write a report. So many of these operations were going on all over the world at this time and we just didn't confine them to paper; there's nothing in the files about that at all.

PETER KEMP

Peter Mant Macintyre Kemp (1915–1993) was a British military officer and writer. He was born in Bombay as the son of a judge and was educated at Trinity College, Cambridge. As a man of the political right, he fought with the Nationalists in the Spanish Civil War in 1938 and was called to the War Office in the spring of 1940. In 1943, he was recruited by the Special Operations Executive (SOE) and was parachuted into Albania to join the British military mission there. He traveled on foot to Kosovo and, after 10 months in Albania, escaped over the border to Berane in Montenegro in early February 1944. He later worked for the SOE in Southeast Asia. After retirement from the army, he took a job with a life insurance company but left its employ in 1980. Kemp was also active as a journalist over the years, and reported on Albania and Kosovo after a visit there in 1990. His wartime experiences, including much on Albania, were recorded in the volumes No Colours or Crest, *London 1958, and* The Thorns of Memory, *London 1990.*

I only played a small part in the Albanian episode. I went out to Rome in the autumn of 1949 to replace John Hibberdine, who was responsible for liaison with the Albanian exiles. Unfortunately, I had an operation in January 1950. The Italians gave me a lot of ether and this went to my lung, starting up my TB again. I was in hospital in Rome all that spring and in May I went back to England to King Edward VII Hospital in Midhurst.

I had been in SOE with Harold Perkins during the war and we were great personal friends. In March or April 1949, when my TB

Peter Kemp (1915–1993), British writer and member of the Special Operations Executive in Albania during the Second World War. Photo ca. 1958.

was better, I went to him and offered my services. I was looking for a job. Perkins had been responsible for dropping me into Poland in 1944.

It was simply coincidence that I should have offered my services to "Perks" just at the time when this operation was getting started and he was looking for officers with Albanian experience. I went to see the "firm" doctor, Dr. Lancaster, and he passed me, so that was all right. "Perks" told me that they needed John Hibberdine for something else and they were looking for someone to liaise with the Albanian National Committee in Rome. I didn't need much briefing. I knew most of the background and most of the people involved.

One of my first jobs was to go and see them through customs at Northholt airport. The three main delegates were Abas Kupi, Midhat Frashëri and Said Kryeziu. I was living in a flat near the BBC off Langham Place and I gave a buffet supper for them. There was strict rationing and my wife had with some difficulty managed to get some ham mousse from Harrods, only to be told that it was useless, since most of the Albanians were Muslims. However, Muslim or non–Muslim, they drank plenty of our alcohol. Malcolm Muggeridge was there and he announced in loud tones that Albania was an absurd country that ought to be partitioned between the Yugoslavs and the Greeks. Julian Amery, Billy McLean, Dick Brooman-White and Victor Gordon-Lennox were also there. "Perks" got TB himself around this time and he was replaced by Brigadier Nicholson, a real pain in the neck. He had a big walrus moustache. Alan Hare used to call him the walrus. Nicholson handed over to another officer from the Buffs. As far as I was concerned, the whole operation lost a lot of its merit once "Perks" was no longer involved. In London I was their "nanny" or bear-leader. I took them round and showed them the sights, the Tower of London. They were here for one visit of a month or so. I remember we took them down to a pub on the river and gave them a tremendous lunch there. Then they went back to Italy.

I went out about October or November. In Rome we had these occasional meetings. I had to pass messages to them, and they gave me messages if they wanted anything passed back. I have the impression that we didn't discuss tactical operations at all. I wasn't involved in the para-military side. It was just liaison. It was a no-job really. I can't think why I was needed. I was just holding their hands so that they had some connections with the Foreign Office. John came back and then Archie Lyall took over. He was an author and great fun. It was a job which, if I had been really fit, I wouldn't have wanted to continue with, not the sort of job for a 35-year-old to stay long in.

I didn't care for Mike Burke. I remember him being an all–American footballer. I think the British and Americans were at cross purposes. They wanted to push the Balli Kombëtar and we wanted to push the monarchists. There was always a bit of friction. But we felt that Abas Kupi had done all the real fighting. Maybe the Balli Kombëtar would have done a bit more, if we'd given them more arms. Abas really fought them from the word go, from the time Mussolini invaded in 1939. We knew that he was a good friend of the British. The others were more problematic. That was one of the causes of contention between us.

I remember feeling that these people had got it all wrong and they probably felt that I'd got it all wrong.

I was there on contract to MI6 and in Rome on my own. I had frequent meetings with the Albanians in cafes and asked them how it was going. I knew that David was at the fort in Malta and I assumed it was training but I wasn't put in the picture. I knew that we were sending people in from Malta. It all came to light when it was published by that dreadful fellow Bruce Page and his Insight team.

I don't think that the Albanian National Committee was very secure. I don't think that they had the slightest idea about security. They probably talked to this person and that person. A well-placed journalist in Rome could find out all sorts of things, not mention the Italian communist party and their Albanian comrades. I think that Nicholas Elliott may have had something to do with it, peripherally, although it was Harold Perkins's baby.

Interview conducted March 5, 1983

SAID KRYEZIU

Said bey Kryeziu (1911–1993) was a Kosovo Albanian anticommunist resistance fighter. He was born in Gjakova and was the brother of Gani bey Kryeziu and Ceno bey Kryeziu. In 1933, he went to Paris and studied briefly at the Section Diplomatique of the university there. He left France in 1939 and was in Belgrade until 1941 where, though under the watchful eye of the Yugoslav government, he helped Albanian emigrants return to Albania to fight the Italians. In April 1941, after a brief clandestine visit to Albania, he and his two brothers, Ceno and Hasan, were arrested by the German authorities in Belgrade and turned over to the Italians. The prisoners were sent to Ancona and from there to the Italian concentration camp on the island of Ventotene. On 8 September 1943, after 14 months of detention, they were released and managed to find their way back to Kosovo, arriving in mid–January 1944. From Peja, Said bey, his brothers, and resistance fighter Llazar Fundo took to the hills to begin armed resistance to the Germans. He was in close contact with the British mission in Albania, in particular with Julian Amery in the summer of 1944, who described him as tall, dark and oriental in appearance, and a passionate believer in social-democracy. Though arrested by the Albanian communist partisans, Said bey was released and managed to flee to Rome. On 26 August 1949, he took part in Paris in the foundation of the National Committee for a Free Albania. The latter was disbanded in 1955 when Albania was admitted to the United Nations. Said bey Kryeziu assisted in Italy in selecting anticommunist fighters for the Albanian operation. In 1959, he emigrated to the United States and died in New York of heart failure.

Aposta Tanef was a man who did everything that the Yugoslavs wanted, an alcoholic, who died without achieving any glory.

I was approached in Rome by Low, McLean and Amery. I was staying in Sicily then with the Albanian community. I came back to Rome when they sent me a telegram. The point was to undertake any kind of work against the Tirana government.

We went to London from Paris, after proclaiming the committee and we had a very good reception at the Berkeley Hotel. Julian Amery was very kind to us. Kemp was a brilliant man, a great friend of Albania. He was anxious to protect us against our neighbors. He was in my house with my brother and father during the war, just before the fall of Mussolini.

We gave no press conference in London, but Peter Kemp gave a communiqué to the *Times* and the *Guardian* on September 11. Frashëri, Kupi and Kotta flew to New York. Kupi and Frashëri had Albanian passports issued in Cairo and Kotta had a French travel document. Pali and I had to stay behind, because we had very feeble travel documents, only identity cards issued by a church organization in Rome, and it took a long time for the Americans to issue visas on a paper that was not even a passport or anything like it. Eventually, we got the visas. Pali and I flew to New York via Montreal, but the American immigration officer in Montreal asked us why we were going to the United States and Pali made a terrible gaffe. He said we were going "for political reasons." So they wouldn't let us go on to New York. We had to stay in a hotel in Montreal and two days later appear before an American immigration court. I showed them the English newspapers with our names in them and Robert Low interceded on our behalf also, so in the end we were allowed to carry on. The other three did not have this problem because their documents were better.

So we arrived with no one to meet us and speaking no English. We stayed in an unknown hotel overnight before the others came and found us the next day. They took us to the Lexington Hotel and then to Washington.

The Free Europe Committee gave a big party for us in Washington. Virginia Hall was there and several people from Poland, Czechoslovakia and other countries. And we had a very good talk with Llewelyn E. Thompson at the State Department. This was encouraging, because no one from the Foreign Office had received us in London.

It all meant a lot to us, because we were lost people, abandoned people, only just out of refugee camps. It was a high point in our morale and in the morale of all Albanians. We really believed that something would be done to free our country.

Frashëri and Kotta stayed in New York, because that was to be the seat of the committee. It was very hot and I think Frashëri was suffering from strain and heat. The other three of us returned to Rome. Kupi and I were in the military junta. Pali was in charge of the newspaper, almost all the Albanian exiles were in Italy at that time.

The committee was started too late. This gave the communists four years in which to eliminate the opposition physically, to break the opposition's back. All this time they were supported by Yugoslavia. They should have recruited a larger number of fighters. And the British should have reacted more strongly to the Corfu Channel incident. And in 1949 the United States and Britain were in a position to impose an anti–Hoxha policy on both Yugoslavia and Greece. Instead, the Yugoslavs formed their own committee under Tanef and it was against us. Our allies were too cautious. And they should have set up a government in exile, not just a committee.

It is impossible to beat the communists with such small groups of people. The communists are much more organized than you think. And of course they had very good intelligence, not to mention Philby. The Yugoslavs were giving Hoxha information about us. They would still rather have Hoxha in power there than us Albanian nationalists. Hoxha has renounced his claim to Kosovo. We have never done so. And a communist will always prefer another communist. Our aim to get rid of the Hoxha government was against Tito's interest.

I think too that Stalin would have been ready to give up Albania. It was not in the Soviet sphere of influence. There was no agreement to the effect. It was an island, not connected with any other country and fighting everybody.

They should have been ready to fight Hoxha openly, not in a clandestine way. It is impossible to beat the communists by secret means.

The Americans were in a great hurry in Germany. In Munich, the Company 4000 men lived in good conditions, though their pay was low, just pocket money. They got training, but it was inadequate. They were heroes, and more should have been done to prepare them for such a very dangerous task.

Interview conducted January 10, 1984

Bido Kuka

Bido Kuka was an Albanian anticommunist fighter from Nivica in the Kurvelesh region. As a supporter of Balli Kombëtar, he escaped from Albania in November 1944 and lived as a refugee in Austria and then in Italy. He volunteered for the Albanian operation in 1949 and was trained in Malta from July 1949 to 1952. Kuka was sent into communist Albania three times from 1949 to 1951, initially on September 20, 1949, as a radio operator, a second time in the summer and autumn of 1950, and a third time in the summer of 1951. He managed to get out of the country alive each time. In January 1952, Kuka moved to England, where he settled.

There are four other Albanians who were in Malta with me now living in England. One is Mr. Bardhyl Gerveshi, who was a friend of "Doc" Zaehner. He got him a job in a wood mill in High Wyckombe. The three others are Baki Hyseni, Nezir Tomorri and Ago Dauti. I was in Malta from 1949 to 1952 and I went into Albania three times, the first time as a radio operator, the second time as leader of a small group of four men.

The first time I went in was by boat, with two English sergeants, Captain George Young and nine Albanians. It was on September 16, 1949. I learnt about Frashëri's death after we came out into Greece. I was in a group under my second cousin, Ahmet Kuka. All the people who went in during 1949 were "democrats," not the king's men.

We landed near Karaburun Mountain, by Sazan Island. They took us to the beach in a rubber dinghy. There were a Cypriot sailor and a girl with them, too. The Cypriot was called "Salvo." We had American 30-round machine pistols. They worked beautifully. We asked Captain Young for 500 rounds each, but he made us take food. He said that they would catch us if we had no food. And we had 50 sovereigns each. In 1951 we only took 30 sovereigns.

Interview conducted September 20, 1981

* * *

I left Albania with a group of friends in November 1944. We went via Yugoslavia into Austria and a refugee camp near Klagenfurt. Then we were moved to Modena and Florence. By June 1945 there were about 300 of us. Then we were moved to camps at Cinecittà (near Rome), Bari and Santa Maria di Leuca, then to Reggio nell' Emilia (near Bologna). We spent most of 1946 there, then problems started among the parties and the Ballists were transferred to Barletta, where we stayed until October 1947, then back to Reggio nell' Emilia. Then about 15 of us were arrested and taken from prison to prison, including Regina Coeli prison in Rome, and we ended up at Fraschetti camp near Rome. There was apparently a risk that we might be sent back to Albania, especially since the Left was very powerful in Italy and many thought the Communists were going to win the elections. Our camp commandant told us that, in that event, he would arm us and take to the hills with us.

We also heard that the British intervened to help us. So in July 1948, three months after the elections, we were freed and taken to Cinecittà where we spent the winter. Andoni, Frashëri and Zef Pali all came to the camp and told us early in 1949 that some good boys were needed to go to Albania and fight. I went with my friend Sami Lepenica (Abduli). He and his cousin Hysen Lepenica wanted me to join their group, but Andoni would not let me because I was not from their area. It was no thanks to him. I would have preferred to fight and die with my friends. I was a soldier of Balli Kombëtar and I did what I was told. My life isn't worth anything.

On July 14, I flew from Rome in a British military plane with Sami to Malta. We were told there would be a man to meet us with a red handkerchief in his breast pocket. So when Alastair Grant came towards us as we got off the plane, I said it couldn't be him because he didn't have a red hankie. Then we saw that there was another man there, Rollo Young, and he did have a hankie in his top pocket.

Young made a sign to one of the immigration officers and we were allowed through. He also stopped one of the customs men who wanted to open my suitcase. There was a car waiting for us outside and it took us past Rabat to the fort. We spent two weeks there by ourselves and then the others came at the end of July.

We trained during August and the first half of September. Sami and I were on radio work. Others were trained in map reading, use of explosives and intelligence. The radio weighed 40 kilos. I was with the first group of nine that was put ashore on the Karaburun Peninsula on September 20, five of us from Kurvelesh and four others from Vlora.

We had some rough seas and we put into a small Greek island near Corfu for 24 hours. I remember some Greek guards coming to look us over and we Albanians had to hide below the deck from them. There were two sergeants, a Greek-Cypriot, Captain Young and one beautiful girl. We spent three or four days on the boat and landed early one night.

We all landed in the same place and walked to Dukat, a very mountainous area.

We had the feeling at once that the communists knew we were coming, but the going was very difficult and we were not much bothered. We went on to Mount Tragjas and that is where we split. We saw no communists before the split, but the Vlora group must have run into some very soon afterwards, because we heard about it as soon as we got to Gjorm, a village not far from Tragjas.

A young girl ran out of the village towards us and shouted, "Brothers, you're all going to be killed." She told us that Beqir Balluku, the communist general, was nearby and that he had surrounded the whole area. She also said that the Lepenica group had been attacked and three of them killed: Lepenica, Abduli and Sheno. We asked for food and they brought us some bread and milk.

When we heard that the area was surrounded, we decided to lie low. So we stayed near Gjorm sleeping in the open. Then we set off for Kurvelesh, which was four days' march away, after sending a radio message to Corfu telling them that we were having problems and advising them not to send people in who did not know the area very well. We reached Nivica, which is our hometown, and spent a week there resting and collecting food.

In Nivica we split into two groups. Ramiz Matuka, Hysen Isufi and I set off towards the Greek border; the other two, Ahmet Kuka and Turban Aliko, went by another route. We had four armed encounters on the way. In one of them we were walking along a ravine at night and some people asked us to stop. They shouted, "Who are you?" We shouted back, "Who are you?" They said they were police and then we opened fire, but they were in defended positions and we did not make much impression. But Matuka was hit and killed. The two of us carried on and crossed into Greece. We had been about four weeks in Albania and we crossed into Greece in mid–October, leaving our radios behind.

We did not tell the Greeks we had been put into Albania by the British. They asked about our uniforms and I said that had been parachuted to us. We had side arms, but there was nothing strange about that. We said we were ordinary Albanians fleeing the country. A Greek major told us about Frashëri's death and then we were taken to Niko Ceci, who was an Albanian working for the Greeks, in Janina police station. Ceci was no friend of ours. I said that I was Enver Zeneli and showed him my forged Albanian identity card. The two of us kept to the same story and we were put into Janina police station for about a week.

Unfortunately, during that week, other groups trickled across the border and some of them told the Greeks the truth. So Ceci came back to me and said, "You're not Enver Zeneli, you're Bido Kuka." I replied that if I had told him I was Bido Kuka, he would have looked at my documents and told me that I was Enver Zeneli. Anyway, in the end they notified the British embassy in Athens and we were taken down there by British military plane, four of us out of the original nine. Safet Kapaj stayed in Albania in his family house.

We stayed two or three weeks in a lovely house in Kifissia, near Athens, and we reported to Jani Dilo and Captain Young, who came to see us. I told them how difficult it was in Albania. Then we were flown back to Malta, where we spent the winter, until the summer of 1950 when two small groups were put across the Greek frontier overland. I was with Ahmet Kuka and Dev Mainutaj.

We stayed two months in Kurvelesh, sleeping in the open. I would never stay in an Albanian house, even my own house, because in every family of four or five including my own, the chances are that one person will be a communist. Also, it could put them in danger if they gave me food. After any encounter with our groups, the police would take any food that they found to nearby houses and ask where it came from. They would even try to identify the bread.

We made contacts as best we could and told people that they would soon be liberated from the communists. People generally believed us. We made propaganda in the area. Then it began to snow in the mountains and we went back into Greece. We did the same a year later. I remember it was summer because there were melons. It was Haki Gaba, Ahmet Kuka, Aziz Azizaj and I. We spent six weeks near Vlora, where Azizaj lived. Then on January 2, 1952, all of us flew to London and I slept that night in Wellington Barracks.

Interview conducted July 20, 1983

SAFET MALUSHI

Safet Malushi was an Albanian anticommunist fighter from the Korça region. He escaped to Greece in 1944 where he lived as a refugee. In 1949 he accepted an American proposal to take part in the Albanian operation and was based at an abandoned airfield near Janina. He first went into Albania on July 15, 1949 and spent two months in the Korça region. Malushi was in communist Albania eight times from July 1949 to the late summer of 1951.

I am a Tosk from the Korça area. I left Albania in 1944 and spent four years in Hadji Kyriakon camp, near Piraeus. In 1948 I was allowed to work in construction and on farms. I lived in an apartment with three Albanian friends. Then we were approached by Greek officials on the Americans' behalf and I refused. I only agreed when I was approached again by Faik Bukmiri, a former Zogist officer. He worked with the British in Cyprus. I only agreed when I was asked by an Albanian.

There were about 130 young Albanians living by Janina Airport divided into three groups: Hamit Matjani's, Xheladin Sokalari's and mine. It was seven miles from Janina and we stayed there from 1949 to 1952. No planes ever came there. It was a disused airfield on the west of Janina. There was another one on the east side. We started the training in early June 1949. Hamit's group was the largest; he had about 50.

Asim Jakova was the link between the Greeks and the Americans. He used to visit us. Jakova had been representative of Kosovo in the Albanian parliament. He now lives in Florida.

Colonel Hysen Selmani was the right hand of the King in Alexandria. He came to Athens and spoke to the three of us. There was also an American there called John with his wife. We never met any of the British-trained people. They were kept separate.

The first three men went in on July 15, 1949. We had very little training, only six weeks. We were Sokolari, Midhat Moglica and I. Moglica is in Detroit now. We wanted to get a first opinion. Did the people like us or not? We were armed with German machine guns and British grenades. We visited people we knew near Korça, zigzagging our way through groups of Greek communists. We were in for 63 days. The Americans thought we were lost. We had no radio. It was for reconnaissance and propaganda. People were very pleased to see us. They were crying, they were so pleased. I told them, "The Americans and the British are working with us and we will set you free." We came back to Greece very encouraged.

We stayed with people we trusted, or in the forests and in the mountains. There were patrols going past my house every night, checking the houses. There were a lot of Greek communists there, too.

I came out of Albania in September 1949. The weather was getting bad. We reported to the Americans. The first time Hamit Matjani went in was in April/May 1950. The three of us had gone in in July 1949 only to see what was happening. We reported to the Americans, but we had no idea what was the purpose of our mission. We were kept in the dark in case one of us was caught and questioned about the purpose of our mission.

On other trips, I went with 7 or 8 people. In the summertime of 1951, I went in for the fifth time. There were eight times altogether in the period from 1949 to 1951. We always went in during the summer, always in American uniform. The border was impassable after October. I made several trips in 1950 and 1951. I never lost a single man. This was because I never went the exact way we were ordered to go by the Greeks and Americans. I never trusted anybody.

In 1951 I had nine with me and Matjani had seven. We passed Mali (Mountain) of Leshnjes. We spent a day observing the Albanian border patrols. We saw that the posts were manned by units of 15 to 35, every few miles, with stronger groups guarding the open areas and smaller groups guarding the mountain paths, which could only be crossed by a handful of men on foot. They started patrolling as soon as it got dark.

All the missions were designed to build up an organization inside Albania. Matjani was on his way to Elbasan. My job was to escort him and his men through Kolonja, Skrapar, then close to Korça and to the borders of Elbasan. My job was to protect Matjani so long as we were on my territory. Then he and his men went on into his territory and I turned back to my territory. That time he didn't stay too long, because there was a communist traitor in his group. One of the nine was a spy sent to give Matjani over to the authorities. Muhamet Kama stayed in Albania and gave the communists all our names. There was another man in Janina who was his good friend, so we had doubts about him, too. We suspected him of poisoning our food. He confessed to being a Tirana spy, then he retracted and the Americans took him away.

In 1950 my brother Gani came out of Albania with about 30 others. They left because the traitor gave my name to the communists. My father and elder brother Fahri were beaten to death trying to escape.

On the last mission King Zog sent two of his officers from Egypt, Zenel Shehu and Halil Bradvica. They got a radio operator from Greece, Tahir Prenci. He had been trained by the Americans in Cyprus. Hamit Matjani and Xheladin Sokolari took the three of them across the border close to Tirana, walking from Greece past Korça and Elbasan, towards the end of 1952. Then Matjani and Sokolari came back to Athens to the safe house. They collected pictures of King Zog and the Free Albania Committee newspapers.

My brothers Gani and Xhafar were told in early 1953 that they must go into Albania and bring out some 12 soldiers recruited by Shehu and Bradvica. Apparently, they had nothing to eat and they were starving. All this was sent by Prenci by Morse. And it may be that he was in the hands of the communists already. It is strange that he was never brought to trial. So they went in with Hamit Matjani and Naum Sula. In fact the 13 men didn't exist.

Irfan Ohri was sent from the king in Alexandria to Greece and he begged the Americans not to send the three men in. However, the Americans insisted. The next thing I remember is hearing my brother's voice on the radio confessing everything. I heard it from Athens.

I had asked Matjani not to go and not to take my brother. I told him that Gani did not know the Tirana area well enough. He might parachute and land 15 miles away from the others. He would never be able to find them. Matjani said that he needed Gani's experience.

Of course, they all gave the police the names of the people they were supposed to contact and I estimate that 400 people were killed in Albania because of the failure of that last mission.

Interview conducted August 8, 1983

BILLY MCLEAN

Lieutenant-Colonel Neil Loudon Desmond McLean (1918–1986), known as Billy McLean, was a British military official. He was born in London of a family from the western highlands of Scotland. He was educated at Eton and Sandhurst and was commissioned into the Royal Scots Greys in 1938. After duty in Palestine and Ethiopia, he was recruited by the Special Operations Executive (SOE) in 1943 to go into Axis-occupied Albania and support resistance movements there. Together with David Smiley, he was one of the first British officers to enter the country, which he did on foot from Greece in April 1943, and established a base in Leshnja near Erseka. By mid–June 1943, he had made contact with Enver Hoxha in Mallakastra. He was recalled in a period of calm, but returned to Albania, to the Biza plateau east of Tirana, with Smiley and Julian Amery on April 20, 1944, after the German invasion. McLean, an enthusiastic anticommunist, had close contacts both with Abas Kupi, whom he admired and wished to support, and with Enver Hoxha and the communist partisans. He established and maintained a radio link with British military headquarters to coordinate activities and arms supplies. In late October 1944, he and Amery were evacuated from Albania, and were forced by higher authority in the SOE to abandon Abas Kupi and his men to the mercy of the communists. From March 1949, after World War II, McLean was actively involved with Smiley and Amery in the Albanian operation. He was also active as a military adviser in Chinese Turkistan, Vietnam, Algeria and Yemen and, from 1954 to 1964, served as a Conservative member of parliament for Inverness. After retirement, he was appointed to the Queen's bodyguard in Scotland, the Royal Company of Archers, and died of heart failure in London.

During the war, Alan Hare was attached to the communists. We were attached to the nationalists. When we came out, the main question was what was to happen to the Albanians who had worked with us. We were forbidden to help them get out, but we told them that, if they could get out themselves, we would do our best to see that they were received as friends and allies. Abas Kupi had lent us a lot of money in sovereigns to pay the expenses of the mission. He was with us at the end and we had to tell him that we were being withdrawn. We had to tell him that we could not take him with us. It was very unpleasant.

In Bari we had some difficulty over the Albanians because of the general attitude in the office at the time, especially those people working under the Balkan air force, headed by Bill Elliott. They were all for the partisans. They believed that this was the way of the future and that the communists would only be upset if we looked after our Albanian friends. But Harold MacMillan turned out trumps. So did Louis Franks, who was financial advisor to SOE, and Philip Broad, a Foreign Office man. But the general mood was strongly against us, they wanted to hand these chaps back. One of the problems was that Albania was not mentioned in the "spheres of influence" agreement initialed by Stalin and Churchill in Tehran.

The general mood of the time, not so much in the Foreign Office, funnily enough, but elsewhere, was that the communists and partisans were showing the way of the future and so we had to be realistic and support them, especially since they were fighting the Germans so well. In SOE this view was widely held. Air Marshal William Elliott held it. And they were egged on by people who were communists, openly or secretly, or sympathizers with communism. The majority view was that we should help the communists in Albania and so make friends with them.

Originally, we were ordered to surrender ourselves to the communists. We knew that they would probably have shot us or tried us, so we had no intention of doing that. In the south we were only three officers—Amery, Smiley and myself—with a couple of wireless operators. There were other missions in the north. Air Marshal Elliott took a practical view that communism was the way to the future. He was a nice chap, but with all the wrong ideas. There was also a General Sewell in Bari. He didn't know very much about anything. The next one was the head of the Balkan section who was Bill Harcourt. He was a sound chap, well meaning, but he didn't pay much attention. The section head was Philip Leak. He went into Albania and was killed. His place was taken by Elliot Watrous. He had very progressive pro-partisan views. And we were very annoyed with him because we felt he was hostile to the nationalists. He used his best endeavors to support the communist cause against the nationalists at every level. And there was one

Abaz Kupi (1892–1976), Albanian anticommunist resistance fighter during the Second World War, speaking here at the BBC in London in the 1940s.

liaison officer who was particularly against us and the nationalists, who worked very closely with the communists. One of the officers who was there was worried about the whole thing and had a row with him. This chap admitted that he had joined the communists and been instructed by the Party to come to Albania. He was the British second-in-command in partisan headquarters. His name is Reg Hibbert. We felt that he was a very bad man.

We had a way of communicating directly with Anthony Eden. David Smiley and I went to see him in London when we came back to report the first time, before the second mission. Jubi Laxtra (?) arranged the meeting. Eden asked us to stay in touch and send him a telegram if there was anything that we needed. It annoyed a lot of people, but it was useful.

Harold MacMillan said that Abas Kupi could come out, that we would welcome him, even that we should rescue him, but luckily he had made his own arrangements. Otherwise, I don't know what would have happened. Anyway, he was well received. Then they tried to pay Abas Kupi back at the nominal rate of the gold that he had lent us, a rate 15 or 20 times to his disadvantage.

As far as I remember, the long-range desert group then tried to do some reconnaissance in Albania, but they met with a pretty hostile reception. Then there was an UNNRA mission and other aid missions. They stayed for a year and had a very hard time. The two English people involved were Charles Brocklehurst and Fanny Hasluck.

She was the Albanian expert in SOE in Cairo. She was a very intelligent and difficult old lady, but marvelous. Brocklehurst would be very accurate about how the communists behaved when they got into power, whom they put into prison and whom they shot, what happened to the refugees.

We then all went off to the Far East. Julian went to China, David Smiley to Thailand, Alan Hare to Ceylon and Thailand. I went first to Ceylon and then to Sinkiang. I came back home early in 1946 and within a year I was in touch with the Albanians again, who were then scattered around Italy, Greece and Egypt. Smiley and I knew Balli well. Julian knew the king's people. The first problem was to help them as individuals, over finance and visas. People were very slow and difficult about helping them, but there was never any danger of their being handed back. That never really came up.

In early 1948, there was a great panic on among the Albanians in Italy, because they arrested about ten of them. Our Albanian friends wrote to us, told us what had happened and said they were afraid that the Italians would hand these people back to Hoxha. It would have been in exchange for Italian officers held in prison in Albania. We told various friends in parliament and the Foreign Office that this was disgraceful and in the end they weren't handed back. We had some contact with Orme Sargent about it through Alan Hare's mother, Lady Listowel. We pointed out that there were several of these arrested Albanians, including Abas Kupi and Ihsan Toptani, to whom we were under great obligation both personally and nationally. They'd saved many people's lives and looked after us during the war. If it had not been for the politics of the thing, they would have received British medals. They certainly deserved them. We wanted to get them a grant of money and eventually this was done, I think through MI6 funds. So the main problem during 1947–48 was dealing with Albanians' personal problems and making sure that there was no backsliding on the decision not to hand them back. There was never a great danger of this, I think, because by then we were on such bad terms with Hoxha because of the Corfu Channel incident. We would not have handed them back, but the Italians might have done so and the Foreign Office had to decide how much pressure to put on the Italians to stop this happening. My impression is that the Foreign Office comes out of the story not too badly.

In 1948, privately, the four of us used such contacts as we had with Conservative members of parliament, including Anthony Eden and Harold MacMillan, as well as with senior Foreign Office men like Orme Sargent, to take a more far-reaching political initiative. But we put forward the view that something should be done in Albania. Various schemes were considered. There was some skepticism. I remember one Foreign Office man saying, "That's all very well, but church mice (meaning the British) don't make wars." The answer continually given was we hadn't any money and couldn't do anything.

Then, about the beginning of 1949, rather more interest was shown by the British government in our view that an uprising could be organized in Albania to chuck the communists out. The Foreign Office was more interested in using the scheme to relieve pressure on Greece, with incursions into Greece by communist guerrillas operating from Albanian bases. Our original representations concerned the liberation of Albania. The Foreign Office reply was more along the lines of the effect of such an uprising on the Greek civil war. That was why they took it up so strongly. A third objective would have been to destabilize the Soviet empire by striking at what appeared to be its weakest link. However, my view, both then and now, is that one should not expect Albanians to mount such an operation and risk their lives solely in order to help the democratic forces of Greece win their civil war. If we wanted to get the right Albanians, we had to offer them a real prospect of a free Albania. I am not sure to what extent the British and American governments agreed with me on this.

The British and American governments wanted us to make the initial contacts, because the Albanians trusted us as a result of our having fought together during the war. This meant a lot to the Albanian émigrés. All three groups were involved—the king, Balli and Independenza. Julian Amery and I went to Athens to talk to the Greek about it, then to Cairo to talk to King Zog, then to Rome to talk to the Balli and some of the king's people. This took nearly two months during the spring of 1949.

First of all, Julian and I went to Athens, with Harold Perkins. Julian wrote a report for his friends and presumably "Perks" did likewise. Julian and I were private citizens, although we were Conservative parliamentary candidates by then.

Ernest Bevin, I heard, was not unsympathetic to our enterprise, but whenever MI6 wanted a quick decision, they waited until Bevin was out of the way and sent it into Attlee, who was famous for giving quick and clear decisions. Bevin's answers tended to be more vague. The Foreign Office and the ambassadors knew what we were doing and approved, though they were careful not to get too involved. It was obvious to us that the local MI6 representatives were doing all the arranging for us, such as travel and accommodation. It was clearly their responsibility.

We were taken on temporarily and informally, on an unpaid basis, for advice and help. We reported back to the Foreign Office and to our political friends. We went there to help and, to be honest, they couldn't have done without us. Or rather they could have done without us, but it would have cost them a lot of time and money. We were the only ones who knew the people. We knew them intimately. We had fought together. The idea that we put across to the Albanians was that at last the British government had seen the light and realized that Hoxha was a bastard, so that it was now vital to put together a committee of all Albanian democratic forces, who would then be supported by the British and Americans, materially as well as morally. The political side was to be completely open, the military side secret.

I remember that the British side was anxious to restrict the committee to political groups that had fought against the axis powers, while the Americans wanted to bring in the pro–Italian party. We felt that this would weaken the committee, probably not vis-à-vis the Albanians, but vis-à-vis the Western world. The Americans were keen on the Italian side partly because of the Italian vote in their country, partly because they controlled Italy and wanted to use that base to extend their influence over the eastern Mediterranean. They also no doubt genuinely wanted to make the committee as broad as possible. We resisted this, not to deny the Americans their due, but so as not to upset such good friends of ours such as Abas Kupi, who had fought against the original Italian invasion, and the Balli Kombëtar, who hated the Italians. Also, there were very close connections between American and Italian influential bodies—the Church, the Freemasons and of course the Mafia. Italy was completely controlled by the Americans, both governmentally and in terms of interest groups.

We had one diplomatic problem. We could not invite King Zog onto the committee, because if we did, we would have been forced to make him head of it and let him control it. Then there would have been no Balli Kombëtar, no real committee. It would have been a royalist committee. He was probably the most capable man, but he was a source of division within the Albanian émigrés. So the only solution was to exclude Zog and to bring in his "right hand" man, Abas Kupi, instead. My view, although I am not sure that it was Julian's, was that we had to set up the committee first and then go to Zog and ask him to bless it. If we had gone to Zog first, he would have insisted on running it. It would not have been on to make him one member of a collective leadership, not after he had been king of Albania for 15 years.

I was not in on the military side of things. All I did was to offer a lodge in Scotland for training. Our friends in London were interested in it, but in the end they turned it down. It was in Rossshire, about 20 miles from the nearest village.

I think that everyone would like the story to be told, as far as it can be told, by you; I think that this would be good because, apart from the Philby betrayal, it is quite an honorable story.

Diary of Billy McLean for 1949

26 January. London. 3 p.m. Orme Sargent with Julian Amery at Foreign Office. 6:30 p.m. Dick Brooman-White. Those meetings would have been to discuss the operation in principle. Julian and I had been writing to the Foreign Office, to Orme Sargent and Charles Bateman, ever since the war ended, on various matters concerning our Albanian friends. Brooman-White was a regular member of MI6.
27 January. 12:30 p.m. Lunch with Dick Brooman-White.
28 January. 3 p.m. Foreign Office.
7 February. 6:30 p.m. Julian Amery. (I was seeing Julian a great deal at the time anyway.)
11 February. Lunch with Alan Hare at Buck's.
14 February. Drink with Brooman-White at his flat.
3 March. 1 p.m. Meeting at flat with Petrit Kupi, son of Abas Kupi. (I was chosen as Conservative candidate for Preston at the beginning of 1949.)
15 March. Dick Brooman-White for a drink.
22 March. Alan Hare.
3 April. Alan Hare for lunch.
7 April. Lunch with Dick Brooman-White and others.
14 April. Lunch at Buck's with Frank Wisner.
25 April. Meet Ihsan Toptani.
27 April. 12:30. Meet Julian Amery. 1:15. Meet Dick Brooman-White.
28 April. Lunch with Alan Hare.
29 April. Lunch with Dick Brooman-White at his flat, 25 Chesham Street. 8 p.m. Dined with Anthony Eden.
2 May. Fly to Greece with Alan Hare and Harold Perkins, all together on a commercial flight.
4 May. 5:30. Brigadier Godfrey Hobbs. He was military attaché. Drink with Whinney.

6 May. Meet Clifford Norton, the ambassador: the Nortons, Pat Whinney, Eric McCloud, John Baddeley, Miss Riddle. Certainly, McCloud was something to do with the British section and John Baddeley was, too. I think they were working with Whinney. Then there was Bob Minor, second secretary at U.S. Embassy. He later became Consul-General at Istanbul. I don't know what he did, but a very nice chap.

12 May. 10:30 a.m. Meet George Papandreou. 11:30 a.m. Meet Pipenelis, secretary-general of the Greek Foreign Office. I think he was in the picture. Julian must have come out some time then, because I remember lunching with Bonasaki and him.

15 May. Fly from Athens to Janina, where we met the Northern Epirus committee. Julian has probably got a note of this with their names. They wouldn't have been party to it, but we would have talked around the subject. Belvis, old man, Tu Lapas, Dr. Lekas, Dr. Stewart of UNSCOB, corps General Sakalottis (crook), Baron Oremi, Colonel Dean, Interpreter Papendeas. And there was a chap called England who was a policeman. Then there was the director of information. We saw the governor-general of Epirus, Aliens Bureau, Archbishop of Epirus Spiridon, Mayor of Janina Oublahisis. 6 p.m. England, the policeman. I don't say he was party to it, but he must have been talking a lot of sense and we must have asked his opinion on things.

17 May. Leave Janina for Athens.

18 May. Leave Athens for Rome. Dine with Said Kryeziu. Derek Verschoyle, he left and died. Osborne the minister at the Vatican (?). Ermenji must have been in Rome.

19 May. Dine with Said Kryeziu.

20 May. Lunch with Abas Ermenji and Midhat Frashëri. 7 p.m. Derek Verschoyle. 8:30 p.m. Dine with Alan Hare and Perkins.

21 May. Lunch with Abas Ermenji and Perkins. 6:30 p.m. Meet Said Kryeziu. 7:45. Dine with Versohoyle. 11 p.m. Midhat Frashëri and Abas Ermenji. At this time Alan Hare, Perkins and I were in Rome and I think Julian was in Athens, but he didn't come to Rome at this stage. Perkins was with us all the time.

22 May. 1 p.m. Meet Said Kryeziu at hotel. 8:30. Dine with Bob Minor.

23 May. 10 a.m. Abas Ermenji. 1:30 p.m. Perkins. 2:45. Said Kryeziu. 3 p.m. Abas Ermenji. Alan Hare leaves.

24 May. John Hibberdine arrives.

25 May. Leave for London.

27 May. 11:30 a.m. Tony Rumbold in Foreign Office for a meeting. 12 p.m. Charles Bateman at Foreign Office. 5 p.m. Tony Rumbold and Charles Peake.

28 May. 10:50 a.m. Dick Brooman-White.

3 June. 1 p.m. Meet Harold MacMillan at Turf Club. He must have wanted to be filled in. At that time he was in Opposition, but he had been minister of state in the Middle East and, when we came out from Albania, he was minister of state in Naples and was tremendously helpful with the Albanians, trying to save them. And had kept up an interest. He was someone who was likely to be supportive and had been supportive in the past. And Anthony Eden was the same. Eden gave me a letter of introduction to the ambassador in Rome, which was quite helpful because, apart from one's activities, one had to explain one's activities and it did seem to have a certain amount of blessing from on high with the Conservatives. At no stage did I see any Labour ministers.

9 June. Meet Alan Hare at White's. 4:15. Meet Tommy Last, who was engaged in a minor way, rather a nice chap.
14 June. 6:15. Alan Hare.
15 June. 3 p.m. Dick Brooman-White.
16 June. 12:30. Alan Hare. 1 p.m. Brooman-White.
17 June. Bob Low-Grosvenor. I think he came before this, but I may be wrong. He wasn't in Rome in May when I was there.
21 June. 11:45 a.m. Meet Henry Hopkinson. I presume in the Foreign Office still, but it may have been the Conservative Party, the conservative foreign affairs research group. 12:30 p.m. Office—Alan Hare, Bob Low and Ihsan Toptani. 7:45 p.m. Bob Low at Buck's.
22 June. Charles Bateman. 12:30 p.m. Tony Rumbold, Foreign Office.
23 June. Harold MacMillan.
24 June. Back to Rome with Bob Low and Bob Minor. 7:30 p.m. Abas Ermenji, Midhat Frashëri, Alan Hare.
26 June. 11:30 a.m. Midhat Frashëri, Alan Hare. 7 p.m. Abas Kupi, Alan Hare.
28 June. 6:30 p.m. Meet Nuçi Kotta, son of Koçi Kotta.
4 July. 6 p.m. Meeting with all those Albanians, sometimes Balli, sometimes other groups. It looks as if we're getting into serious negotiations, every day meeting several times.
5 July. 10:15 a.m. Bob Low, Said Kryeziu at Excelsior Hotel. 6 p.m.—all. That means there must have been masses of Albanians there.
7 July. 10.30 a.m. Said Kryeziu. Lunch—all and Selim Damani. 6 p.m. Meeting. Leave for Cairo. Five plus Selim. Full agreement. We went with Alan Hare and Perkins to Cairo. Not Julian. I think Bob Low.
8, 9, 10 July. Cairo.
13 July. Leave Cairo for Alexandria. Dine with Bob Low, Alan Hare, Julian. So Julian must have come out and joined us in Cairo.
14 July. Alexandria. 10–12 noon—Zog, Bob Low, Julian Amery, Alan and self. 6 p.m. Zog and dined. Probably all of us with Zog.
15 July. 9 a.m. Zog—looks as if it was just a morning meeting.
16 July. Lunch with Julian.
17 July. 10 a.m. Meet Zog. Left Alexandria at 4 p.m. by car to Cairo.
18 July. 3 p.m. Leave Cairo to Rome. Presumably means us three—Alan, Julian and myself. Probably Perkins, too.
19 July. Rome. 12 p.m. Said Kryeziu. Lunch with John Hibberdine and Julian Amery. 7 p.m. Said Kryeziu for dinner.
20 July. 12 noon. Midhat Frashëri and Zef Pali.
21 July. Lunch—Embassy. 8 p.m. Abas Kupi, Said Kryeziu.
24 July. Alan Hare, Bob Low arrive in Rome. 3 p.m. Dined with Bob Low, Alan Hare, John Hibberdine.
26 July. Julian and self audience with Pope. 1 p.m. Lunch with Abas Kupi, Said Kryeziu. Dined with Bob Low, Alan Hare and Julian Amery.
27 July. 12.30 p.m. Said Kryeziu. 2.30 p.m. Abas Kupi. 6 p.m. Midhat Frashëri, Zef Pali. 7:30 p.m. Abas Kupi and Said Kryeziu. 9 p.m. Train to Trieste. I think I went with

Julian and we stayed with Terence Airie who was the general there and also to see Archie Lyall, who ran our information services and later took over the operation in Rome.

29 July. Archie Lyall.

30 July. Trieste to Rome. 5 p.m. Midhat Frashëri and Zef Pali. 7 p.m. Abas Kupi and Said Kryeziu.

1 August. 10 a.m. Leave Rome for Paris. 2 p.m. Arrive at Le Bourget.

2 August. Go to London.

3 August. Lunch with Julian.

5 August. 1 noon. Meet Tony Rumbold at FO. 1:15 p.m. Dick Brooman-White at In and Out Club?

7 August. 12:45 p.m. Peter Kemp.

8 August. 12:30 p.m. Tony Rumbold at FO.

20 August. Go to Rome with my fiancée.

20 September. I return to London. Everything was arranged and agreed before I left Rome. I wouldn't have left the Rome meeting until it was done.

19 September. Came back from Milan to London. Lunch with Julian. 4 p.m. Dick Brooman-White.

29 September. Dick Brooman-White at his flat.

20 October. 6 p.m. Dick Brooman-White. 6:30 p.m. Bill Deakin, Peter Kemp.

30 October. Back to Rome.

8 November. Lunch with Abas Kupi and Said Kryeziu. Meeting with Gaqi Goga and Nuçi Kotta to introduce them to my wife.

9 November. Lunch Abas Kupi and Gaqi Goga. Talk with John Hibberdine.

10 November. Meet Michael Burke.

13 November. Abas Kupi and Gaqi Goga.

14 November. My wedding. The Albanians there were John Hibberdine, Abas Kupi, Gaqi Goga, Said Kryeziu, Abas Ermenji.

16 November. Leave for London.

3 December. 7:30 p.m. Dick Brooman-White.

Seeing here Mrs. Aubrey Herbert. Although they weren't in on the actual scheme, Mrs. Herbert was a great supporter of Albania and revived the Anglo-Albanian society. It took a bit of time to revive. There was a bit of a slip when some of these people sent to train, they were known as "Mrs. Herbert's Australian Evacuation Scheme." It was very unfair for them to do it. She heard about it and was very upset. I'm sure if she had been told, she would have agreed. Auberon was freelancing a bit. He was all over the place. He sympathized with it. He must have known roughly what was going on, but not the details. Then I dropped out of it.

But I came back in 1952. I was involved slightly when the committee moved to America. We were asked by the Foreign Office to help, as friends. The reason was that we'd been pushing the Foreign Office, especially Orme Sergeant and Tony Rumbold, to give the Albanians a decent deal since 1945. I don't think the Foreign Office were properly in touch with the exiles. They had just been left to rot. The FO hadn't given them a thought. The only people that they still knew and liked were people like myself, Julian and Peter Kemp, because we had stuck by them as good friends. Otherwise, they would have thought that the operation was a trap. They could never really have got on good terms with them except by using our past goodwill. We'd never let them down.

Alan Hare was in the secret service then, so it was Julian and I in particular. David was away in Germany, but we'd obviously recommended him. Alan Hare did not have the same position with them because he was captured by the communists and therefore didn't know the nationalists. The Americans didn't know them either.

Our job was to get as many Albanians together and say, "Look, we really think it's worthwhile. Although it's not perfect, it's the first step to getting freedom for your country and I think you should take it. Don't look a gift horse in the mouth. Go for it. And we wouldn't advise you unless we thought it was in your interest."

Perkins seemed to be in charge. Alan was the official Foreign Office "friends" advisor and we were the freelance agents. We were doing what we wanted to do and we weren't paid.

I didn't meet Philby until 1962. Derek Verschoyle was a very unhelpful "C" man in the Embassy. He disapproved of the whole thing. The Englishman Queen Geraldine refers to was Perkins, or maybe Julian or Alan Hare, but not Philby. I don't think Philby was involved at any time in the thing in Rome or Athens.

I don't think Gaqi Goga met Philby at my wedding. I think he met John Hibberdine. My guest list includes Somers-Cocks, John Hibberdine, Mona Sammy, Charles Briggs, Abas Kupi, Gaqi Goga, Said Kryeziu, Abas Ermenji, Madame La Motte, Ida van Linden (?), Ida Susea, Nina Belmonte, John Angles, Ana Marinovitch, Arturo Roderiques, Esterhazy, Taffy and Rosy Rodd, the Ros Petrarovitches, Mario Bamfield, Lucio Daquari. But John Hibberdine, who was left behind, would probably have known Philby because Philby was at that time in the secret service.

Pat Whinney is a rather stiff chap, but he's very nice. I don't recollect the long meeting Pat Whinney mentions. I don't recollect Oakley-Hill being there. But when I was getting married, Julian may well have gone back. We had a lot of conferences there and my notebook wouldn't put everything in. I almost certainly wasn't there.

(The account of Geraldine's meeting.) I think that's more or less true. I can't remember who led it. I think it was Perkins and Bob Low. We were advisors. It was something along those lines. Zog was very annoyed and rightly so. We didn't put it at all diplomatically to him. Certainly, I do remember it was a bad start. I remember him saying, "On what authority is this committee formed? Is it themselves? On whose authority?" It was a very good point.

And he said, "Anyway, in this committee

Bob Low.

you've got three presidents and you can't have three presidents in one committee." The meeting did go badly, but they had been warned that the king wouldn't like it. That it had to be put more tactfully. They went lumbering in like bullies, thinking that they could get the king as they had got all these other people, not realizing he was a man of considerable skill. All the others, except Kupi, wanted to do without the king at all. They rather resented having to go to the king.

I don't remember Gaqi Goga at the July meeting. The two Englishmen would have been Alan Hare and myself. I think Goga must be referring to an earlier meeting. The American military attaché was in touch with Zog and I think Gaqi Goga would have mentioned me by name, because at that time I knew him quite well.

I think Goga may have got the sack from the Royal Court. He got into trouble in Egypt because he wanted to marry a Pasha's daughter. He was Orthodox and he was already married to a girl from a good family in Albania. A Christian marrying a Muslim was frowned upon by King Farouk at that time. And the Pashas were not very keen on their daughters marrying unknown Christian Balkanites. So it could have been at that time that Zog said, "Well, you can't be my ADC any more."

By the time we left for Cairo, there was full agreement. The date of the agreement was July 7/8. Then we saw Zog on July 14. And we saw him again on July 15. The first meeting was the one that started awkwardly. Then we met again in the evening and dined, so everything must have been all right. This was just Julian, Alan, Bob Low and I. The others didn't come. I don't have Perkins down.

Interview conducted December 12, 1981

Sefër Muço

Sefer Muço was an Albanian anticommunist fighter from southeastern Albania. He had been with Balli Kombëtar and escaped from Albania at the end of World War II. As a refugee in Italy, he was recruited for the Albanian operation and flown to Malta. He received training there and in England, and was smuggled into Albania in early November 1949 with a group of fighters. He spent five weeks in the Korça region before crossing back into Greece. He was in Albania two other times, from July to September 1950, and in the Berat region in 1951 for three weeks. He later settled in England.

I spent seven days in Cinecittà before being flown to Malta. There were 29 of us, all Balli Kombëtar. Three went on ahead—Kuka, Dilo and Hysen Lepenica. Sami Bardha and Zeni Mançe were the radio men. There were about 16 of us in my flight. We landed in Malta at night and cars took us to Bin Jema.

Conditions were very nice at the fort. I remember, though, that they wanted to send us into Albania on a reconnaissance mission without guns. Abas Ermenji persuaded them to give us guns. My group was five, all from Korça: Petrit Butka, Sami Bardha, Përparim Ali, Zeni Mançe and I. We moved from one boat to the other in the

Adriatic and we were rowed ashore by two sergeants, one called Kelly, on November 6. There was a group of six from Gjirokastra with us: Haki Gaba, Bardhyl Gerveshi, Xhemal Asllani, Pëllumb Sino and Ago Dauti.

We went round villages near Kolonja and Korça. It was quite easy and there were no problems. We talked to people. I gave them newspapers and political leaflets. They were pleased to see us. The leaflets were to be passed from hand to hand. We slept in the hills, never in houses, or else among trees. We were offered beds in houses, but I made a point of never accepting a bed, never believing people. That is why I went in three times and survived.

I was group leader and I sent phonograms to Jani Dilo in Corfu. Abdyl Sino was there, too, and Muça Doko. We were in Albania about five weeks. Then I decided that we could not stay any longer. There was rain and snow. One evening we were talking on the radio and Dilo said to me from Corfu, "You will move 64." It was a numbers code and I had a book with me. He meant to Greece. I remember that it was snowing and my men jumped up and down with happiness shouting "64! 64!"

When we crossed, we were interrogated by a Greek colonel. I told him that all I could give him was some telephone numbers. He took them away, checked them and told me that they all belonged to the British embassy. Then the Greeks took us down to Athens by car and we stayed there for eight days, until Dilo and Alastair Grant came to collect us.

We left the radio in Albania, in a hole covered with stones. It was very heavy. It weighed 38 pounds, half of it the radio and half the generator. The generator made a very loud whirring noise when it was being used: "Yaw! Yaw! Yaw!" This was dangerous and we tried always to use it near a running river to disguise the noise.

The people said to us, "We are glad to see you, but it is not possible to make a revolution like this." Some said, "We'll join you if you give us guns." But we had no guns to give them, only guns for ourselves, German or English. All of us returned safely to Greece and Malta at the end of 1949.

On July 15, 1950, I went in again. We flew to Athens, then to Janina, with Zaehner and Sino. We were two groups of three: Muharrem Hito, Nezir Tomorri and Xhemal Asllani; Përparim Ali, Zeni Mançe and I. Our mission was delayed because of an incident in a coffee house in Janina when a man threw pepper all over Abdyl Sino. We all had to go back to Athens because of that.

One evening in Athens, we were given some cheese, liver sausage and whisky by Zaehner and he asked us if we were sorry not to have gone into Albania. We said we were and he answered, "That's good, because you'll be going back in soon." We traveled back up to the border area in embassy cars.

A Greek captain and Sino took us up to within one mile of the Greek border. The three of us made for Korça and the other three went to Tepelena, near Gjirokastra. Another group of three—Bardha, Butka and Doko—were due to join us. We waited for them for a week, but then the communists caught Bardha and they nearly caught me.

Bardha went to his home and his mother talked too much. She told people that her son was staying with her and that we were expected to join her there. This news reached the communists by word of mouth. Then a friend of the family asked Bardha to come and see him and bring the three of us, too. The communists waited by the house all night and when Bardha came there they caught him. But they didn't catch us. This was between Erseka and Kolonja. Butka and Doko retreated into Greece.

I stayed in Albania 55 to 60 days. It was harder than the previous year. They had created special anti-guerilla police brigades. An Albanian major made contact with us and said he wanted to meet me with my men. The message was passed to me by some shepherds. But I didn't believe it. Maybe it was true, maybe not. Anyway, I survived again and crossed into Greece in September and returned to Malta in October 1950.

I spent the first part of 1951 in Malta, but I was ill and I did not take part in the mission that was sent in that August. Tefiq Kokla was the leader of the group and the others were Ali Turbohova, Muharrem Hito, Baki Ermenji and Muço Çeprati, who was the Morse operator. They went in by boat. They met communist forces. Kokla was killed and Çeprati captured. The other three escaped into Greece at weekly or monthly intervals.

About that time, I went to England to a parachute course with Zeni Mançe, Fadil Duro, Sami Butka and Abdyl Sino. The idea was that we would join the Kokla group by parachute. It was a three-week course. I jumped twice from a balloon and twice from an aircraft. During the course, Sino told me that Kokla and Çeprati were lost. After that, I returned to Malta and stayed there until December 1951, when the training camp was closed down.

All the trainees came to London and we spent the first half of 1952 in Bicester. Early that summer, I got a card asking me to take a train to Paddington, where I was to "remember my previous instructions." I didn't know what this meant. When I got off the train I saw a man beckoning to me. I followed him, without saying anything to him, until he got into his car and beckoned to me again. I got into the car.

I joined three other Albanians, an English major (Sherman) and two captains. They told me that the Albanian National Committee had ordered me to go into Albania again. I was not pleased, because the other three (Medi Dobrusha, Muharrem Hito and Hetem Çuli) were not my friends and it was not to my home region. But I am a patriot. I fixed this idea in mind and I agreed to go. From London I went to Jackford (?) and stayed three weeks. It is four hours by train from London. I met Tony Northrop there and was very pleased to see him.

Then the three of us went to Athens and Çuli joined us straight from Lavrion. I refused to go in by parachute. I insisted on walking. It is more difficult, it takes longer, but it is much safer. And I was in Albania for three weeks with the three others. It was more dangerous than in 1950, much more dangerous than in 1949. There was not enough bread, everything was strictly rationed and people were frightened. But God was with me, and I was lucky. The main thing was that I had a gun and I did not believe what people told me. You can never believe what anyone in a communist country tells you. People say different things depending on what they've been told to say. That's why other groups were destroyed. My group never took risks and none of us was ever lost.

During our stay there, a pilot made a mistake. He was meant to fly along the River Vjosa and drop leaflets over Gjirokastra and Vlora. Instead he took the River Osum, where we were hiding in the mountains. We woke up one morning and the whole valley was white with these leaflets. Immediately, the communist party ordered the police, soldiers, civilians, boys and girls to go out and collect up these papers and burn them. So there were police and other people all around us. Where were we to go?

Colonel Hill asked me why we had come back from Greece so soon. I told him about the leaflets and he said, "No, we only dropped leaflets over the Vjosa, not near Korça." I took some of the leaflets out of my pocket and showed them to him to prove what I said. He took them and showed them to the Americans. Then he told me that the pilot must have made a mistake. I said it was a mistake that could have cost us our lives.

I stayed one night in Malta only on my way back to England. Then I stayed with Mrs. Reader (?), the sister of Colonel Jeffries (?).

I fought the communists since 1943. They burnt my house, destroyed my property. My wife died in a camp in 1981. She had been there since 1945. Two of my sons were moved from a camp to prison in 1975. They stayed in prison until Mehmet Shehu was killed. Then they were sent back to the camp, to a government farm. It is a very bad government. It started with blood and it will finish with blood.

Interview conducted August 1, 1983

HALIL NERGUTI

Halil Nerguti (b. 1920) was an Albanian anticommunist fighter from Gjegjan in the Luma region. He escaped from Albania at the end of World War II and was a refugee in southern Italy for several years. In May 1950 he was recruited for the Albanian operation and sent to Bavaria for military and guerrilla training. He was dropped into northeastern Albania in November 1950 and stayed there until the end of the year, when he and his men crossed over to Prizren in Kosovo. In March 1951, he returned to northern Albania with more men and crossed back into Kosovo at the end of the year. There he was arrested and sent to prison in Serbia. He remained in Yugoslavia until 1963. He is the author of Jeta ime për Shqipërinë dhe mbretërinë e saj [My Life for Albania and Its Kingdom], *Tirana 2003.*

I was recruited from a camp near Bari in May 1950. Frashëri, Goga, Kupi and Kryeziu came to the camp and said they were looking for young men, young and physically fit, to fight against the communists and free Albania. They wanted every group to take part.

We were taken on a special train to Dachau, dressed in American uniforms and accommodated in barrack huts. Conditions were quite good, with two men only in each room. One of our instructors was an old German major who had been in Albania during the war. There was also a German medical officer. As well as guarding the ammunition dump we had some military training—automatic weapons, rifles and grenades. Every evening they showed us films about guerrilla warfare, how to live in the open and deal with the enemy. We were allowed out of the camp in the evening.

I was one of the first to be taken from Munich to the training school in September 1950. We went in trucks and it was a four-hour drive. The place had been a military academy in the Nazi period. It was a secret zone and there were 34 Albanians altogether. In the school the guerrilla training was far more intense.

We went on night exercises in the hills surrounding the school, practicing guerrilla techniques and the use of two-way radios. We also did parachute training. And there were three hours a day of physical training—drill, runs and route marches in full kit. We also had political instruction, in how we should act when we got to Albania, how we should approach people and talk to them. We were given pictures of all the main leaders in exile, including King Zog and Frashëri. We were told to find out first who was in favor of which party and then give them the right picture. The head of the school was an American colonel who had been a parachutist. He had a glass eye that he used to take out from time to time.

I decided to risk death because I wanted my nation free again. I knew what I was doing. There was no pressure or persuasion from the political leaders. Our eyes were open. I was ready to fight and die if I had to, as I had fought against the Italians and Germans. I knew that it would be harder to fight against an Albanian enemy, because they knew the language and the people and the country better than our previous enemies did. But we felt no inhibition against fighting against fellow Albanians, men who, a few years earlier, we had fought side by side with. We felt that they too were representing foreigners, I mean the Russians, and they had killed many of our friends and family. Many of my cousins were arrested and either shot or sent to the camps.

We knew that they would retaliate against our families. In fact, they did against my family. They shot my brother Hysen and my father died in one of their camps. But we still had to do what we did. It was necessary for the nation. And it was the right moment. There were internal quarrels in Albania at that time. Xoxe had been arrested, the Yugoslavs were on the way out, and the Russian party was not yet in full control. The nationalist movement was still alive. So we could have hopes. The whole thing was realistic. Unfortunately, we were betrayed. Every time one of our groups landed, they were waiting for us.

Toptani and the four others were meant to contact Bilal Kola in the Mati area, where King Zog was born. Kola never surrendered to the communists and we had information that he was still fighting. In fact this turned out to be untrue. Kola had already left and been arrested in Yugoslavia.

All 34 of us were flown from Germany to Athens on October 30, 1950. We stayed a few nights in a house near Athens and on November 3 we made our first attempt to drop into Albania, only the weather was bad and we had to go back. They gave us our equipment in Greece. They gave us uniforms either of the Albanian army or of the police. At that time the Albanian police usually had German weapons, captured during the war. The army had Russian weapons. The cloth for our uniforms was made in Yugoslavia, the same as they wore in Albania. At that time Albania had no textile industry. We had some gold Napoleons and some U.S. dollars. They also gave us poison capsules and they told us not to surrender. The poison capsules were for the men who might not have it in them to shoot themselves through the head.

There were nine of us who left for Albania on November 11. We were supposed to be dropped near the village of Dega, but unfortunately (or fortunately) the pilot could not spot the right signs. All they could tell us was that we were roughly in the Dega area. He did not think that he would be able to find the exact place. So we told him we would jump, so long as he was sure that we were not over Yugoslavia, because that would have been a waste of everything. So we jumped and we landed near Zarrisht, a six hours' march from Dega.

The pilot was meant to turn back and drop our equipment where he had dropped us, but he didn't do that, he just dropped it further on, the result being that it landed in another village entirely and we just had to abandon it. We lost our radios, our food and our spare ammunition. We had only our pistols and machine guns as well as a few medicines.

The other group led by Toptani got their material, but they were surrounded very shortly after they landed and destroyed. One was killed, one was wounded, two escaped. Toptani got away but was betrayed and captured six months later.

The Albanian authorities must have known about our arrival, otherwise the Toptani group would never have been surrounded and destroyed so quickly. This happened because they were dropped exactly in the right place. We were lucky in that we were dropped in the wrong place, otherwise we'd have been surrounded, too.

The Albanian authorities may have known about the camp in Germany from Albanian exile sources. They could have got facts about the operation in general from there. But Philby would have been the only possible source of precise times and places. Even we did not know these details. The decisions were taken by the American authorities in Greece.

On November 4, we were visited by Gaqi Goga, Said Kryeziu and Zef Pali. They were worried about the whole operation and, I think, they wondered whether we ought to go ahead with the parachute drop. There was some sort of misunderstanding between them and the Americans, including one of our American instructors, and after this, three of the fighting groups decided not to go, 12 men out of the 34. They thought that something must be wrong. They were taken away to a Greek island to isolate them from the rest of us.

When we landed in Albania, we didn't go into the village. We went into the forest nearby, keeping away from the roads. Next morning, some villagers alerted the authorities, telling them that they had seen parachutists landing. The police were there very quickly and they surrounded Zarrisht village. They thought we were there, but luckily we weren't, we were in the forest. And we made our way across the hills to Kishaj, a village near Kruma. We called at an isolated house with two or three families in it. They were surprised and frightened, but they received us quite well and they gave us some food, or rather we took some food, enough for eight days. We retreated back into the hills.

Then we set off towards Domaj and after a week's march we met some shepherds just outside the town. They helped us and we stayed there a month. It was well into December already and snowing. The roads were blocked and we were out of reach. But still, we never stayed the night in a house. That would have been too dangerous. We only stayed in remote huts and stables.

We were making for Gjegjan village in the Luma district, where my home is. My brother Ymer and my father were already under arrest. I wanted to find my mother, my brother's wife and their family and get them across the border. But there was no way we could get to Luma because of the cold and the snow, so we crossed into Yugoslavia.

We stayed two weeks with an Albanian family in Prizren and we were joined by my other brother Hysen, who had deserted from the police. Ymer, my elder brother, has been in prison ever since. Two years ago I heard that he was alive, but I've no idea whether he is now. I met a few friends, Albanians living in Yugoslavia. They found us a place to stay in town and we moved into it with our equipment. We sent messages to Rome, writing on the back of envelopes with special white pencils that left invisible marks on paper. We asked them to wait until spring before sending any further groups and told them that our equipment was lost. We got a reply that more stuff would be made available to us through the American consul in Skopje.

On March 17, 1951, the Yugoslav police discovered that there were Albanian parachutists in Prizren and we knew we had to move out. So I went out and bought weapons, enough to arm the 14 Albanians from Yugoslavia who had joined us, and at the end of March, the 18 of us set off from Prizren back into Albania. The Yugoslavs blocked the roads to stop us getting out, so we had to move back to Trepetitz. We were reported and surrounded. We had to fight the Yugoslav police, but we managed to get out of the circle and back into Albania, across Koritnik Mountain.

It was very hard for us to get enough food for 18 people, so we decided to split into four groups, which was the normal way of traveling across country. One group under Ramadan Cenaj went to Mirdita. I took a group towards Luma. Myftar Planeja took four men to the Has region. Rexh Berisha took the last group towards the Doda fort.

Our aim was to last out until spring, to wait for reinforcements from Athens and then get back into action. We agreed on a rendezvous some weeks later at Ganniqe Mountain, so that we could report to one another. I sent two of my men, Albanians from Yugoslavia who had joined us, to this rendezvous, but they were intercepted on the way and shot.

I went back into Yugoslavia to report this and some days later I got a message from Gaqi Goga, a letter with a secret pencil message. It said, "Wait, I have sent two parcels." He meant two people, Tahir Vata and Liman Peposhi. They were dropped in the Has region, they survived and joined up with us. Then we got in touch with Gaqi Goga again and he told us the dates when equipment would be dropped. We signaled to the plane with torches and they dropped us machine guns, pistols, ammunition and food in the valley of Laski in the Mirdita region. All this time we were recruiting people whom we trusted and we gave some of them the weapons, telling them to keep them for future use. We also received two more people with radios. This was in June 1951.

We hid the equipment with the help of villagers. All this time, we were expecting more stuff, more people and more instructions. At this stage, we had good radio communication and we spent the summer there. In October, we got a message advising us to go back to Yugoslavia, so as not to spend the winter in Albania. We were also told to contact the Yugoslav authorities, because by now they had broken relations with the Albanian government. It was thought that they would be ready to help us.

Two Yugoslav officers came to Pashtrik on the border and two of us, Liman Peposhi and I, went to meet them. We asked whether the Albanian exiles we had brought with us would be allowed to return home to their families. The Yugoslavs agreed. Two of the exiles had been shot going to the mountain and two others were shot in Mirdita. The others were allowed to go home.

So there were eight of us, the four original members of the group and four who were dropped later, two without weapons and two with the radio. The Yugoslavs split us into two groups at our request, and we spent the 1951–52 winter in Kosovo. Three of us went from Prizren to Chachak in Serbia, because no one knew us there, and we hoped to get back into Albania in 1952. The Yugoslavs put us up in a hotel in Chachak for one month and they were quite helpful.

Then in December 1951 three Yugoslav officers came and arrested the three of us. The others in Prizren were not touched. They sent us to Mitrovica and kept us for six months in jail in very bad conditions, sleeping on the floor, very little to eat, no exercise, no washing or shaving facilities. They wanted us to give up our mission and sign an undertaking to that effect. We refused.

My brother Hysen was free in Prizren. When he inquired about me, the Yugoslavs asked me to write him a letter saying that I was all right. I did this, but I included a secret sign in the letter, so that Hysen knew the truth. He and the others eventually went back into Albania in August 1952 and later he was caught and shot.

In late August 1952 the second group moved to Macedonia and crossed into Greece. They contacted Rome and the committee sent $1,000 to the Yugoslav police, so in September 1952 they let us out of prison. They sent us to Rashka, a town in Serbia, and gave us asylum with several other Albanians. And I stayed in Yugoslavia until 1963.

I got married to a Kosovar in Yugoslavia in 1954 and had a son. I could not bring my family out from Albania. After a bit my brother Hysen asked the Albanian authorities for permission to go back there. They agreed, left them in peace for six months and then arrested them.

The committee made no attempt to get me out of Yugoslavia. I think that this was because of the confusion in the committee at the time and the failure of the Shehu/Matjani mission.

It is true, I have had a difficult life, but I do not regret going into Albania. I feel proud that we Albanians tried at least to get rid of the communists and that I played a part in the attempt. I would do it all again if I could, only with better organization.

Philby is responsible for great suffering in Albania. There are a hundred families still in jail there today, just on account of my mission alone. Others were shot, like my brother. And he caused us to lose faith in our allies. We realize now that we Albanians have very few friends and that the big powers don't care very much about us. We were a small part of a big game, pawns that could be sacrificed. We were used as an experiment.

Interview conducted July 24, 1983

Anthony Northtrop

Anthony or Tony Northrop (1922–2000) was a British military figure. He was in Albania twice during World War II, for a total of 16 months. In 1950 he was involved in the Albanian operation and was sent to Malta where he

> was active in training the Albanian fighters. In November 1951, he returned to England and from early 1952 gave training courses for Albanian fighters in Devon.

I remember one of the trainees trying to commit suicide by swallowing his cyanide pill. It was not so much out of fear as from complete despair at the operation's successive failures. He was taken to Imtarfa Hospital near Rabat. The main doctor was Colonel Nichols. They were never entered into hospital under their real names. They all had Italian or Greek names.

This man went missing one day. He had been acting rather peculiarly. So I left the fort to look for him and I found him in the main square at Rabat sitting on a bench. As I approached him, he took the pill. I grabbed him by the throat and shouted at him not to swallow it, but I couldn't stop him swallowing it, or rather part of it. Then someone phoned my wife, she came down in the car and we got him to the hospital literally in five minutes, where they used a stomach pump on him. This was around April 1951.

I first went into Albania in December 1943. I was with Alan Palmer and Norman Wheeler. Then I came out and the second time went back in on my own.

I went to Malta in May 1950. Smiley wasn't there and Howard had to fill me in on a lot of things. We lived in the de Trafford house in Rabat, a lovely and isolated house overlooking a large part of the island towards Valletta. It was 15 minutes' drive from the fort along a rough track. My wife helped with the welfare of the men, giving them a woman's touch, but she was not on the payroll.

Some people had known me in another capacity and they were confused by my "cover." Perkins felt very strongly about it all. Jessica Aldridge was his right-hand woman. She came out to Malta several times. She was specifically assigned to the Albanian operation. Usually, I met them both in London and she would come to Malta on her own to see how it was all going. Perks was connected with Perkins Diesel Engines. He was a very good boss, forceful and difficult, but ebullient and well intentioned. There were some people in Broadway who, unlike Perkins, wanted the operation to go ahead for political or career reasons and they had no concept or understanding of the difficulties involved, what a man has to go through when he is put across an enemy frontier or landed on an enemy shore. It's not much good putting a man into the field if he can't get any further. There was a feeling among some people in the office, for whom I don't have much respect, that we had to get the operation underway whatever the cost and quickly. My own view was that there was no point in sending people in unless they were capable of delivering the final blow and doing the job that they were supposed to do.

The time that elapsed between recruitment of a man and sending him into the field was quite insufficient. I know, because I've done it myself. And there was no officer material, with perhaps one exception. There was motivation, yes, but not the necessary skill or experience. Some of them I trained told me that they were sure they were not going to come back. And in my mind I had to agree with them. I knew it was very high on the cards.

I thought that there were people in Malta keeping an eye on us, probably Italians, and I advised London of this. Jimmy Blackburn confirmed to me that there were Italians quite definitely sounding him out.

I remember when one of the Albanians died and the Commander in Chief, who saw me from time to time, refused to have anything to do with the funeral arrangements. He told me that I was on my own and he didn't want any trouble with the Maltese authorities. In the end I had to get hold of Jimmy Blackburn and we took him out to sea in the *Henrietta*.

Several times I went to Athens and Rome to meet the Americans and talk to them about their side of the operation. I remember Joe Leib particularly. And one night we had a very fine dinner at Pat Whinney's house outside Athens with Perks and Jessica Aldridge. This was to celebrate the first successful incursion.

The Albanians told us that two of the men caught during the first operation, perhaps the Lepenica brothers, were taken to Korça and dragged through the streets. The 1950 operations were overland, but most of my men were taken in by Jimmy Blackburn by sea. In my time there was one abortive attempt, when Blackburn had to retreat because of patrol boats, and two actual landings.

Part of my job was to convince the trainees that there was a real chance of changing the Albanian political situation. Several of them asked me about this from time to time. Did I think it was a real possibility? Even at the time I felt that the chance was very slim, but I could not say this to the men. My job was to instill confidence. Still, I don't think I fooled them. And I must say that they were very brave men indeed, because they must have known certainly by 1951 that their chance of being caught was quite high. And I feel sure that the main aim of the operation was to test a theory rather than to liberate Albania. I don't think we had much idea of what people in Albania were thinking at that time. I knew Hoxha personally during the war and he locked me up for a period. When I first met him, I thought what a charming man he was, very affable and presentable. My own view was that by 1950 he was very firmly established. It was not true that he could have been dislodged by one little push from a few well-trained men. Of course, exiles always exaggerate the unpopularity of the regime they have left.

I do not think that Philby was the main reason why the operation failed. I think that our reading of the situation was wrong. Hoxha was very much more firmly established than we imagined. Philby or no Philby, I don't think it could have worked. The job needed officer cadres. I don't mean that there was anything wrong with the men themselves, but they lacked leadership. My men were fine as ordinary members of the team, but not as decision makers. This would have been a problem too if we had succeeded in getting a foothold inside the country. Where would we go from there? I discussed this with Perks. It really needed a cadre of better people, more time and better planning.

I also felt that, once they were there, they ought to have carried out acts that would really have convinced the local population that something was happening. I mean significant acts. My idea was not for them to blow up a bridge or a house, but to get straight to the communist leadership and kill the well-known figures. If some of the leaders could have been eliminated, even in a suicide mission, that would have been worthwhile. And I'm sure that some of my men would have been ready to do it. You'd have had to make a stir both inside and outside the country. This was difficult, since the United States and Britain were doing everything to keep the operation quiet. It would nevertheless have been possible to mount a more public operation and still deny official involvement.

One doesn't like to say it, but probably those that did come back survived because they didn't go far enough forward. It doesn't mean that they were afraid. They just had no way of carrying out their tasks, so they lay low.

The allies did not want to make the operation a public affair. This damaged its chances of success. In order to gain support, our men needed to publicize their activity and show that they were serious. The fact that Hoxha was firmly in control does not mean that he was popular.

Our son Anthony was born in November 1951 and we left Malta just before Christmas. I had to leave in fact two days before Anthony was born and then go off somewhere else, leaving her to have the baby in Malta. This was something that persuaded me shortly afterwards not to prolong my career. Anthony Newman took over from me.

I was aware of the parachute training activities around Bicester in 1952, but I took no part in them. My own view was that those doing the training ought to have had some personal experience themselves of being parachuted into hostile territory, so that they would know how the Albanians felt about it. I trained some of them at Chagford in Devon. I taught courses of five or six men every three months or so, courses in espionage and sabotage. It was on a smaller scale than Malta.

Blackburn was putting them ashore from time to time. He was also a very good bomber pilot. There were some stories about him that were not to his credit, but my view was that none of it got in the way of his job, which he was very good at. I trusted him myself. He lived on the Henrietta all over the Mediterranean. Perks put me in touch with him. I told him that I didn't care what he did, so long as it didn't mess up the operation. I asked Perks not to be mean about payment, to make sure that we had his exclusive services so long as he was with us, that he wasn't doing any trading on the side.

I was offered the job in early 1950 on my return from the West Indies. Perks explained it all in his Broadway office. I was trained in this sort of work in SOE headquarters in Cairo. And I did a parachute course in Haifa. I was born in 1922. And I had spent 16 months in Albania. I was asked whether I was interested in the job and whether I was sympathetic to the course. I was happy to accept, frankly, because I don't like communism. And I particularly didn't like Hoxha. I knew him well, and Shehu. I lived with them for some months with Reg Hibbert, Victor Smith, Alan Palmer, Norman Wheeler. I must say that I rather liked Hibbert and I got to know him in Rome.

We were on the run together for some weeks in January/February 1944 around Korça and Elbasan. We arranged a coordinated attack on a German position. The partisans would attack it and the RAF would bomb it from Italy. At the last minute Hoxha called off his part of the attack, so that the air strike was ineffective. After that, I canceled all further supply drops to Hoxha, whereupon he locked me up in a house, imprisoned me, in fact. Another thing that angered me was that one night we bedded down, several senior partisans and I in the same house. I was woken up by a villager who said that there were Germans searching the village. I asked him where General Hoxha was and he said that he had taken his men and retreated out of the village. I took a dim view of the fact that they had left me behind. I got out just a couple of minutes ahead of the German patrol.

I was given a cover as a major in the Royal Ulster Rifles. My training in explosives was not out of date. My only job was to familiarize myself with the actual operational details. I remember discussing whether to send the boys in by land, sea or air. I said that it would be wrong to send them in by air. They did not have the right training. They told me about the Balli Kombëtar and what we hoped to achieve. It was mostly Perks and Jessica Aldridge.

I flew out to Malta from London without Jean, so that I could settle in. I had stayed at a hotel below Valletta on the sea front, driving every day to the fort. I looked for a house. Grant was in charge at the fort. I remember nothing about "Blondie" Stover except that he wasn't a very good cook.

My first job was to read the signals. They were deciphered by Grant or, in the case of personal messages, by me. Then I used to see the Albanian group leaders, to explain the training for the day. Often, I took part in it myself. We practiced using our Schmeiser automatic weapons in the moat. It was a very good submachine gun, only subject to the fact that it tended to slip when on safety. Most of their work concerned the use of explosives and description of the targets. Grant and I trained them in explosives, which was their main military task. Their weapons were only for their own protection. Grant had a problem over a love affair that he confided to my wife. He was a very likable chap, but a bit of a softie, not really tough enough for a job like that. He knew the job, but he was not the right man for it. There was physical training and coding. And I always checked that there had been no serious quarrels during the night between the men. There were frequent verbal disputes, provoked by depression and the uncertainty of their existence. I did this because I felt I knew Albanians and they trusted me.

Willingness to die is an essential element in this sort of operation. I don't mean that they ought to have a death wish. But they have to be ready to die if necessary. They have to see the mission as more important than their own survival. There were one or two, I thought, who would have put their lives entirely at the mission's disposal. But most of them were hesitant when it came to the point. They wanted to do something, they wanted to fight, but then it would strike them in the small hours of the night that in two or three weeks' time, they were going to find themselves alone on a beach in hostile territory. At that point, yes, most of them were worried men. It was not a long period of training and it's quite natural for me in that position to be keen as mustard up to a certain point where suddenly it dawns on them what they've let themselves in for. I certainly remember some who were convinced that they were not going to make it.

Some of the men I dealt with in London took a very harsh view of this lack of dedication, as they saw it. They described the Albanians as a lot of cowards. These were people who had not been in the field themselves and they ought to have known better. It was a measure of London's impatience at the delays and failures. The same people were in favor of sending them in by air, because it was the quickest way of getting them into the field. They seemed to imply that the "pixies" were expendable. It made me very angry. In fact, knowing the men as I did as well as the terrain where they were landed, I'm sure that a lot of them just lay low and tried to get out to Greece as soon as possible. I don't think many of them carried out their assigned tasks. They got to Greece and explained that they'd done their best. And I think that by their standards they had.

I'm thinking of a couple of instances where I had quite violent disagreements with my superiors about this. This was because they had a program, they wanted the job done, it was taking too long, it wasn't going very well and they were under pressure. I remember from my own missions that it can be very dangerous to try and increase the tempo when things aren't going well. This feeling was there as soon as I arrived. Perkins warned me about it and advised me to be understanding in my treatment of them.

There were some men who, at my suggestion, were not put forward as candidates for an operation. They just stayed at the fort and never went into the field. After a few months of tension and anti-climax, they became very depressed.

The accounts of the survivors had a bad effect on the others. They came back to Malta with stories of what a bad time they'd had. For instance, they all believed that two of the men caught during the first mission had been dragged through the streets of Korça behind a jeep.

When I trained with them, I did exactly what they did. I mingled with them, went on runs with them, sat with them while Grant was giving them lessons in explosives. They were quite small, as most mountain people are, but generally in good shape, fit enough for the job. There was no doctor in the fort, so anyone who was sick went with a British escort to Emtafa Hospital in British uniform. The medical officer who saw them knew that they were a special bunch. This was something that I had to take up with the commander-in-chief, because any normal MO was going to ask questions about these peculiar people who don't speak English and aren't Maltese. So a special MO was brought in and briefed in my presence, to make sure he didn't ask questions.

One enterprising corporal in the RASC looked me up in the Army List and found that I wasn't there. He did this because he had heard about the "funnies" up at Fort Bin Jema and that I was in charge of the "funnies." I immediately asked for a check on him to be made and the general saw me about it, asking what we were to do. The man had written to his MP. The general said we had a problem. He had been asked from London who I was, because I wasn't in the Army list. What was he to say? It was traced back to the RASC corporal. It died a natural death only because I left Malta.

On another occasion I went to see the C in C and asked a corporal in GHQ to tell his office that I was there. He did an extraordinary thing for a soldier to do. He looked at his watch and said, "I'm off duty now, sir." I saw a military police sergeant a few yards away and I said to him, "Put this man under open arrest." I was proposing to charge him after seeing the C in C. As soon as I left, I realized what a stupid thing I'd done. It was bound to bring me into the limelight. Anyway, by the time I got back to the guardroom he was very contrite and he apologized, so I let him off and everything ended all right.

I kept myself out of the social round. A school friend of mine called Robert Browning invited me on board the *Magpie*. I tended to see Navy men rather than Army men. At another party a woman came up and said, "Oh, are you in the Army? The last time I saw you, you were in the civil service." My wife explained that I had just been called back into the Army to do a specific job.

There were rumors all the time about what we were up to. We were called "the funnies" and I was called "the funny major." They wondered why I didn't have a driver.

The operation suffered from a fault inherent in every bureaucratic system, where decisions are taken along general political lines, with little attention being paid to the individuals actually involved. Generally speaking, my view is that, if I've accepted the king's shilling, I'll do the job whatever the cost. But I have this one aversion to men who are prepared to sell their subordinates down the line when they haven't been in that situation themselves. If they've done it, they can talk to me about politics and expediency, but if they haven't, I object most strongly.

If I had to do the operation again, I would spell out very clearly what the objectives were. You have to do something very dramatic, something that everyone sees. And, unhappily, that means violence. If Enver Hoxha or one of the men around him had been disposed of publicly, say, by a man running up to him with a couple of grenades and blowing them both to pieces, it would have had a great effect. But it wasn't on. So it's a long and very hard road to bring down a government by paper propaganda. Anyway, the government would never have allowed such a "noisy" operation to take place under their auspices. They were determined to keep a low profile. Perkins explained to me that the level of violence that I was proposing was simply not politically acceptable. I told him that in that case the thing would not succeed.

When Blackburn was due to take a team in, I was advised of his estimated arrival time and he contacted me as soon as he reached Malta. He had no permanent residence. He just lived on the boat. We had to be very careful about getting the men on board the *Henrietta*, because strictly speaking, they were leaving Malta illegally. It was made absolutely clear to me by the military that I was on my own and that I would have to get out of any trouble as best I could. The only problem we had was when we had to bury this man at sea.

I left Malta towards the end of 1951, while there was an operation going on. We met Joe Leib and Perkins in Rome. It was when CIA and OPC didn't speak to one another, although they both spoke to me. Leib lived in considerable style in a house on one of the Seven Hills. There were a lot of women around. I remember that he used to "treat" me, as he put it. I was never allowed to know the venue. We went to dinner once and then there were paraded some quite exotic-looking young women. He said to me, "Choose whichever one you like, Tony, and she's yours until breakfast time." It was real American hospitality.

I was not very impressed by the Americans I met in the secret world. I would have refused to take part in an active operation with any of them. And I didn't much like being involved in sending others into the field under that sort of sponsorship.

On election night in October 1951, Leib organized an amazing party in Rome. When the radio stopped broadcasting the results, he decided to take us into town to celebrate Churchill's victory. It was about four o'clock and everything was closed, but Leib found this one club with a light still on and he opened it. They began by laying on wine, food and girls for the three of us and very soon other customers arrived, too.

I had a drink with Burgess in the basement bar at HQ a couple of nights before he defected.

Interviews conducted in March and April 1984

* * *

Anthony was born on November 11, 1951. I left Malta around October 20. The dinner at Leib's house on October 25 was a sit-down affair for about ten people, including

Jessica Aldridge and Perks and a couple of other Brits. Jessica was the only woman there and we left after dinner. I stayed on in Rome for a few days to attend John Hibberdine's wedding and then I went back to London.

Several of my boys in Malta heard the October 1951 trial on the radio and this was the reason for their despair.

In Rome we discussed our past operations and the advisability of continuing them. It was also a question of how they would continue. There was no indication to me at that time that the whole thing was folding up on the British side. We noted that the British-trained men had fared better.

We also discussed parachuting and I was against it because of the proposed height of the drop. So as to ensure that their men landed precisely on target, and to protect the plane, the Americans proposed to drop them from a height which, in my view, was too low for an untrained parachutist to jump at with heavy equipment. Top-class men would never jump at less than 400 feet. The chute would take 180–200 feet to develop. This left only 200–300 feet for the fall, which was very little. At 400 feet you're very close to having your chute open after you hit the ground, so to speak.

There was no way in which men of this general caliber, physically and mentally, could be trained in just a few days to drop safely at such low altitudes. A rush parachute course lasted ten days and it included two practice jumps. Parachute jumping without this basic training was in my view suicidal. It can be done. It was done during the war. But it would have greatly reduced the risk of death or injury to have put them through a course. It would have enabled them to avoid elementary errors. If they had never done it before and they were poor material and they were being dropped from low heights, then it was suicidal, quite apart from the fact that the whole mission was betrayed.

If you're flying at tree-top level, you have to rev your engines very high, so as to be ready for a sudden push upwards. This is quite terrifying for someone not accustomed to parachuting. You're sitting by a hole in the fuselage with air rushing in and the noise is deafening. It's no reflection on their bravery. It used to frighten the life out of me and I was properly trained. So if you've never done it before, then you'll be thinking all kinds of things, but not what you've been told to think about.

The men who dropped me were excellent. They dropped me and the equipment inside the signal fires. In this case there was no reception committee and, I imagine, no discussion between the crew and the men being dropped. Quite apart from the fact that the crew were Polish and the parachutists Albanian, they were not allowed to meet and talk for security reasons.

When I went in, I knew where I wanted to go, all the maps were available in Italy. I sat down with the pilot and discussed how he ought to fly the plane. He dropped me within 50 feet of my target.

This is why we rejected the idea. If they had been commando types or if there had been more time and facilities for training, then it would have been different. As it was, while these men were brave and highly motivated, they were not suitable for the job.

It is no easy matter to fly an aircraft at 50 and then suddenly pull up to 500 feet or so and find the precise moment in your arc of ascent to put your men out of the door. It must have been very difficult to navigate in Albania.

In peacetime it has to be without a moon, though with a clear sky, and it is a succession of mountains and valleys. There must be a point of identification, a river or a tall peak, and there must be no trees, otherwise the man can get his chute caught in them. They must have had some practice of navigating during the leaflet raids, but it was obviously not enough.

Another aspect of the operation's bad security was the policy of sending men to their hometown or village. It was the only place where they might have a chance of being helped and of recruiting others. It meant, though, that as soon as one man fell into the communists' hands and gave them the names of the other men being trained, they knew immediately where they were going to be dropped. This would be known as soon as each group left Munich for the training school and their names were leaked to them through Rome. They would know that a group would be unable to operate other than in its home area.

The parachuting had the advantage of getting the men to their home area as a group, without having to give each group a guide through every place on the way. The Albanians generally knew only their home area. Outside their own valley they were lost. That is why they either needed guides or they needed to be landed directly on the exact spot where they lived, which meant being dropped from a low height, to make sure that they landed where they knew where they were.

If we had trained them, we'd have taken them to Abingdon and made them do a tower jump, a balloon jump and two jumps from an aircraft. They should have been given that opportunity.

I told Perks that on an island the size of Malta it was absurd for us to try and conceal our own existence. If anything, I said, we should advertise ourselves. The more we tried to keep our operation under wraps, the more talk it generated. We could, for instance, have kept them locked up in the fort day and night. This would have made them all the more conspicuous. And it would have been very bad for morale. I used to let them go into town in groups of three, with one man designated to look after the other two.

In Rome we discussed where their operation had got to, where ours had got to, and tentatively what we were going to do in the future. After it was over, I flew to England. I did not know then what I was going to do, but early in 1952 (February/March) I started training men in Chagford in Devon. I did three groups of four or five men, training them for two or three weeks at a time. I have no idea what they did then. I did not need to know anything about that. Several of them were men who had also been with me in Malta. I remember being worried about the undue haste with which it was being done. I argued that it made sense to train them for longer periods, that it would make the difference between a halfhearted mission and a serious one. I said that with six weeks training, it would be a better operation altogether. As it was, some of these men who had marched 25 miles across the Devon moors weren't even fit to go to bed, let alone into action. They just weren't up to it physically.

It sounds amazing, but I remember asking my superiors, "Have you ever marched 20 miles in a snowstorm? And in enemy-occupied country?" It's one thing to walk 20 miles in nice weather over a place where you have no fear. It's quite another to do what these men were going to be expected to do. So if they couldn't do it across the Devon moors, they certainly weren't going to be able to do it in Albania.

These were men who, if they had come before a British army selection board in World War II, would not have been chosen for a commando course. They'd have been given something less demanding. I cast no aspiration on their bravery and their motivation which were both obviously high. I say simply that their potential to carry out the mission was limited by their physical capabilities.

Interview conducted July 19, 1984

LORD ST. OSWALD

Rowland Denys Guy Winn, later 4th Baron St. Oswald (1916–1984), was a British military and diplomatic figure, also known as Rowland Winn. He served during World War II with the 8th King's Royal Irish Hussar Regiment, primarily in the Middle East and in Southeast Asia. On 19 September 1944, he was parachuted into Albania, whereby he broke a leg. He fought in the Korean War from 1950 to 1952 and was awarded the Military Cross. In 1957, Rowland Winn succeeded his father in the barony and took his seat in the House of Lords as a Conservative member. From 1973 to 1984, he was a member of the European Parliament.

I was parachuted into Albania around September 1944 into an area held by the partisans. The drop went badly from the beginning. The pilot was new, the aircraft was substandard and there was no moon. I was also rather clumsy. Anyway, I broke my leg as we hit the ground. I tried to force myself to stand up, but when I put my weight on the broken leg, the tibia went squish and scraped its way along the fibia. I fainted with the pain.

The partisans said that a German patrol was expected in the area. What were they to do with me? They could either leave me to be captured by the Germans or they could hide me. I knew that I would have very little chance of being treated as a prisoner of war, so I asked them to hide me.

They got a local horse doctor to look after me. He worked out with a stick that my broken leg was considerably shorter than the good one. He said that he ought to pull the broken leg and set it back in its proper place. I asked about an anesthetic and they gave me a bottle of raki. I anesthetized myself as far as possible and he pulled the leg and set it as best he could.

Then they carried me on a litter to a partisan base, where I met Reg Hibbert and several other British soldiers who were with the partisans. In the course of a discussion, he told me that life was not going to be very pleasant for me. He said that he had arranged with James Klugman, who was with SOE in Bari, for Smiley, Amery and McLean to leave the nationalists and move into partisan territory. Then, he said, there would be a "mistake" and all three would be shot. "I fixed it," he said, explaining that as a communist he had decided that it was necessary to dispose of the three British officers in order to ensure Hoxha's triumph in the civil war.

I tried to send a telegram to Bari, asking them to warn Smiley, Amery and McLean, but it was intercepted by Hibbert's sergeant. Anyway, I had underestimated the cunning of my three friends. They received the order from Bari, but they disobeyed it. They escaped by taking a boat across to Italy.

Interview conducted March 1, 1983

ABDYL SINO

Abdyl Sino was an Albanian anticommunist fighter in exile. He had been with Balli Kombëtar forces during World War II and escaped to Greece, where he lived as a refugee. There he got a job with the American mission for aid to Greece and from late 1949 was involved in the Albanian operation for radio communications from a base in Corfu. He was then transferred to Malta where he worked as an interpreter for the British in training the fighters. He also helped train fighters in England and Germany. In 1952, Sino worked for the Americans at a radio monitoring station in Cyprus, and later for the Albanian service of the Voice of America. From 1964 to 1980 he lived in Vienna.

My first involvement in the Albanian operation was in Corfu in the Villa Bimbelli, which overlooked the Albanian coastline. Ihsan Toptani and I and another Albanian were there, also Alan Hare and Captain Cadell. There were two sergeants dealing with signals. I remember only their first names. One was called Lewis, the other Laurence. There was another sergeant who dealt with supplies. This setup was designed to communicate with the boys that had been sent in to Albania. Before that I had been in Athens, while the first group were being trained in Malta in mid–1949. I was working with the American mission for aid to Greece. I was with Balli Kombëtar, which means "national front." The royalists were cooperating with Balli Kombëtar, but not the "Independenza" who were pro–Italian. We didn't want any connection with them. Abas Kupi was the royalist recruiter and Abas Ermenji was the Balli Kombëtar recruiter.

In February 1964 the Americans moved us from Cyprus to Vienna, because of the trouble in Cyprus. I stayed in Vienna from 1964 until the end of July 1980. Then I retired after 28 years.

Abdyl Sino, an Albanian anticommunist fighter in exile.

The British arranged with the American

"aid to Greece" organization to pick me up and send me to Corfu. A royalist Albanian and I stayed at the British Embassy one night. Then the two of us and Toptani flew from Athens airport to Corfu. This was at the end of October or beginning of November 1949. It was so close to Albania that you could see the guards on the other side. So it was a very good spot for communications.

Unfortunately, we got very few messages from them. It didn't work. We had set times when they were supposed to come on the air. The boys landed three or four days after we came to Corfu. We were told that the operation was on and we started listening in at certain set times. Only one of the groups managed to get through and reach its destination (a long way from the coast) in the Skrapar district. They set up a base without being spotted and made contact with us. They were all landed near Vlora, called Avlona in Italian. The other two groups were spotted as soon as they landed. About three weeks later we realized that the operation had gone wrong and we went to Malta to prepare for another landing. My royalist colleague was Mustafa Doko. The three of us went to Malta.

Three groups were landed, with four or five men in each. The successful group came on the air from Skrapar after about a week. They did not know about the other two groups because they had landed at different points. They could not come on the air sooner because of the heavy equipment that they had to carry across the country. They had carried their pedal generator, machine rifles and other equipment across this rocky country. They had money and the names of people that they were supposed to contact. My personal view is that it was nonsense. People were waiting for our agents, but when they arrived they were immediately asked, "Why are there only four of you? We can't fight the communists with four or five people. If we see larger numbers, better equipped, and supplies of arms, then we'll start." When they arrived and came on the air, they told us simply that they had seen people who did not seem enthusiastic. They were tough boys, between 20 and 40 years old, some of them experienced World War II veterans.

One group was landed near Vlora and was spotted the next day as soon as it got light, climbing into the mountains. They were followed and ambushed. One was killed on the spot, the other managed to escape into Greece. The other two survived for a few weeks, were captured and were never heard of again.

The second group reached Skrapar and made contact. They were the only group that made contact. They stayed in contact for about three weeks, then sensed that they were under observation, took some of their things, left the rest behind and made for Greece. They managed to cross into Greece all in one piece. The third group made for the Gjirokastra area, saw that there was nothing they could do and also crossed into Greece.

Jani Dilo was there in Malta. There were about 30 Albanian trainees. The training was done mostly by Alastair Grant and myself. There was Captain Wilkie, who stayed just for a few months with Bill Collins on radio training.

The big American was called John Papajani. His code name was Palmer. He was the CIA representative. He stayed a couple of months during the training and left. He contacted me years later in Cyprus through Jani Dilo. Jeffrey Kelly was there helping with the signals and a man called Osgood. All my family, my brother and my parents, were killed by the communists. As soon as they captured one of our men, they got my name out of him and immediately arrested all my family. Or probably they already knew that I was involved, because Philby had given them the details. They knew exactly, right from the start, what was going on and who was in the operation.

In Malta I was an interpreter, helping with the training for the subsequent operations. Every few months a group of 12 to 16 would be taken by boat and either landed in Albania or infiltrated across the border. Some sort of agreement was reached with the Greek government, when Papagos was prime minister, and we started infiltrating people by land. The boys were kept for a few nights at a house in Athens specially rented, which at once aroused the Greeks' suspicions, and then flown up to Janina. Things were complicated in Janina because of the Greeks from northern Epirus, who had come there from across the border and who contained a number of communists and infiltrators. Probably they had been told about our operation because, when we arrived at Janina airport all dressed in uniforms, there were journalists and photographers out to meet us. Everyone was taking pictures. I turned to someone and said, "What is this? Are we going to a wedding?" The security officer told us not to worry. Professor Zaehner was with us speaking his marvelous ancient Greek, which nobody understood, and drinking a little too much. We went to the Greek security office, the *Alagopon*, which means the aliens' bureau. They took our Albanian fighters and locked them up in a cell. It was the summer of 1950, very hot, and after a few hours the boys were sick. I told the Greek officer that we had come to invade Albania, not Greece. He told me everything would be all right, everything "kala." Zaehner and I and a British officer whose first name was Michael stayed in the local hotel. I thought it was quite wrong. I thought that people knew who I was and once I was attacked in the street there.

I saw that it was not going to work. So I went back and I told Zaehner, who was not in very good shape, that we could not continue. Everybody knew that our boys were in the *Alagopon* cells. People from North Epirus were going to the *Alagapon* and asking what was happening, who these people were. I said that we ought to go back to Athens. So we flew back and returned to the same house, waiting for transport to Malta. We stayed a couple of months, eating and vegetating. We couldn't let them go out. They had no documents, no civilian clothes. Officially, they hadn't even entered Greece. Finally, some arrangement was made through the Greek army to get the boys back up to the frontier and into Albania, not by air this time, because of the danger of being spotted at the airport, but by military truck. We left early in the morning and we arrived late in the evening, this time we camped outside the city in the fields. We stayed there for a day and the next morning we moved up towards the border. It was near the two main towns in the south, Korça and Gjirokastra.

We divided them into two groups, one to go right, the other to go left. The Greek army lent us some mules and we got right up to the border, which is marked by a river. This was in September 1950. We had one Greek army sergeant, probably from intelligence, a few Greek soldiers and we walked with our mules and horses along the border, like going to a wedding. People did not seem to understand what the communists are.

There were some corn fields by the border, the river bed was dry and we made them cross. We waited about one hour, to give them enough time to get inside the country. We just watched them walk off into the dark. We slept the night in the fields. The next day Michael went to the border during the day without me. Then we set off in another direction, about 40 or 50 miles to the east of the place where we had sent the first group in. Then I walked a bit along the border and by chance I found a piece of newspaper. It showed me that the Albanian border guards knew that we were in the area and had set up ambushes all along the frontier. That same day I went back to Janina and took a plane to Athens and another to Malta. As soon as I got to Malta I found an urgent message: "The boys who crossed the border the night before last have been attacked." They had been ambushed and they were back at the border.

But we did not know how many had managed to get back to the border. So what were we to do now? I flew back to Athens immediately. The boys had been brought down there by the Greeks, but not all of them. They told us that the communists had let them walk a few miles in and then opened fire. Three of them managed to get back, the other disappeared. We don't know what happened to him.

Tony Northrop was there, too. He took over from Smiley. Later we found out what had happened to the fourth. They caught him, got all the information out of him and put him in prison. But they forgot that he was a trained fighter so after a couple of weeks or so, he escaped and disappeared into the country, where he was hidden by relatives. He lived there for a few months and finally made his way back to Greece. I never saw him again, because he went straight from Athens to the United States. His name is Sami Bardha. We found out about him from Albanians who crossed into Austria from Yugoslavia. I met dozens of them. So this boy managed to get away and the other three we took back to Malta.

The British training was perfect in its way, but there were too many cooks. The Americans were training in West Germany, the Italians in Naples and Bari. The Yugoslavs were training, the Greeks were training. None of this had anything to do with us. Nothing was coordinated. As far as I could see, the only question was, who is going to get there first?

The Italians were sending in their "Independenza" people, former supporters of the Italian administration under Mussolini.

The whole operation was doomed to fail. The Americans were doing independent operations, parachute jumps, without the British. Our operation in Malta was Anglo-American cooperation. The Americans were training their men independently, from the labor battalions in Germany. There were almost 500 people there. I stayed there six months. Abas Kupi was in charge. They were sent in by air. But every time they landed, the communists were there, ready to pick them up. I was a radio monitor in Cyprus during their trial and I had to write up the radio broadcasts of the trial, during which the accused spilled the beans in great detail. I wrote the BBC monitoring reports.

After a few months in 1951 we sent another team from Malta, where Tony Newman had taken over from Northrop. We sent two groups in by sea. One went to the Gjirokastra area, by the Greek border. It was more or less the same people that had gone there before. The second group went to the Skrapar district, between my hometown and Elbasan. But by and large, they were told that the West underestimated the strength of the communists and that it was no good sending groups of four or five against them. "If you had sent more people," they were told, "we would all have joined you, the whole division. But not when you are only four or five. So get out of here as soon as you can, otherwise you will suffer, your families will suffer and we will suffer, too." One group emerged intact. The other group was in Skrapar district, the same group that had made contact with us in Corfu two years earlier. This was in August 1951. But the communists had learnt from Philby and other means that there were groups in the country. They tracked them down and kept them under observation. Then finally one night they surrounded them, opened fire and killed their leader, Tefiq Kokla. Ahmet Lirioni was another caught trying to cross the frontier into Greece.

Kasem Daut Shehu was with us in the first landing when we were in Corfu. He was captured and sentenced to 20 years imprisonment. But they never come out, these people who are imprisoned. It is better to finish them off. They get sent to the coal mines or the chrome mines, where they live like hell.

Our people were really trained and resolute. They were all good trained boys. They were taken on night maneuvers in Malta and out to sea. Most of the survivors emigrated to the United States. But the Albanian communists know who they are, because the ones they caught were tortured and must have given them information. All in all, we didn't lose more than five people. But others were lost from the American operation.

Their line is that everyone who is not with us is against us. And if you are against us, we owe you one lek. One lek is the price of a bullet.

Interview conducted April 18, 1981

* * *

I was ready to go to Australia in mid–1949, with a passport and a ticket, when I was asked to join the operation. I stayed a night at the house of the British military attaché in Athens and then flew to Corfu around October 15. There were about 15 of us altogether in Villa Bimbelli. It is a large house on a hill facing Albania in a garden full of olive trees, between the northern tip of the island and Corfu town.

The British officers were Alan Hare and two others called Morgan and Cadell. Mustafa Doko and Ihsan Toptani came and joined us from Italy. Also there was Jani Dilo and some radio technicians, typists and administrators.

It was very boring and bothersome work. The boys were meant to come on the air at a certain time every day, but usually they didn't. We got very few messages. When they came, it was plain Albanian speech, numbers interspersed with a few words. We then had to take the numbers to the code book, the "bible," and turn them into a proper message. They were all taught by Bill Collins in Malta and when the training got better, they used Morse rather than plain speech. His best student was Muço Çeprati.

The radio was too heavy. How could such a thing be carried over rough country, through mountains and forests, as well as the guns and ammunition and everything else they had to take? I had very little knowledge of such things, but I said to them, "They're not going to open a front in Albania. They don't even have a base, they need something lighter, so that they can move fast when they're in danger." Also, it was too noisy. This was dangerous and it got in the way of the speech, though not of the Morse.

Alan Hare took us into town a few times in his big Humber station wagon. We also went swimming and boating. But that's not what we were there for. The anxiety and the waiting drove us crazy.

In July 1950 I took the Kokla group to the border. As soon as we arrived in Janina we had trouble with the North Epirus group. They were there at the airport and they were photographing us as we got off the plane. I said to the Greek officer, "What is this, for the newspapers?" He said, "No, it's all right, they're our boys." In fact it was Nico Ceci and company.

But then they drove our men off in a truck and took Zaehner and me to a hotel in Janina. The next day I saw some of the North Epirus people following me. They had influence with the aliens' office and I heard that our men had been put into a cell. I went to see them and it was true. They were locked up in a small room in terrible heat, with not enough water, sweating and suffering.

It is very hard to deal with the Greeks in such matters. General Papagos knew about us and was with us, but every second Greek is a prime minister. You can make an agreement with one Greek authority, but then there's another that either doesn't know about it or doesn't agree with it. So they get in your way.

Zaehner wouldn't help. He was only a professor. And I couldn't help. I was only an Albanian. Then one day I was in a tavern opposite our hotel, drinking coffee, when a man came up behind me, hit me twice and threw pepper in my face. Two Greek officers were there and they just watched. After that, we decided to withdraw. Zaehner and I took the boys back to Athens.

Smiley was in Athens and he spent the next two months running here and there, trying to sort the problem out. In the end, it was worked out so that we had nothing whatever to do with either the border police or the aliens' office, only with the Greek army. So up we went to Janina again in Greek army trucks (escorted by Reg Voyce). This was after two months in Athens with Grant and Zaehner. We weren't allowed out of the British house in Kifissia. At last Zaehner came to see us, gave us a party and told us that we were going up to the border again. It was very good news.

We waited with our trucks outside Athens until it was dark. Some Greek officers and I checked the border during the day, then that night we pushed the boys across, with the help of the Greek army. I crossed the border myself from time to time, always in British uniform. The next day we drove back to Athens and flew to Malta. As soon as we reached Malta, we got the news that the group had run into trouble and been attacked. This was Sami Bardha, Butka and Doko. Sami Bardha was also captured, but he managed to escape and get back across the border. He went to live in America.

I was in England when the Kokla group went into Albania in the summer of 1951. I was the interpreter on a parachute course at Abingdon, lasting 18 days. We lived in barracks and the boys were dropped from balloons or planes. My job was to wait for them on the ground and shout instructions to them as they fell, through a loud-hailer, which was a metal funnel.

After that we went back to Malta and at the end of 1951 we all came back to England. The Malta station was closed down. I visited the boys in their barracks in England and then I was sent to Munich to Company 4000 for six months. On August 2, 1952, I was posted to an ordinary monitoring station in Cyprus.

Interview conducted September 10, 1983

COLONEL DAVID SMILEY

Colonel David de Crespigny Smiley (1916–2009) was a British military officer and writer. He was an army officer of the Royal Horse Guards in World War II, who was recruited by the Special Operations Executive (SOE) in 1943. He was sent into Albania from Greece in April 1943 together with Billy McLean, as one of the first British officers to organize anti–Axis resistance. There he developed close contacts both with Abas Kupi and the Legality movement, and with Enver Hoxha, Mehmet Shehu and the communist partisan movement. After a period back in Italy, Smiley returned to Albania on April 20, 1944, with McLean and Julian Amery to the Biza plateau, east of Tirana. He withdrew from Albania in September 1944 and returned to England the following year. From 1949 to 1953, David Smiley, now deputy commander of the Royal Horse Guards, worked for MI6 and was involved in setting up the training camp in Malta for the Albanian operation. There he taught the recruits guerrilla warfare tactics and wireless communications. Smiley was later active in Germany in 1952–1955, Sweden in 1955–1958, Oman in 1958–1962, and Yemen in 1962–1966. He published his war memoirs in the volumes: Albanian Assignment, *London 1984, and* Irregular Regular, *Norwich 1994. Smiley returned to Albania in November 1994 to inaugurate the British military cemetery in Tirana.*

Harold Perkins, my contact in the "firm," asked if I would go down to Malta and set up a training center for Albanians and organize their infiltration into Albania. I rather jumped at it. I was second in command of my regiment at the time, the Royal Horse Guards. My colonel retired, but I was only 32, so they said that I was too young to take over. I would have to wait as second in command for another three years.

These little men—Albanians are usually rather small—were recruited mainly through Abas Kupi, who was head of the Legality movement, and Abas Ermenji who was head of the Balli Kombëtar. They produced the men to be trained. Back in Spain I've got photographs of every man and every team. There were about 36 or 48 of them.

There were very few people on Malta allowed to know what was going on. Being a soldier, I was given a cover as deputy chief of staff and I was given an office in garrison headquarters. I used to go there every morning, pretending that I was a soldier, and then I would go up to Fort Bin Jema, which was where we kept these fellows. It was an ideal place, tucked away down a rough track miles from anywhere. I had five British officers.

I started in the Xara Palace Hotel. Then when my wife came out I moved to St. Andrew's House, the local brigadier's residence. I was only in the hotel for two or three weeks, then in the house with my wife and two children.

Bill Collins was a very good friend of mine. He only retired this year. He was my wireless operator in Albania, then in Siam. He literally saved my life when I got rather badly blown up. He came as wireless operator and instructor out in Malta. Then he

Billy McLean (1918–1986), British officer and member of the Special Operations Executive in Albania, here on the left and Abaz Kupi (1892–1976) on the right, in Albania during the Second World War.

went back to Government Communications in Bletchley. He was a gunner sergeant and his code name was always "Gunner."

Alfred Howard was a quartermaster from a guards' regiment, a typical sergeant-major type. Alistair Grant was quite a good weapons-training officer, but he was having a terrible love affair at the time and a bit off balance. He didn't stay on in the firm. They got rid of him quite quickly. We introduced him to a very pretty nurse, whom he eventually married.

I kept in touch with "Doc" Zaehner, a don at Oxford in classical Persian. He was sent to us as an interpreter, but I have no idea where Persian came into the affair. He was a very charming and amusing man. We had interpreters, one of whom has just settled in England. He was with the Voice of America and in Vienna for years. His name is Abdyl Sino, 14 Fortescue Drive, Chesterton, Bicester, Oxon 0X6 8UT. He has a wife called Margaret and a son called David. Another interpreter, who is now in Italy, was Ihsan Toptani, who came out of Albania with Abas Kupi at the end of the war and got a job with the Caversham monitoring service. Then he became a professional photographer and the last I heard was that he was living in a caravan outside Rome. He is a very good linguist, speaks German, French and Italian as well as English.

Another interpreter was Jani Dilo, Woodward Hotel, Broadway and 55th Street, New York, N.Y. 10019. Corporal John Topliss was a senior clerk. Captain "Rollo" Young was also in Albania and quite knowledgeable about it. He too was recruited by Harold

Perkins, who ran the Polish section of SCE. I won't mention my previous assignment with MI6. It's still far too hot. And there was a cook called "Blondie" Stover.

The course was in guerrilla warfare and wireless, how to handle "Tommy" guns and grenades. All the cipher traffic with London was done by my wife, who had been a FANY during the war. She was officially on the strength as my cipher clerk. They used the same wirelesses as we had had in SOE. It was kept in a suitcase and called a B2, but instead of having very heavy six-volt batteries that would have to be lugged around on mules, we used a bicycle-frame generator.

The GOC in Malta knew that I was doing something funny, so did the senior admiral called Sir John Power. Mountbatten may have known, too, although he was only the third senior admiral. There was a MI5 man called Bill Major. He arranged for them to get through immigration. They all wore battledress and had the "cover" of belonging to a pioneer unit, because after the war there were a lot of non–British men in pioneer units doing various things. We were worried that they might get picked up by the military police in Valetta or somewhere and ruin their "cover" but they behaved very well. The only problem was when some were picked up for wearing gym shoes with their battle dress. Bill Major had to sort that one out.

We trained them pretty thoroughly. I wouldn't have let them go inadequately trained. Then they were infiltrated by boat on to exactly the same spot just south of Vlora where I'd been evacuated from with Billy McLean in 1943. It was a very good place because there were cliffs all around and a goat track up and over the mountains. It was miles from a main road and not on the way to anywhere. We imagined that they'd be able to land there completely undetected.

After we'd finished the training and sent the men off, I moved to Greece to a "safe house" near Athens, and another one in Corfu. We had places like this all over Greece. We had a wireless station that was supposed to be in touch with the men in Albania. But very few came up on the air and those who did gave us to understand that there were people waiting for them. We couldn't think what had gone wrong. I was quite convinced there was no security leak either among the British up at the fort or among the Albanians themselves. With hindsight I thought that there was one Albanian who might have been suspicious. He was an American Albanian, a big fat man dressed as an officer. I didn't quite trust him, because I thought he had been fiddling the funds, the gold and other valuables that were part of our operational money.

A few of our men managed to get back into Greece, where they were promptly arrested by the Greeks who tend to hate the Albanians, and we had a hell of a job getting them out of Greek jails. The ones who came back all said that the Albanian authorities must have known they were coming, because there were troops and police in the most unlikely places.

We had organized them into groups according to their tribes and the areas they came from. Although they were all landed in the same place, they had to make for different areas of the country. But none of them got there. The few that escaped doubled back towards the Greek border, which was what they were ordered to do.

So that was the end of the story as far as I was concerned. I went back to my regiment. And it was only a few years later when Philby surfaced that I realized what must have gone wrong. All along he had been the man in Washington responsible for coordinating the British and American sides of the operation. There had been no contact between me and the American training program. That was done at a higher level. And Philby was the man responsible for it on the British side. He was quite correctly telling the Americans everything that we were doing. But he was tipping off the Russians as well.

I got to know them so well. They were such a good little lot. They bloody well knew they were sticking their necks out, but they were brave enough to go in and try this operation. We had information that there was fighting in bits of Albania where the communists hadn't fully taken over. If our men had made it to their own areas and established contact with us in Greece, we might have been able to reinforce them with arms and push Enver Hoxha and the rest of them out. It was worth trying.

Even with hindsight I still think that it could have worked, if it hadn't been for Philby. I don't say that it would have worked, but it had more than a sporting chance. I would guess that of the 36-odd who were sent in, 25 were never heard of again. Some were shot on the spot. One or two were tortured, tried and executed. None of them stayed on in Albania. About ten men made it back to Greece.

Leka was two or three days old when King Zog and Queen Geraldine fled from Albania, when the Italians attacked on Easter Day 1939.

The fort had a very good moat that we used as a pistol range and rooms off it that were good for storage. The Albanians were always referred to in telegrams as "pixies." I handled the boat business in conjunction with the Royal Navy. It was a MFV (motor fishing vessel) painted gray and belonging to the Navy, manned by Royal Navy personnel. We embarked them from a lonely beach and they were taken to a rendezvous on the high seas with a Greek caique manned by two British sailors. This was in the middle of the Adriatic, at night, halfway between Italy and Albania.

I never saw the author of the *Sunday Times* article in my life. He must have been one of those people who came out for a couple of days from London with wireless sets and bombs. I showed the article to Eddie Boxhall and he said, "We would have prosecuted him but he died." He certainly wasn't one of the two men who took the Albanians ashore. Some things in the article are true, but there's a fair amount of rubbish there, too. He wasn't an officer. Julian Amery told me that he certainly wants the story told. He said that this would be in everyone's interest.

All the experts were dressed up as officers, partly from the "cover" point of view, partly so as to impress the Albanians. In fact, I was the only regular officer among them. "Doc" Zaehner was the only one who never put on uniform. He would have looked too out of place. He had enormous horn-rimmed glasses. He could never have been passed off as a soldier, let alone an officer.

Billy McLean and I went into Albania originally from Greece and there was a lot of intermingling between the two countries. I had no dealings with the Italians at all, only with Greece and Malta. But I think that some of the Albanians were recruited from DP camps in Italy by Abas Kupi and Abas Ermenji. The latter is still head of the Balli Kombëtar. Auberon Herbert wasn't involved at all. He just used to turn up at Albanian gatherings for many years. He could have been involved in the English end of the operation in Broadway Buildings, but not as far as I know. I knew nothing about the English end. The less I knew, the better.

Perkins was always known as "Perks." He was a very nice man, a specialist in Poland. He's been dead for some years. I was in Poland after the war, but that's another story. His picture is hanging on the stairs of the Special Force Club in a sort of "rogues' gallery." Oakley-Hill used to work with General Percy, who ran the gendarmerie under King Zog.

This was my third assignment for MI6. The first two had nothing to do with Albania at all. One was an office job, the other was an operational one, something I won't talk about at all. So when I had got recruited by Perks for this job and I went more or less straight from Germany to Malta, with not more than a day or two in London to see Perks. And as far as I remember, he was the only one who came out regularly to see what was going on.

The first time was when I was with my regiment in Germany. Perks and another ex–SOE type came to stay with me and chat me up. Then I worked in London for a bit and, a year later, when I was back in Germany, Perks came and asked me if I'd do the Albanian job. My first job in MI6 was as a seconded officer. They always had a soldier, a sailor and an airman of colonel rank working in the London office. Why they chose me I do not know, though I suppose that my SOE background had something to do with it and of course I knew a number of people in the "firm" personally. I must have been vetted behind my back.

While I was with MI6, I was paid rather more than my army pay and I lived in a very nice house with my own soldier-servant and a Maltese cook. My pay went straight into my account at Cox's and King's Branch. I remember talking to the general commanding troops in Malta and he said that I was getting nearly as much as he was. I think it's fair for MI6 people to be paid over the odds because, apart from the physical risks that they run, they have no future. No MI6 person in an embassy rises above the rank of First Secretary. Their friends and family wonder why they aren't becoming ambassadors. They may end up with a CBE or something, but not much else, not much kudos. Nor can they dine out on what they do. When they're asked what they do, they have to say, "I'm a passport control officer." It's not very glamorous.

When Julian Amery and I left Albania in 1944, we weren't allowed to bring any Albanians with us, but we were allowed to bring three Soviet citizens. They were from Turkistan. I think that Julian managed to turn them loose, so that they weren't forcibly repatriated. We were viewed with deep suspicion by many intelligence officers in those days of left-wing views, such as Basil Davidson and James Klugman.

Interview conducted February 12, 1981

* * *

When the last of the groups had left Malta and been put ashore in Albania, I moved to Greece, with a wireless operator and a couple of chaps. The listening post in Corfu was run by Alan Hare. The men there were still in uniform. It is now a hotel. It was very well situated on high ground looking over the Straits of Corfu. The messages that we got were mighty few and they all indicated that they had run into trouble, some that their arrival was expected. Later several of them got back over the border into Greece, where they were promptly put in jail. One of my jobs in Athens was to liaise with the

Greeks and get these people out of jail. My family and I had a "safe house" in Pacifico, a northern suburb of Athens. The people in Corfu were a mixture of British and Albanians, some working the radios, some collecting the messages and transcribing them.

I've had pressure applied to me not to talk to you, but I'm not only talking to you, I'm also including a chapter in my own book on this subject. I've taken advice from many people that I trust and they all say, "Publish and be damned." I can see no adequate reason on the grounds either of security or British interest for putting a stop on this one. The MI6 censor told me that the writer of the *Sunday Times Magazine* article would have been prosecuted if he hadn't died. He certainly was never on my staff. I knew all my men; there were only six or seven of them and he wasn't one of them, but what he wrote is basically true.

The Albanians were put on board a motor torpedo boat manned by the Royal Navy in Malta. They were then taken to a rendezvous point in the Adriatic with a Greek caique manned by two officers known as the "Bessie boys." We never knew their real names. They were former naval officers. I don't know whether they belonged to the "firm" or whether they were just doing it as private enterprise. They put the Albanians ashore at the same spot from which Billy McLean and I were evacuated in 1943. It was an excellent spot, very secluded, south of Vlora. We codenamed it "Seaview." A lot of people came out from there towards the end of the war. From the cliffs there one could see Sazan Island, where it was rumored that the Russians had a naval base.

No one from my staff went onto the caique, but several went onto the MTB to see them off and keep them happy. They were transferred on the high seas at night, in groups varying between four and six, and they got ashore from the caique in rubber dinghies.

When we were evacuated from this bay in 1943, our rubber dinghy leaked, so I rowed and Billy bailed. It sank about ten yards from the boat and we had to swim for it. We each had a briefcase full of secret papers, which we had to hold up with one hand out of the water, while the sailors yanked us on board. The local people were literally starving. We had lived for ten days on one dead mule and water sucked up out of the rocks with a sponge. The MTB captain was able to get right up close to the rocks and the sailors heaved some crates of bully beef and other types of food onto the rocks for the Albanians and Italians left behind. This was October 1943.

The second time was in October 1944. I was taken off a sandy beach in the north of Albania with a number of British NCOs. I went out the first night. Billy and Julian Amery went out the next night. That was when they sent this chap on the boat to make sure that we did not bring Abas Kupi with us. The people in SOE headquarters in Bari at that time were very biased towards the communists—James Klugman, Basil Davidson and a chap called Eyre. There was a very strong communist lobby in SOE headquarters. James Klugman, to give him his due, never claimed to be anything else. As for Reg Hibbert, I have my views, but I don't really want to talk about him for the moment. The trouble was that in the Balkans, as elsewhere, the feeling of the time was that anyone who had fought the Germans was our friend and that anyone who had not fought the Germans was more or less the opposite.

The Albanians did fight the Germans, but not as much as they claimed to have done. I went on a couple of operations with them myself and saw how a small engagement, with two or three killed on each side, was turned into a big battle, with hundreds of casualties by the time reports reached our headquarters. They would ambush a truck on the road, kill half a dozen and claim to have killed 40 or 50. Then signals went flying back from the British officers attached to them saying that they were doing a wonderful job and killing hundreds of Germans. The non-communists, unfortunately, did not have anyone with them to report how many Germans they were killing. There was only ourselves with the Abas Kupi team. I agree that Abas Kupi started too late, but he was holding out for orders from King Zog, while the Foreign Office was preventing Zog from giving the orders, so as not to annoy Tito by recognizing Zog.

We had asked permission to bring off Abas Kupi, Said Kryeziu, Ihsan Toptani and others—people who had helped us a lot. They looked after shot-down Allied airmen and lent us money when we ran out. The man on the boat was either from SOE or from the military police. I went at once to Lord Harcourt, head of SOE in Bari, to protest about it. So did Amery and McLean, when they arrived the next day. They flew up to Caserta to see "Jumbo" Wilson. Macmillan was there, too, and they both said that Kupi must be rescued at once. They were ready to send a destroyer. But by the time they got back to Bari with this good news, the Albanians were already there. Ihsan Toptani had gone into Montenegro, where there are good sailors, and bribed some men to take them across and they had been picked up by a British minesweeper in the Adriatic. The engine stopped halfway across and they drifted for a couple of days. We took a very dim view of the abandonment of Kupi and the others.

Zaehner was a wonderful man. He got on with everybody. But he was not much good as an interpreter. I asked him whether he spoke Albanian and he said, "No, not a word, but I do speak classical Persian." He was a great help around the place and excellent company. He had a reputation as a heavy drinker, but he did not overindulge while he was with me. He was a devout Catholic, a lively wit, a raconteur.

Several of the staff from Malta came with me to the house in Athens. In Malta my cover was a deputy chief of staff on the garrison headquarters. When I went to Greece, I was given the cover of G1 (Ops and I). It was not very popular with the regular MI6 chap there, who worked in the embassy. He thought I was treading on his toes. He thought that our blundering around was bad for security. And the regular British soldiers asked themselves, "Who's this bloody chap from the Blues who doesn't seem to do much work?" But I had to have a cover with the Greeks. I had a nice house down by the coast and we took part in Athens social life, went to embassy parties. No one knew what I was doing.

The Governor of Malta at this time was an unfortunate choice, a former railway porter and a trade unionist. When he arrived at the airport, he didn't take his hat off to the guard of honor. The Maltese did not like someone like that being sent out to govern them. Someone ought to have told him about the hat. The general commanding the troops knew about me. There were two generals: William Reville-Smith and William Heath. They overlapped while I was there. I played polo with them both in the afternoons as part of my cover. Admiral Sir John Power knew, too, and the Director of Naval Intelligence and Admiral Mountbatten, who was commanding cruisers, and the local MI5 chap Bill Major, who was a major by rank, too. He was the man who dealt with any of the Albanians' misdemeanors, though they all behaved extremely well. I only remember one being picked up for wearing gym shoes with his uniform instead of boots. There was no drunkenness. They were very patriotic and brave little men.

Julian Amery thinks that the main purpose of the operation was to take the pressure off Greece. I don't agree. I think that the idea was to topple Hoxha and to get a friendly government in his place. Greece was incidental. I would hate my Albanian friends to think that I did what I did merely to help the Greeks. They would have objected strongly to being used as cat's paws or pawns in some great Balkan game. If it had been put to me in that way, I don't think I would have taken the job on. I was a soldier. It was not up to me to ask political questions. On the other hand, I could have turned the job down. The question put to me was, "Would you like to help your Albanian friends to kick out Enver Hoxha?"

I was only in Greece for two or three months and it was very low key. Really, once we'd finished the training, my job was done. I can't honestly think why they kept us on. Once I left Greece, that was the end of the operation as far as I was concerned. I just drove my car up to Germany and rejoined my regiment as second-in-command.

Interview conducted March 16, 1982

* * *

The training was basically in use of radio, small arms and demolition. Rollo Young came out about halfway through and was there when one of the batches went in. He was on one of the boats, known as "conducting officer." He was a career MI6 officer. John Hibberdine was originally taken on for this operation, having been in Albania in SOE, and he stayed on after it ended. He served in MI6 all over the world.

Eddie Boxhall went through the roof when the *Sunday Times* color supplement article appeared. It was just about the time when I was looking for clearance over my own book. He told me that nothing could be written about the Albanian episode, because it would confirm what Philby had written in his book. I think that he was out to make himself indispensable as the MI6 "censor" and that is why he took such a tough line. He stayed in the job until he was over eighty, until last year. I saw him in his office in Century House. He spent his entire time reading books by former SOE and 1,116 officers. He told me that my case had been considered by the highest authority. He gave me the impression that he was trying to help me, although I don't think he really was.

He warned me against you very much. "Don't tell anything to that chap Bethell," he said. The Foreign Office obviously hate your guts because of your Russian book. I gave the chapter to Air Chief Marshal John Barraclough, a friend of mine, and he showed it to Maurice Oldfield, who said that he saw no reason at all why it should not be published. I take more notice of people like Oldfield and Julian Amery than I do of Eddie Boxhall.

They don't like anyone to confirm anything that Philby said. In fact, Philby is wrong to say that the Albanians involved were mainly royalists. Abas Ermenji was the main recruiter, not Abas Kupi. I thought that it was revolting of Reg Hibbert to say that we were wrong to try and help Abas Kupi. Kupi did a great deal to help us during the war. He lent us money when we were broke, money that was only grudgingly returned to him and very late. He was promised air drops if he fought the Germans. He started to fight, but there were no air drops. And SOE sent a man on the boat that took us off to make sure that we did not bring Kupi with us.

I spent a year with the partisans. There is no doubt that they exaggerated their military exploits. They would fire a few shots at a German convoy, run away and then claim that they had "ambushed" it, killing goodness knows how many. Billy and I trained and more or less raised the First Partisan Brigade. And they had very few weapons until we started dropping them to them. We supplied them with mortars and anti-tank rifles, then trained them how to use them. Each *cheta* had about 30 men and they were eventually all collated into the First Partisan Brigade by Mehmet Shehu, about 500 men.

Then the Italians came and chased us. Shehu's men just ran away. I thought at the time that I had never seen so much cowardice displayed in my life, but then I realized that those were their orders. They were ordered not to engage the enemy, to accept all the arms that the stupid British gave them and keep them for the civil war. In this first period, 1943–44, they only fired enough shots to convince the British officers with them that they were on our side, to make sure that the drops kept coming. Meanwhile, they were eliminating groups of Balli and royalists wherever they could.

Billy and I went into Albania originally with no contacts at all. We dropped into Greece and walked into Albania with a left-wing ELAS group, who handed us over to the partisans. They made damn sure that we never met any Ballists or royalists. They referred to both groups as "fascists." Only several months later did we manage to find the Balli and then we carried out a successful ambush of a German convoy. I commanded the Ballist group myself. The partisans never took my advice, they always knew best. They were keen to find out how to fire a gun, but not to learn about tactics or strategy.

Brigadier "Trotsky" Davies came in in 1944 and took over our mission. He told us that, since we had been the first in, we ought to be the ones to go and report. When we departed, we took with us a document which was a blueprint of the communist tactics of waiting for the civil war. We explained all this to Anthony Eden and he told us to go back in and raise the non-communists in the north, men who until then had not done much fighting.

Abas Kupi at first said that he would not fight until he had a written order from King Zog telling him to. It would have been easy to get such a letter, since Zog was in England, but SOE did not want to do this, for fear of antagonizing the partisans. You see, the SOE office in Bari was so penetrated with communists.

Kupi said that he would not fight until he got weapons. We said that he could not have weapons until he started to fight. That was the kind of thing that went on. Julian Amery sent a letter to Anthony Eden about it from Albania, but it went straight into the wastepaper basket. A secretary in Bari told me who had done it. It was Jim Eyre who was an RA major and a communist. He stood as a communist in the 1945 election. James Klugman was quite open about being a communist. I liked him. Basil Davidson never admitted it, but I think he was. And Reg Hibbert, too, I think. I'm not saying he held a card, but his sympathies were with the communists. They always referred to the three of us in conversation as "the fascist spies." Hibbert's memo is thoroughly biased.

Eventually, Kupi did start to fight, without waiting for any drops, and then the drops never came. This was the double cross. The Bari people decided that the partisans were the only people worth helping. Earlier on, the whole of the North was with Kupi and the Ballists. We should have helped them earlier on. And I'm not at all sure that Tito would have stopped them winning.

I'm not sure that the Albanians had any anti-aircraft potential. They only had the arms that we dropped them and what they captured from the Germans. The use of Polish pilots was a safety measure, but maybe an unnecessary one. The Germans in fact walked out of Albania more or less unscathed, because by then, the civil war was in full cry. Otherwise, they would have been massacred. Rollo Young told me that the "Bessie boys" had originally been professional smugglers.

In the end, the partisans probably did do more, because they got all the weapons and supplies to do it with. Kupi got very little and I don't think that the Balli got a supply drop ever. They basically all went to the partisans. We went into the country in April. The first drop was in May and they continued from then on, from May 1943.

There were five of us, Billy and I, Williamson the wireless operator, a corporal in the Black Watch, and Duffy, a sapper. We were the first team in. By the time we left and handed over to "Trotsky" Davies, there were five or six missions established all over the countryside. SOE headquarters switched from Cairo to Bari as soon as we captured the south of Italy.

The Americans were always overflying Albania on their way to bomb Ploesti. Some of them had to bail out over Albania. Kupi collected them all up and we got them back by submarine or motor torpedo boat.

The only money we had at the mission was gold sovereigns. We were broke at the end and they wouldn't send us any more from Bari, so Kupi lent us some to keep us going, to buy food and mules, to pay mulemen. I think he got it back in the end, but Billy and Julian had to put up a fight.

The fort was in many ways ideal. It had a deep dry moat that we used for small arms training and plenty of accommodation. Moira worked in the fort, enciphering and deciphering the signals being sent by John Kelly and Collins. Meanwhile, I was being a bit of a playboy, spending every afternoon playing polo, giving the impression that I was just a useless cavalry officer doing a not-very-arduous job as deputy chief of staff. We used to finish work at 1 o'clock and have the whole afternoon and evening free.

There were only three people in Malta who knew what was going on. One was the commander-in-chief, Admiral Sir John Power. Another was Major Bill Major. He was very helpful getting equipment through customs. The third was Vice-Admiral Sir John Inglis. He later became director of naval intelligence, but he was then only a captain. He helped with the naval side of things.

The Albanians behaved extremely well. There were no drunken brawls or fights. The only problem was when some were arrested for wearing gym shoes with their uniforms instead of army boots. We explained that they were poor refugees who didn't speak any English and didn't know any better. Bill Major helped sort things like that out. They were not thugs or mercenaries, they were serious young men, patriotic, who wanted to kick the bloody communists out of their country.

At that time, an idea was still on the cards. Halit Kola and Bilal Kola were still fighting in the north of Albania in 1949. The communists had still not got complete control.

We discussed whether the Albanians ought to be allowed out of the camp. Eventually, we decided that we couldn't lock them up in a prison and forbid them to go anywhere. I don't think they would have accepted it. They weren't prisoners. They were being trained for a difficult and dangerous job. We reckoned that they would not be conspicuous, because at that time Europe was full of thousands of displaced persons of every nationality, a lot of them wearing British or American uniform.

At 1 o'clock we used to drive for lunch to our house called St. Andrews' House in St. George's Bay on the other side of the island. In Athens I lived in a suburb called Pacifico and I was known as G1 (Ops and I), attached to the military mission. Ihsan Toptani had the only house in Albania, as far as I could see, with a basin, a plug and a loo that flushed.

As deputy chief of staff I arrived at the Castille every morning sharp at 9. This was the army headquarters in Valetta. I collected any letters, popped into a couple of offices to say hello, and drove to the fort in my staff car in lieutenant-colonel's uniform.

Papajani was not very popular. I don't know who his friends were. I was just told that we had to have an American there. I wasn't very pleased about it, but I did what I was told. I had to accept it. He was rather an awful fellow.

Interview conducted March 13, 1983

MOY SMILEY

Moyra or Moy Smiley (d. ca. 2012) was the wife of David Smiley. She was trained in enciphering and supported the Albanian operation in Malta while her husband was training the fighters.

Our son Xan was born on May 1 in Germany. We came from Germany to England towards the end of May. David was briefed and he flew to Malta during June. Meanwhile, I did a refresher course with the firm's enciphering department for a month and flew out to join him with Xan in July. My cover was that I was interpreter for the "little men." I used to drive up to the fort before dawn every day, do what I had to do and get back to the Xara Palace Hotel, or later to St. Andrew's House, by about nine o'clock. So, as far as most people were concerned, I was no more than an ordinary soldier's wife.

I was a corporal in the East Africa Command in Nairobi during the war, in charge of the enciphering office. I was trained there by Stanley Mullin, a schoolmaster who later became editor of *Soldier* magazine. I was a member of First Aid Nursing Yeomanry (FANY). All this ended four years before Malta.

I was asked to do the job in Malta because I was trained and had the necessary security clearance. It made sense, since I was married to the commanding officer, for the firm to give me this job on a part-time basis and pay me by the hour. Later on, when the traffic in coded messages increased suddenly, they sent out a full-time firm employee and we worked together for a month or so. I don't think she really approved of me. She went back to England after a month or so.

Xan was my third child. I had two children by my first husband. We had a girl to help with the children, so there was no problem over that. And most mornings I only did two or three hours work. Just occasionally, I came back in the evenings. Most of the officers in Malta stopped work for the day before lunch. I stopped before breakfast. There was something to do every day, but the work was far from arduous. I was reachable by telephone if there was anything urgent.

The messages were received by Bill Collins and given to me to decipher. Collins would only have known about field coding, the use of one-time pads. Our system was more complicated. We had no machines, we used groupings of numbers, with the first line giving the key to the relevant page in the cipher book. These books were very secret and had to be burnt in an emergency. Machines existed then, but we were too small an operation to need one.

Mainly, it was family life and social life. The only problem was that David seemed to be doing very little work. He was hardly ever in the office. I worked alone in a room inside the fort and one of the officers would come and collect it. Usually it was "Doc" Zaehner. The radio room was in the keep.

We led a rather ordinary colonial life with our house; our baby son; my two children, Anna and Gavin; David's batman, Ron Little; and the Maltese cook. We had excellent bathing and riding. Princess Elizabeth was there, expecting Prince Charles, and Prince Philip was a serving lieutenant. His uncle Lord Mountbatten was the "number three" naval officer in Malta. They all played a lot of polo. The Mountbattens had a big house in Valletta.

Some of the visiting Albanians came to St. Andrew's House for meals. And there was a very unpopular American, John Papajani, always trying to change money or sell something. He was big and fat. Ihsan Toptani and "Doc" Zaehner visited us, too.

Interview conducted February 20, 1984

CYRUS SULZBERGER

Cyrus Sulzberger (1912–1993) was an American journalist and writer. He was a member of the family that owned the New York Times. *During the 1940s and 1950s, he was that newspaper's leading foreign correspondent. He visited Albania as a young man. The report of his visit to the court of King Zog was subsequently published in his book,* A Long Row of Candles, *London 1969.*

I was working for the *New York Times*, wandering round the world as a troubleshooter, based in Paris. There was no other American journalist of this type. I was just about the only Balkan specialist in U.S. journalism. I used to have leaflets in Albanian that our people dropped over the country.

I got into a bit of trouble with those articles on the "invasion" of Albania. They got angry and asked me what my source was. Telegrams were flying all over the place, especially to Belgrade, Rome and Athens. I told them it was none of their business. Quite a few government officials mentioned it to me and I gave them all the same answer. I can't think why they were so upset. There were plenty of people around the Balkans who were well informed on the matter and obviously the Russians knew about it down to the last semi-colon. I just wish I'd had the source that they did.

I met the man Philby in 1938 in Spain, where we were both war correspondents. And I saw him once in Washington with a group of other British officials at Frank Wisner's house, 3327 P Street. It's his wife's home now. She is married to a newspaper columnist called Clayton Fritchey.

Interview conducted in Paris February 29, 1984

Ihsan Toptani

Ihsan bey Toptani (1908–2001) was an Albanian historical and public figure born in Tirana. He was the son of Abdi bey Toptani, a signatory of the Albanian proclamation of independence. He was educated in Graz in Austria, where he attended secondary school from 1920 to 1928 and finished a doctorate in political science in 1940. As the scion of a leading landowning family, he led a comfortable existence on his return to Albania in 1942. He played an important role in efforts to unite the various resistance movements during the Italian and German occupation, but to no avail. He was also in close contact with the British officers on mission for the Special Operations Executive (SOE) in Albania. In October 1944, he fled to Brindisi in southern Italy with Abas Kupi and worked for Newsweek *in Rome. In 1949, he joined David Smiley in Malta and helped recruit anticommunist fighters to infiltrate Albania. In September 1949, he also joined the National Committee for a Free Albania, chaired by Midhat bey Frashëri. Toptani worked in Paris for some time before moving to England. In London, he worked for the BBC monitoring service and obtained British nationality in 1958, before retiring in 1967 to a country home in Surrey. For years, he was respected as the doyen of the Albanian community in Britain and is said to have been the last Ottoman bey living in Britain.*

The young men who went into Albania after 1949 were heroes and martyrs. They are the forgotten people. Their story should be told, but I do not want to compromise my signature of the Official Secrets Act with revelations that were based on little more than guesswork.

I was brought up in central Albania around Tirana and Kruja. My father died in 1942, but I inherited from him a political tradition and a wealth of personal contacts. There were no proper schools in Albania before the war, so he sent me to Austria, where I learned English and studied political science, including Marxism.

During the war, I used my contacts to try to convince non-communist groups to work together. Through my brother-in-law, Ferid Dervishi, a follower of King Zog, I met Abas Kupi and developed a natural cooperation with him. I was also a good friend of Midhat Frashëri. The two men distrusted one another and did not want to meet. In 1942, I was able to bring them together. I enabled them to meet, if not to cooperate.

When the British came to central Albania, I was an unofficial liaison man moving between the British, the royalists and the nationalists, trying to strengthen the alliance against both the Germans and the communists. I used my knowledge of English, which was rare in Albania, and my friendship with Colonel Oakley-Hill and other British who had trained the king's gendarmerie.

The British officers who were with the partisans were not allowed to cross nationalist territory. For instance, an officer called Colonel G. C. Nicholls was wounded in an ambush and kept by the partisans in a hideout. They would not take him down from the hills so that he could see a doctor. This meant that he got frostbite, which turned to gangrene. Eventually, he was brought across the lines, partly through me, and he was operated on. But it was too late. He died.

The British were not really interested in the future of Albania at any time. There were just interested in Churchill's order to kill as many Germans as possible. The Albanian nationalists said, "We have nothing against that, but at the same time we don't want to cause too much damage to the country just for the sake of a slogan. We don't want to kill two Germans and have three Albanian villages razed to the ground." This was why they were passive for some of the time, but it did not mean that they were pro–German.

The communists were not inhibited in this way. They were ready to see destruction. Indeed, destruction of Albanian property and lives helped them. It discredited the Germans and, by depriving Albanians of their homes and property, it brought them recruits for their bands in the hills. It was also more in line with British policy, which was to mobilize the Albanians against the Germans.

There were cases of nationalists and communists fighting jointly against the Germans. Then the communists would open fire on the nationalists to give the British officers there the impression that the nationalists were fighting on the German side. Generally though, the British were not interested in the civil war, only in the war against Germany. The nationalists, on the other hand, thought that any damage done to the Germans by them would be insignificant in the context of the war effort as a whole.

Albanian landowner Ihsan Toptani (1908–2001) who was in close contact with British officers on mission for the Special Operations Executive in Albania during the Second World War.

It was in the communists' interest to make people homeless, so that there was nothing for them to do except join their ranks. However, even though their actions were not as spectacular as they claim, I agree that they probably did most of the fighting.

Some Balli Kombëtar men worked in the occupation authorities, but this was simply to keep the communists out of power, not to help the Germans. They wanted to be on the spot after the Germans left. They were the only organized party who could do this. The royalists were not a party and were far less organized.

I left Albania three days after McLean and Amery on a boat from the Mati river estuary. Originally, we were all supposed to cross over to Italy with Abas Kupi in the British boat that came for the British officers, but when we got there, there was an order than no Albanians were to be embarked at all, not even Abas Kupi. So we had to find a boat for ourselves.

On October 28, 1944, I left Albania with Abas Kupi, his two sons, his two bodyguards, his secretary and three crew. The motor broke down and we were adrift for six days before being picked up by a Canadian landing craft.

We got to Italy on November 6 and were sent to a refugee camp at Santa Fara, near Bari, with several hundred other Albanians. Then Abas Kupi went to Cairo and I went to Rome where I worked on a magazine until 1947. Generally, there was no work for refugees in Italy. They had to rely on UNRRA. So when I lost my job in 1947, I could not get another. I had to live on the money that I had brought with me from Albania, 300 gold coins. Eventually, in March 1949, I went to England and worked at Caversham as a radio monitor.

All this time I had been on good terms with Amery and McLean, so when the committee was formed, I was asked to join as a consultant. I was the one who announced its formation over BBC radio to the Albanian people on August 6, 1949.

Auberon Herbert went to Rome as a freelance supporter of the Albanian cause. Only he did me a bad turn. He told Balli Kombëtar people in Rome that I wanted the pro–Italians to join the committee, whereas my line had always been that they should not join until they expressed regret for having supported the Italian occupation. Most of the Independenza party were Catholics. Hasan Dosti was a Catholic, too, although he was Balli Kombëtar.

In 1949, the Albanian security services were not so well established. The population had more hopes. It was feasible to think of doing things inside the country. Now we know it's impossible. The communist system has everything wrapped up very tight, tighter than anyone in the West can possibly imagine.

If it was to work, it would have had to have been organized on a bigger scale and with the cooperation of both neighbors. Yugoslavia would have had to cooperate. And Greece would have had to cooperate wholeheartedly. But Greece was not keen on the idea of building a free and independent Albania. Greece considers herself still at war with Albania. And Yugoslavia has her problems with minorities. So it was all very difficult.

Ermenji was in favor of using non–Albanians. Of course, if Tito had cooperated, we could have had bases along the northern frontier of Albania and plenty of Albanians from Yugoslavia would have volunteered to overthrow Hoxha. Groups could have infiltrated and withdrawn on a large scale, collecting Albanians from inside the country and creating a snowball effect. It would have broken the Hoxha government's morale. The population would have been ready to fight against Hoxha if there had been somewhere to go to. The atmosphere would have been different.

The British-American decision to keep the operation secret worked against the operation's success. An open challenge to Hoxha would have given the people hope and encouraged them to rebel. But maybe Greece would not have been ready to help at all in those circumstances. The Greeks had their own fish to fry.

Interview conducted April 16, 1983

Sali Toptani

Sali Toptani (1926–2006) was an Albanian historical figure. He was a scion of the wealthy landowning Toptani family of central Albania. He served in the army in communist Albania in 1948–1950 and escaped to Italy in 1951. He later emigrated to the United States and died in East Horsely in Surrey, England.

I was born in 1926. As a member of the Toptani family I always had problems in Albania. I was considered a "reactionary" element. I served in the army from 1948 to 1950 and was dishonorably discharged, even though I broke no rule whatsoever.

I remember in 1950 hearing the trial of some of the infiltrators being broadcast from loudspeakers in Tirana's main square. It was one of the few entertainments we had in Albania in those days.

I remember being called to a public meeting at Ihsan Toptani's house near Tirana. The meeting turned out to be about a man who was accused of feeding anti-communist leader Musa Picari, who had operated in central Albania in early 1945. The man said that he had acted according to the Albanian rules of hospitality, that he had fed everyone who came to his house, including the communists. The officer told him to shut up and shot him. Then all the other soldiers leapt on top of him and pumped him full of bullets, just to show how enthusiastic they were.

In late 1945 there was a currency reform. I remember hearing one morning that a relative of mine, Veli Bey Juba, a big landowner and son-in-law of Esad Toptani, had been arrested for currency speculation. I went round to the house the same afternoon to see what I could do only to find that he had already been tried and executed.

All our family property was confiscated. We were allowed to hang on to our own home for a year after the war, but then it was taken away and made into a school.

My own impression about the operation that began in 1949 is that it depended to some extent on personal gain and prestige. The Albanian leaders in exile were pleased to have American and British sponsors. They half hoped they might achieve something, but they must have realized at an early stage that the idea of liberating their country by such means was hopeless.

As soon as I arrived in Rome in 1951, I heard about the operation and about men being parachuted into Albania. (Of course, I already knew about it through the trials.) It was common gossip in the Donay Cafe and many other places where Albanians met.

Interview conducted July 1, 1983

KEVIN WALTON

Kevin Walton (1918–2009) was a British military figure and Royal Navy officer who involved in the Albanian operation in Malta, where he arrived in February 1951. He accompanied several runs with Albanian fighters who were landed on the southern Albanian coast. One of his duties was as a rower for getting them ashore.

Everyone in Malta wondered why we were allowed to move about so freely in the Mediterranean, whereas other people weren't. They assumed we must be smuggling. It was a very good cover, but it made my life complicated sometimes. One evening in 1951, I was with Peter Wyatt, the fleet pilot in Valletta, and Bill O'Brien, the fleet intelligence officer. The subject of our alleged smuggling came up and Wyatt said that if that was the case, he didn't want to know me. O'Brien knew the truth, but he just sat there and said nothing. Some years later he met me and asked me if I'd been anything to do with the boys at the fort. When I said yes, he agreed that he owed me an apology. Both Wyatt and O'Brien were naval captains. O'Brien was the only naval man we had anything to do with.

I had been an instructor at the Outward Bound School at Eskdale in the Lake District. A friend sounded me out and brought me down to London, where I saw Frank Slocomb at Nell Gwynne House in Kensington. They gave me a contract up to September 1951, after which I was to join an Antarctic expedition.

By this time the *Henrietta* was in a lot of trouble. She had two 900-horsepower unsupercharged Mercedes engines, beautiful engines so long as you know how to run them. She was refitted at Teddington in 1950 to replace *Michelangelo* and brought down to the Med past Gibraltar that autumn. Jimmy Blackburn had an engineer with him, ex–merchant navy, who didn't know how to work the engines. He used the wrong oil. So the *Henrietta* arrived in Malta with useless engines. A new pair had to be flown out from Stuttgart at vast expense, all paid for by the Americans. First I went to Stuttgart to see the new engines. Then I flew down to Malta in February 1951 after the engines had been fitted.

Blackburn had "Darby" Allen on board and a chap called Ron whom he'd bailed out of a French prison on a smuggling charge. He and Ron had been up and down the Med in the *Valfrere*. MI6 were after Blackburn for carrying unauthorized passengers. Many people said he was smuggling, but in my view he was absolutely straight. He was at Wellington School. Then in the war he was a bomber pilot until he told the RAF he wouldn't do it anymore. Then they used him to drop agents into the Balkans. He was cultured, well-read, shy and very moody. He didn't have many friends. None of us could have friends. But I had great respect for him. He wasn't smuggling, although a lot of people thought he was, especially the real smugglers who were jealous of the way he moved about so freely. We did one "pixie run" in the summer of 1951. Then we didn't want to go back to Malta, so we cruised round the Greek islands, put into Pantelleria for a few days and did some practice landings on the Tunisian shore, near Sousse and Sfax.

In summer 1951, I flew back to England to find my replacement and I came up with Martin Whitworth. He was ex–Navy, a rowing blue working for Thornycrofts in the Isle of Wight. I invited him to join me. He was cleared by Slocomb's mob. And we spent a month working together in the Med, with me showing him the ropes, before I flew back to England in September, leaving Blackburn, Whitworth, Gordon Dyke, Ron and Jack the cook. He was the only one who couldn't cook. They spent the 1951–52 winter refitting in the South of France and I spent it in South Georgia.

In March 1952, I got a telegram in South Georgia inviting me to rejoin the team by first available boat. I hitched a ride on a whaler from Grytvyken to Montevideo and then on the *Montcalm* at about seven knots to Liverpool. And I flew back to Malta.

We did a "double pixie run," four men into Albania and four the next night, in July 1952. I rowed them ashore, since Whitworth was now the engineer. Perks had seen me in London and he gave one of his "toys" to help me get away in case there was an Albanian reception committee on the shore. I couldn't see why anyone would be expecting us, but now, after reading your book, I see that he must have known about Philby and that he had every reason to be worried. Of course, I knew there was a risk, but Perks knew it was quite a big risk. If I'd been captured by the other side, I could have spilled a lot of beans. I find it incredible that I was sent into the field after Philby had been recalled from Washington, when it was more or less known that he had blown the operation.

So he thought up this idea, a sort of baby trench mortar worked by compressed air. You had it in the boat between your legs and if there was any trouble on shore you pressed the button and it threw out an object about the size of a tennis ball that burst with a bank and a very bright flare. This was to scare them and give us time to row away without actually firing at them.

Perks and I tried it out in the "firm" garage in Queen Anne's Mansions, a huge 12-story brick building just round the corner from "Broadway," an office block with a garage at the back guarded by security men. We fired it, without the flare of course, up into the high roof of the garage. All this was in the summer of 1951, when I came back to recruit Martin Whitworth.

"Darby" Allen and I did the rowing and we carried them up the beach beyond the sand, to make sure they didn't get their feet wet or leave any footprints, and we smoothed the sand over as we walked back to the dory. Every time we went ashore, Blackburn gave us a money belt. The idea was that, if we were caught, we could buy our way out. He always examined the belt when we got back to make sure that the seal was intact. I've no idea how much money was there, but it was very heavy.

Blackburn was a brilliant skipper and navigator. He would take us up to the target area at 22 knots almost blind, with no radar. Two or three hours past Corfu he'd turn her towards the shore and say, "There's the beach in front of you." He was uncannily accurate. I'm not surprised he was such a good bomber pilot. Also, she was a very suitable boat for the job. And we were helped by having American money to get her into good order. She was 74 feet long, a German R-boat used to rescue airmen from the North Sea, steel framed and oak timbered, a very good sea boat. She could operate in heavy weather, too, at times when even destroyers were putting back into port.

Interview conducted November 29, 1984

PATRICK WHINNEY

Commander Patrick Fife Whinney (1912–2004) was a British intelligence officer. During World War II, he worked for the SOE when he landed and collected agents from the French and Italian coasts. After the war, he joined the diplomatic service and was the MI6 station chief in Athens from 1948 to 1953. With his experience in secret landings, he was recruited to be part of the Albanian operation.

Any help that I can give, you shall have, to the best of my ability. We are, however, talking about events of over 30 years ago and my memory is undoubtedly patchy. I think you should know that although I was at that time the head of the local office and therefore responsible in the ultimate for all operations of that sort, the bulk of the detail was carried out by Oakley-Hill who had been sent out from London for that purpose. He had been in the Albanian gendarmerie for some years. Unfortunately, for your book I am almost sure he has died.

To weaken past links still further, both my two I/Cs have since died; likewise one other officer, Alabaster, who was also directly concerned, and Jack (an ex–RSM of the Brigade) who helped on the administrative side. Depressing, isn't it?

All the people you mention were certainly known to me—bar one, James McCargar, who I cannot place.

There were, however, others involved—especially on what we used to call "the sharp end." Sam Barclay and John Leatham were engaged on sea ops. Both are still breathing. Voyce, my driver, who had some amusing frontier experiences is also among those now defunct. He drove the ambassador (after he left me) for some twenty years or more. A real Cockney and very funny with it.

Since you have had long discussions with Julian on the subject, I wonder if you have "tapped" Billy McLean. Both of them came out of Athens for a truly memorable meeting with the star resisters in May 1949. Scheduled to last four hours, it went on for something like 16 hours with no break at all. Accustomed as I was to lengthy conferences in that part of the world, I remember becoming a little anxious when the clock had made one complete round with no sign of conclusion. Darrell assured me that was normal.

My CIA opposite number was Tom Karamesinis. He went on to become quite important in CIA. His number two was Henry McLean, known as "Mac." He was very bright and effective, but he was sacked from the CIA for drunkenness.

Doc Zaehner was brilliant, eccentric, well off and quite irresponsible. Everyone liked him. Frank Salwood (?), my number two, and his wife Corah put him up for a time and she one day found a drawer in his bedroom completely full of money, hundreds of pounds. He told her that it was his pay. He never spent it, he said. He had no particular use for it. He and my secretary Iris Riddle were the two most short-sighted people I've ever met. Both wore pebble glasses an inch thick.

Interview conducted March 9, 1983

* * *

I arrived in Athens as MI6 station chief on June 13, 1948, and I left in September 1953. It was a fascinating period both because of the civil war and because of the importance of British influence in Greece at that time. Clifford Norton was ambassador when I arrived and he was in favor of playing second fiddle to the Americans. He was rich and his wife was a power in the London art world. He told me at our first interview that he wanted the Americans, not ourselves, to play the dominant role in Greek politics. And my heart sank. Still, this was what was done, until Charles Peake took over in 1951. He turned the embassy upside down and decided that Britain was going to play first fiddle from then on.

When the Americans moved in to take over the British intelligence role, in Greece as in many other parts of the world, they did something that we would never have dreamt of doing. They imported first-generation Americans of the nationality in question. It was not popular in Greece, but it paid off. An example was Tom Karamesinis, who was my CIA opposite number towards the end of my stay. He was completely bilingual. He had the money and people listened to him. He was anti–British, not because of his own personal views, but because Washington had told him to be careful of the British. And this was because of Kim Philby. At this time there was no cooperation at all between the British and Americans. The other CIA station chiefs were John Baker, Henry McLean and Alfred Ulmer. John Baker was the only one who talked to us at all. He was a nice chap, but rather heavy and dull. McLean was much brighter, very indiscreet and with a wealthy wife, but he drank too much. Al Ulmer was very bright, a typical CIA man in that he was prepared to shift his ground very quickly but once you knew that, everything was fine. After he left the CIA he was Niarchos's man in London for a period and he married a "Miss Miami." Another key person was Bronson Tweedie, who was London's station chief.

There was no liaison at all with the Americans. They were simply not allowed to talk to us. We were ready to talk to them, but not the other way round. This was because of Kim Philby, who was under a cloud as soon as Burgess and McLean defected in May 1951. Before that, I did have some liaison with John Baker over the desk of Fouli Kalinski, the head of the Greek commandos and brother-in-law of General Papagos. Papagos was trained in Brussels, a very austere man, and his sister married Fouli Kalinski, who was head of the "sacred battalion" in Egypt during the war. He had a white moustache, white hair, blue eyes and perfect manners. In fact, he looked like a Scottish landowner.

He was stone deaf. I think he had links with Hod Fuller and Mike Burke. Christopher Philpots was my successor in Athens.

We had already conducted a feasibility study of an operation in Albania and had concluded that it would be very difficult. According to local custom, travelers had to go in groups of four or five. Otherwise they were suspect and they were bumped off. Travelers in a small group could come to a village and would receive hospitality there, then proceed the next morning, but once they were five miles or so from the village they were fair game. The same system worked, though rather less brutally, in the Greek mountains around Janina, where I spent some time with Greek commandos. The mountain grapevine always knew where we were and this guaranteed us a warm welcome whenever we walked into a village. We always had a marvelous welcome, slept the night and went on the next day, walking considerable distances.

Sam is a modest chap, careful to get the truth right. John is more fluent and ebullient. We had quite a big station in Athens, seven or eight officers, ten or a dozen secretaries, with a sub-station in Salonika. Darrel Oakley-Hill was sent out to us as a supernumerary to deal with the operation. We were not asked to do much about it. We weren't equipped to do so. We had no Albanians with us. Oakley-Hill knew them all by their first names.

The first big event was the conference held by Amery and McLean. We got a cable asking us to arrange a very hush-hush conference between those two and various nominated Albanians. Oakley-Hill was there, too. So we found a villa outside Athens and the idea was for the conference to last a few hours, from noon to five o'clock, including lunch. They did finish at five, but it was five in the morning.

Robert Low is of Bulgarian origin and he was the lover of Ava Gardiner. I stayed with him in New York in 1951, at Kim's suggestion. He had a house in New York City, equipped with cook and butler. He had everything waiting for me: the drink, the bath, the theater tickets, the dinner reservation and the girl. The theater was *South Pacific* and the girl told me she had seen it six times. He was then one of the reporters on *Time-Life-Fortune* magazines. The next morning, after the Stork Club, we went to see Howard Black, his proprietor. This was just before the Burgess and McLean defection. I was in the U.S. on "firm" business, war planning. Kim had left Ankara and was station chief in Washington.

He came to stay with us in Athens, while stationed in Istanbul, and my wife took an instant dislike to him. So did our Greek maid. She said, "Not only is he drunk, but he is also a very bad man." I personally couldn't get on with him at all. He had a terrible stammer and he was always making mock of the establishment, things that I had been brought up to respect, or even revere.

I had a boss called Kenneth Cohen who once said about Philby, "That man's so bloody clever. He'll cut his own throat one of these days." Kim had written something especially rude, caustic and sarcastic. He was very plausible, though. He had a fight with Felix Cowgill, who was his head of section. The section consisted of Kim, Nicholas Elliott and Rodney Dennys, who all worked under the overall supervision of Colonel Valentine Vivian. These three did not get on with Cowgill, who wanted to keep all the strings in his hand. Vivian's son Michael also came into the office and was with me in Athens. He could have given us some stuff on Albania, but unfortunately he's dead.

Dennys was head of station in Paris up to 1948, not speaking any French. His place was taken by John Bruce-Lockhart. Elliott's father was headmaster of Eton. He has iota of jobs, including Lonrho. He's a rascal, but I like him.

My wife Maria took an instant dislike to him when he came out to visit us in Athens for one night in 1949 from Istanbul. His wife Eileen was very ill after the birth of one of their children and the office was very good to them, spent quite a lot of money to help them over this crisis. He couldn't afford the bills himself, he wasn't being paid enough by Moscow. I can't remember what business we had to discuss, if any. Maria and I had to go out and we left him with dinner and the whisky decanter, all of which he drank. He was so sure of himself, so sure that he was right. It was difficult to warm to him, unless you were prepared to flatter him, which I wasn't, or match him quip for quip, which I wasn't prepared to do because I knew he'd beat me. He was rather like Malcolm Muggeridge, full of intellectual arrogance, which I believe to be one of the main ingredients of treachery and treason.

The Albanian team were under my umbrella in Athens, but I had very little to do with them. They just asked me for facilities. My driver Reg Voyce drove parties of Albanians by truck up to the border several times. My officers and I were not allowed less than 30 km from the border. Oakley-Hill could break this rule, but at a certain stage he, too, had to get off and they carried on to within five kilometers of the border with Voyce, who had driven all the way from Athens. The Greek commandoes then escorted them across the border. Voyce was once arrested after being caught asleep under the tailboard of his truck in a sleeping bag. We had to keep away from border areas because of the fear of our being kidnapped, as happened in the Venlo incident.

Eileen Hill was daughter of the Shell manager in Salamis and she married Sam Barclay. The other daughter had her eye on John Leatham, but he was nimble-footed and he sidestepped. John married a girl who came out to be "au pair" to Brooks Richards. John is a Catholic. He is very intelligent and good, but if my head depended on some decision I would take Sam's.

We helped Sam and John financially. We got a diesel engine out from England for them. I gave them funds to finish off their new boat.

In the "firm" you don't ask about things that you don't need to know. Or if you do, you may get a dusty answer. Philby could only have discovered operational details if he had been in head office in London on a visit. He couldn't decently have asked about that sort of thing from Washington. The reply would have been, "Why do you need to know?" The Washington job anyway is mainly liaison. It's designed to stop overlap and collisions with the CIA.

Once the fact of the operation was known to the other side, it would not have been too difficult for them to circumvent us. It is a small country with a short coastline and a difficult frontier—in other words, not many places to land and not many places to cross.

I'm not surprised that information leaked from the Albanian side. They are a tribal nation and each man trusted another who came from his own tribe.

Gratian Yatsevich was very correct, precise and able. He was on the operational side and he came and went. Oakley-Hill was meticulous and quite fierce with the Albanians, an ex-policeman, quite bad-tempered. Natsenas was the head of KYP, the Greek

CIA. The Greek escorting party wore khaki, either gendarmerie or commandos or Greek army or KYP.

The ballooning was a bit far-fetched. I've no idea whether any of them arrived. Some of them are probably still there lying on the hills.

Philby's job was very important. The entire basis of British-American cooperation in intelligence was the SIS man in Washington and the CIA man in London. Those two men have a heavy responsibility. The thing that really makes me cross is when someone like Philby is called a spy. In fact, he is a traitor with blood on his hands.

Perks was a sledgehammer of a man, a master mariner, able and wily, with plenty of common sense, but not an intellectual. He suffered during the slump in the U.K. in 1931. He was out of work like everybody else and he answered an advertisement to go to Czechoslovakia to run a shoe factory. In 1939 he volunteered to join the Navy, but the Admiralty would not have anything to do with him because of his Czech and Polish connections. He was very angry. He was a huge man with not very many teeth. So he joined the Army and then he moved to SOE.

After he left the firm, he became a security officer in Northern Rhodesia, where he later died.

Interview conducted May 4, 1983

SIR RICHARD WHITE

Sir Richard White (1906–1993), also known as Dick White, was a British intelligence officer. He was director-general of MI5 from 1953 to 1956 and head of MI6 from 1956 to 1968. He questioned Kim Philby in 1951 about his activities, after the defection of Guy Burgess and Donald MacLean, and became convinced that Philby, too, was a Soviet spy. This resulted in Philby's resignation from MI6.

Obviously, I offended the MI6 people because of my suspicions of Philby and it was awkward when I was appointed head of MI6 in 1956. This was the year of Hungary and Suez, so there was no time to look back at what might have gone wrong in 1953.

Philby was certainly responsible for Volkov. He must have done great damage to our interests in Turkey, especially with the Armenians. But when he went to Washington, it was as general liaison officer to the CIA. No doubt he also betrayed the Albanian operation, but overshadowing this is the fact that all émigré organizations are hopelessly infiltrated right from the outset. So it is not easy to pin down the precise extent of Philby's responsibility. He was a coordinator, but he did not have executive responsibility for the operation.

Philby was brought back from Washington in June 1951. I was by that time totally convinced that Philby was the culprit. I was not yet head of MI5, but I was of sufficient senior rank to be able to deal with the then head of SIS at least for his being neutralized, taken off any sensitive work. This was thought grossly unfair, because there was no evidence that could be used in a court of law. This was always our difficulty. And there was the problem that, if I wanted an investigation of this or that operation to see if there were weaknesses, I had to depend on SIS to carry it out. There was almost a state of internecine war between the service.

In the end I think that Sir S. Menzies took the view that he owed it to the Americans not to employ him any further. They were, of course, by this time very suspicious of him, if only for his close association with Burgess in Washington.

Milmo's report concluded that Philby was guilty, but it was rejected by SIS. Nevertheless, the decision was taken to retire him. It is one of those frightful difficulties. When you can't prove something, what on earth are you to do? But when there are such big issues at stake, it's better to err on the side of caution. And that is what I persuaded them to do.

So I don't think Philby had any access to sensitive information after June 1951. However, anything that he had gleaned either in Turkey or in Rome or in Washington would certainly have been given to the Russians.

After his recall to England, so I was told by a friend of his, Philby spent the next two years at his home in Hertfordshire with his wife and four children in a very miserable and humiliated state, as a result of the investigation and of having been let go by his service. During this period, 1951–53, he had no connection with MI6 as such, although no doubt he was in touch with friends who were still in the service. Equally, he would have been free to meet any of his Soviet contacts, although he would have been on the alert, assuming that he was being watched. His information could still have been useful to the Soviets, even though it was not up to date, and even though he had no access to secret material.

Most of his friends thought he had been unfairly treated. And this was quite understandable, looking back, because it really was the most incredible thing to hoist on board. He had such a good record. And you had to remember too how, when he was recruited in 1940, men of every shade of opinion were acceptable. The Russians were our allies. It also involved men of a highly privileged background. This had never happened before. And the natural bureaucratic reluctance to admit that one of their most successful people was a traitor.

He was an impressive chap. He had this stammer that enabled him to think twice before answering a question. I think he cultivated the stammer. He was a quiet, good-looking man, determined, the sort of Englishman that Americans like. Of course, there was his drinking, but it did not develop until late and it did not involve public scandal, as with McLean. He was always discreet, he avoided politics, even when drunk. He was a classic performer. And this helped him in his "cover" as a spy, from our point of view.

On émigré organizations, I think one must try to look into the minds of the KGB. And their first consideration must be the security of the USSR. Therefore, they must put their minds to what the émigré organizations can do to damage that security. They would take that as a priority task. Therefore, they must put great effort into penetrating the émigré organizations. The leaks from émigré sources can be limited, but never completely done away with.

Firstly, the trainees were isolated in a house whose location they did not know. Secondly, they sent no letters to their Albanian friends and family while at the school.

In 1951, the evidence against Philby was purely circumstantial. But it was very powerful. There were his activities in Spain, his attempt to build up a sort of cover life, including membership of the Anglo-German Fellowship. He was making great efforts to show himself as being on that side, against all the evidence of his undergraduate days. Why should he have himself accredited to France? What was his motive?

So I did not have any doubts. But I was fairly alone in this. His own service supported him, partly because they did not have all the evidence. Their attitude was understandable. It was the first betrayal from the dead center of the establishment. I remember having to announce some of this to senior men in the Foreign Office. They could hardly credit it.

Milmo carried out the interrogation on the basis of evidence that I gave him. And he did it pretty well. But where are you with a man who has been trained very carefully, who knows how much the other side knows and who refuses to confess? It was different with George Blake. Once we confronted him, the truth just poured out. Apart from anything else, he wanted to show us how clever he had been. It is the interrogator's job to establish a relationship with the suspect so that this is what he does. But it wasn't possible to do this with Philby. He was too devious a man, too deep a man, with an iron will.

Philby was in Turkey in 1947–49. He didn't go back there in 1951. He was in a dejected condition, then a business job, then a journalistic job.

Through all this I thought that time was on our side. I thought that eventually the item of evidence we needed would come to hand. It couldn't fail to. It did eventually, but it took a long time. You see, he covered his tracks so carefully.

Interview conducted October 19, 1983

MARTIN WHITWORTH

Martin Whitworth was a British naval figure. He was recruited for the MI6 Albanian operation by Kevin Walton and sent to Malta in July 1951. He was responsible for running the boat that transported the Albanian fighters to Albania and for getting the men ashore.

Kevin Walton contacted me in June 1951 when I was with Thornycrofts in Southampton. I had graduated from Cambridge on a state bursary in engineering in 1945, then joined the Royal Navy and spent two years in the Far East. I was with Thornycrofts to get practical experience. Walton found me through the Cambridge University Appointments Board and asked me to come for an interview for a possible job.

I met him outside the RNVR Club in Hill Street, London. He jumped into my car—we were both Riley 9 enthusiasts—and we drove to the flat of Frank Slocum's secretary, Irene Thrupp. Only then was it explained to me what type of work was envisaged. They had presumably checked me out in the meantime and the fact that my father was in the Indian Army and my uncle in the Navy would have counted in my favor. He explained roughly what was required, though without mentioning Albania, only talking vaguely about secret work with boats in the Mediterranean, and this appealed to me. I don't think they did much checking out. These things were done very much by personal recommendation. We didn't discuss conditions at that stage.

I was influenced by a feeling that I had done very well out of Britain. I had been through Cambridge University on a state bursary, which was the beginning of the present grant system. I had got my degree in engineering, then gone to the Far East in the Navy from 1945 to 1947. So part of my reason for accepting this secret assignment was that there was a debt that needed to be repaid. Britain had given me an education and then shown me the world.

I went out to Malta in July 1951, after two or three weeks of clearances and a rather comic medical examination by Dr. Lancaster. I was impressed by Slocum. He had a great facility for remembering everything that I said to him. We used to argue and then he would take his decision, either my line or his, irrespective of how hard he had been putting his case against me.

Slocum was MI6's deputy director for administration. He was in the "Q" Branch of 54 Broadway. He had run boats full of ball bearings from Sweden and won many foreign decorations, including the Croix de Guerre. Perks was a nice, hearty man, rather cold-blooded in his approach.

I was given a letter constituting a one-year contract renewable for intervals of two months. My job was to run a boat, not to worry about politics.

Kevin was still there when I arrived and we lived on board the *Henrietta* in Sliema Creek, which was her Malta base. There always seemed to be plenty to do keeping the *Henrietta* shipshape. We had to change the oil after every 50 hours of running. That could be done in any harbor. We had to do a major overhaul after 500 hours and change the engine itself after 1000 hours. They were the 12-cylinder unsupercharged version of the engine originally designed for the Graf Zeppelin airship. The hull was excellent. She had been used for air-sea rescue duty off the Dutch coast during the war, known as a "Raum" boat. She could operate in very nasty weather. Other such boats were used to escort the French fishing fleets off Brest, to make sure that none of them made a run for England. The *Henrietta*, though, had this special Mercedes engine that gave her a top speed of 26 knots.

We normally carried four "pixies" on each run, landed them in two pairs with our surf boats. Once or twice we did a double run, which meant that a Royal Navy motor launch met us at the mouth of the Adriatic with the second group of Albanians and drums of fuel. Then, after the run was over, we usually went to Piraeus and sailed round the Greek islands for a time before returning to Malta. It would have looked suspicious if we had left Malta and returned a couple of days later. The motor launch caused a lot of talk, though, because she was a petrol boat and people wondered why she was loading up with drums of diesel oil. This happened in the late summer of 1951, shortly after I arrived.

The first four men simply came down to Sliema Creek from the fort by taxi in the early evening. We would set off as it was getting dark and make the landing just over 24 hours later. The double run we did with Kevin Walton was at the end of July 1951 on a sandy beach north of Vlora. There were three men in each surf boat, two "pixies" and one man to do the rowing. The rowers were Kevin Walton, Darby Allen, Arthur Watkin and I. We carried them ashore so that they wouldn't get their feet wet.

The rendezvous with the motor launch took place just south of the Straits of Otranto. The shipping traffic either turns west or east after passing through the straits, so we agreed to meet the launch in a "quiet" spot in the middle where we were unlikely to be observed. The diesel fuel was pumped across from the drums on the launch. Then they didn't even dump the drums because they were Royal Navy property, and no one in Malta could understand why they had left with 20 drums full of diesel oil and returned two days later with them all empty. However, for security reasons they were not told who they were going to meet. I remember that they were quite surprised when they saw us and realized that it was the *Henrietta*. Of course, they had seen the boat in Malta and they knew us; they had thought we were smugglers. When they returned to Malta, though, they must have known that we were MI6. It was a risk, because Malta is a very small place.

Another risky thing was that the *Henrietta*'s papers showed joint owners, Jimmy Blackburn and H.M. King George VI. This was so that Jimmy could sign documents for the boat, on the one hand, and to prevent him from dashing off and selling her and keeping the money. Tangers would have been a good place to sell it. In fact, Blackburn was neither a smuggler nor a crook; he was absolutely straight.

Blackburn was a very self-contained person. He kept his ideas to himself. He was very friendly with Arthur Watkin, a young member of the crew who had joined when he was about 17 years old, after being on the *Michelangelo*, which did one or two runs into Albania in 1950. Blackburn was captain of the *Michelangelo*, too, with Arthur Watkin and a mechanic called Doug. The *Sunday Times* article describes this period. Watkin had been with a salvage company working on wrecks off the North African coast. Blackburn recruited him locally. Jack Smith was an atrocious cook and he couldn't add up his household accounts. He could only add up when he was playing pontoon. It was a lack of arithmetic rather than dishonesty. And there was the radio operator, a fair-haired tall Cornishman, Ron Ramsey, who had run a SOE radio set on board a Greek island ferry during the German occupation. There were Bill Tilbury and Gordon Dyke on the engineering side.

Blackburn was taciturn, but a good man for the job, very competent. It would have been good to have someone a bit more outgoing as skipper, to make it a happier ship, but one couldn't actually fault him.

The transfer from the motor launch was done at night, a few hours after we had taken the first lot ashore. On one occasion they had no photographs on their identity cards. We took their pictures and made the cards for them. We did a hurried passport-photo session and developed the photos in the dark room on board. It can't have been a very professional job, I suppose, but at least they had a picture on the card instead of just a blank space.

We went to the Greek islands to wait for the next moonless-night period. We collected two "pixies" from the "firm" man in Piraeus and put them ashore. Then we abandoned operations for the winter, because the weather broke in mid–September. So we did two drops, one in July and one in August, both at the time of the new moon. We went back to Malta after the August drop.

Then we did a top overhaul of the engines, decarbonizing and grinding valves, changing piston rings. A fitter came out from Germany to help us, because special Mercedes tools were needed to dismantle the engines. This was our autumn occupation. Then in December we went up to Antibes and spent the winter there. Some of us went home for Christmas. We got back to Malta in early May 1952.

We did a run throughout the summer of 1952 at each new moon period, four men a run. The last three runs were to the rocky coast just north of Corfu, south of the Adriatic Sea. We found an inlet where we could bring the boat in and land the "pixies" on a rock. The first time we landed four men, the second time two men, and the last time we collected the two men from the same rock where we had landed them a month earlier.

We were very nervous about that last operation. If the two men had been caught, they could have given away our plans and there would have been a reception committee waiting for us.

The valley system must have been a problem for them. If they were in a "foreign" valley, they would be treated almost as an enemy. If they reached their own valley, people would ask them where they had been for the past two years. I got the impression that the last two men, the ones that we took in and out, were more competent than the others. We had a VHF radio, an "88" set, in the landing boat and we used lamp signals, too. We got the last two men straight onto a flat rock sticking out of the water. They jumped onto it from the boat without getting their feet wet. It was a bit rough and the sea threw the prow of the boat under the rock. We had to fight to get it loose as water poured in and the two men scrambled ashore. The water put the radio out of action, so that we couldn't let the *Henrietta* know what was happening. And it made it hard for us to find the *Henrietta*. It was very dark during the new moon period and at a distance of more than 50 yards she was invisible. We used the radio to guide ourselves back to her. Her paintwork—dark-green hull, light-blue deckhouses and yellow window frames—were designed to make her invisible at night. The decks merged with the horizon. Kevin Walton and I did the rowing. All this took place, according to your book, after Philby had been dismissed from MI6 for alleged disloyalty. It seems extraordinary.

Perks always spent the night of an operation at Broadway and he would get our messages from the *Henrietta*, relayed via Malta, about how each operation had gone. Perks was responsible for the operation, Slocum for the equipment and administration.

Darby Allen left us at Antibes. He was a bit of a pest. He had been broken from corporal several times. I remember him coming on board one night in Antibes roaring drunk and making a nuisance of himself. Bill Tilbury, former policeman, laid him out cold, threw him into his bunk and told him the next morning that he had slipped coming up the gangway. It gave me some insight into how policemen deal with drunks generally.

There was one occasion when we heard a patrol boat in the distance just as we were landing the men and I had to face the possibility that the *Henrietta* would take off and leave me behind. Those were her orders. Losing me would have been bad enough, but not as bad as having the whole boat captured. If they had gone, I would not have trusted myself to make it overland to Greece. I'd have rowed for Italy and I feel sure I'd have made it, at least during the summer calm weather.

GRATIAN YATSEVITCH

Gratian Michael Yatsevitch (1911–1997) was an American military figure of British-Polish descent. After studies at Harvard, he served as the United States military attaché in Bulgaria in 1947–1949. In 1950 he was recruited by the CIA for which he worked for the rest of his life. Yatsevitch soon became head of the American side of the Albanian operation. He died in Maine.

I was born in the Ukraine. My mother was Scottish, my father Polish. I was brought up partly in England, near Potters Bar, partly in the United States at Harvard University. I was a mining engineer by profession. After leaving Harvard, I went to the Balkans for a summer job and stayed for five years, from 1935 to 1940. I was manager of the mine at the age of 23. It was called Zlot Gold Mines Ltd. I am afraid that the amount of gold that we found was limited. Before leaving the mine for the United States in 1940, I blew the whole thing up, because I was sure that the Germans were going to come in.

There were a number of requests from OSS for me during the war, but they were all turned down by my commanding officer. Then the chance of a military attaché job in Moscow turned up in 1945, a few days after the war ended. I went there as an assistant military attaché. Harriman was my ambassador, then Bedell Smith. Then I found myself in an environment where, if I did what I wanted to do, I would only cause the embassy embarrassment, so I had myself transferred to the military government of Bulgaria. I was number two in the U.S. mission. My Russian is grammatically incorrect and heavily influenced by Serbian. I was in Moscow for a little more than a year.

The military government in Bulgaria was liquidated in 1947 and I became the first U.S. military attaché. I was there until the end of 1949. I met many Yugoslav Albanians during my mining days. My first official contact with them was when I was seconded to a U.N. force monitoring aid to the Greek partisans. The Albanian government would not let us in.

At the end of 1949, I was sent to Detroit as an army lieutenant-colonel to control a chemical works. I did not like Detroit very much and I was quite happy to leave when I was recruited into the CIA. The Army did not want to release me, but they were ordered to do so by the Secretary for the Army. Apart from a short period involved in the development of chemical weapons, I spent all my life in the CIA.

They picked me up really because of my Balkan experience. As far as the Albanian operation is concerned, it was "coordinated" between the British and the Americans, nothing more. It was not a joint operation. They were independent but coordinated activities. It was the coordination that involved the contact with Kim Philby. Philby would not have known the detail of what I was doing. This was not because I suspected him, but because there was no need for him to know the operational details of what the American side was doing. The "need to know" principle was adhered to quite strictly so long as I was in charge.

I was in on some of the discussions about forming a capacity for this type of activity during peacetime. It was always important to preserve a capacity for plausible denial, something that is very hard to preserve under an open government. One principle of this was the rule that no British or American agents were allowed into the target territory. British and American agents also had to keep far enough away from the target territory to avoid being captured and put on parade. The idea was to create indigenous revolts against communist authority.

I had to get to know the Albanian leaders in emigration who might become politically powerful after a successful revolt. That is why I went to Cairo to meet King Zog. The royalists were an important element, but Abas Ermenji's people were vital, too.

The professional foreign service people influenced this aspect of the affair and this was really where the coordination came in, the decision over the political coloring that we wanted these groups to have. Very early in 1950 I was with Kim Philby the joint "commander" of the Albanian operation, but I am afraid that I cannot give you any details about it. I consulted my former superiors before this meeting and they told me quite clearly that I must say nothing about the operational side of it.

Interview conducted May 20, 1981

* * *

I was, I suppose, the American commander of the operation. But I would not say I was the joint commander. I always considered the two operations—the American and the British—as separate. They used different people, different places and different methods. They were not joint but coordinated. That is why I met with Philby—to coordinate. I think that is an important point to make.

I took over from Jim McCargar. No, I can't tell you why. I just can't remember. But I was suited to the job as I think I was the only one around who had direct Balkan experience. I had been running a gold mine in Yugoslavia before the war. I had then been in Romania where I got to know King Michael very well. When I took over, which was in 1950, I don't think I ever asked myself the question "has this been well set up?" It was just there, the planning had been done. We just had to get on with the training. Frashëri's death had been a blow because the committee needed the right people. But Hasan Dosti was also a very impressive man. I can't tell you who chose him, but he was not a bad choice.

There was a difference between Jim McCargar and myself. I agreed strongly with Julian Amery that Zog was a very important figure, more so than the Balli Kombëtar. Jim is a liberal type and was keener on the Balli Kombëtar. I was very impressed by Zog. I saw him a great deal. He had four sisters who he had been trying to marry off since before the war. I think he was trying to pair me up with one. I thank God that I escaped that fate. But he really did understand Albanian politics. He combined all the contradictions that make the Balkans so extraordinary. It's very difficult to explain the Balkans to anyone who has never been there. The Albanians are typically Balkan. Two of them may have a feud, I mean, they want to kill each other—but if one of them is traveling, he will visit the other, they'll welcome each other with open arms, have a splendid dinner, and the next day he'll be given twenty-four hours to get away. That's "typically Balkan." That was why it was so difficult to get the right combination of people and agreements between them on the committee. Bob Low did a very good job there. It was before I worked on the operation.

We did have some problems with the committee later, but not the problems that the Albanians talk about. Yes, there was the incident of the tomb in the snow. But that wasn't all that serious. The real difficulty was that they were suspicious about the composition of a future government. That is, if they were successful. I mean they were suspicious about what our intentions were.

[NB]: What were your intentions? Were they different from the British?

[GY]: We just didn't have any. I just don't think we had thought that through. Zog was important not just because he was respected and could deal with the complications, but because he had done what we were trying to do once before. That was in 1924 or 1925. He had been thrown out by Fan Noli and he came back from the North with an army. He also had support from some guerrillas from Yugoslavia. It was a very small force and yet the Albanians rose up. That was the important point for us. I suppose it was the model we were working on. We believed that a small force but the right one— could start up resistance. It could have worked. The time was right. The information we were receiving told us there was a lot of resistance and that Hoxha's grip, especially on parts of the country, was not all that firm.

[NB]: So you already had agents in the country?

[GY]: I'm afraid I can't answer that, but we were receiving direct information.

[NB]: Many of the drops, especially from the British side, were in the south of the country. Surely that was where Hoxha's grip was firmest. It had been his power base.

[GY]: Yes, that's true. I'm afraid, I can't really comment. But I think some people would see that as a mistake. But I do really think that the operation stood a good chance. I think it was well planned. We spent a long time training, getting the right force together. The Albanians were very good, very brave men. Of course, things go wrong on operations like these. Albania is a small country—very small, really, and I'm sure word gets around very quickly amongst the villages. But things started to go wrong too often. After a while it began to seem as though there were troops waiting for them, as though they knew they were coming. It was statistically more than the normal margin of error expected. I just didn't know what was going wrong. I could see no way of blaming ourselves. I'm afraid I can't say whether we moved to the Greek island to enforce stricter security. But islands, of course, are much more secure places than camps on the mainland. But we were also using houses in Greece. Things did keep on going wrong after that.

Looking back, of course, Philby was the traitor. He was representing the English side. I was with him often. I can't tell you where. He wouldn't have known any of the details of our end, much more the British end. The best way for you to tell the story properly would be to debrief Philby himself. I liked him a lot. He was immensely charming, very bright. Of course we talked to him. We all talked a lot because here was a man who we were told was one of the new breed in the British service. The irony is that we felt he was safer to talk to because he was this new breed—more professional and so more trustworthy. I never suspected him. One person did—Bedell-Smith. He was a very frightening man. If he said, be at my office at 3 p.m., one would be there at 5 to 3. Except with Jim McCargar, he always arrived at 3:10. Bedall-Smith suspected Philby.

He didn't tell anyone at the time. I'm not sure if he had any evidence. He was always very worried that we were too close to the British anyway. He thought we told them too much and that was unprofessional. Philby was their representative. But at the time I liked Philby. He drank so much that I am amazed he managed to carry on such a life successfully. My last memory of him? We had been to his place for dinner and he had drunk a great deal but he insisted on coming outside to say goodnight. Unfortunately, he couldn't stand up and fell backwards into the hedge. So my last memory of him is a pair of feet and a hand waving goodbye sticking out of a hedge.

When Philby defected, my emotions were very mixed. I was very angry. Here was the man who had sent a lot of very brave men to their death. He had also ruined an operation. But somehow I also admired him. He had done it so well for so long. I don't think the whole problem was Philby. The Albanians at a low level—operational level—were very talkative. That's what Albanians are like, terribly Balkan and there is nothing you can really do about it.

[NB]: Not even by shutting them up on an island?

[GY]: I cannot comment on that. But I do not subscribe to the theory that somehow the Italians were involved. The Italian Secret Service was very efficient at that time and I don't think there were any leaks.

[NB]: The operation consistently went wrong until the Matjani episode and then things started to look up. Did you feel this?

[GY]: Matjani was very brave, very independent. He wasn't a Zog man or Balli Kombëtar. In fact he was Albanian, a patriot, just the right sort of man. He went in and out more than the six times you suggest. He was successful. I cannot comment anymore about him. He always insisted on walking in (*laughs*).

[NB]: Did you ever meet Matjani?

[GY]: No, I couldn't meet with anyone at the operational level. They could have identified me if they had been caught.

[NB]: Did Matjani come to you and say that some officers should be sent in?

[GY]: I can't answer that, but it is very important in an operation of this sort that one sends the right people in at the right time.

[NB]: Did you go personally to see Zog and ask him for the officers?

[GY]: I'm afraid I can't remember. It could have been me.

[NB]: Was Zog bitter after the capture of his officers?

[GY]: I don't know. I don't really want to comment. He certainly understood the dangers of this sort of work. We remained very good friends after everything was over.

[NB]: Was the Matjani episode the real end of the whole affair?

[GY]: No, but it was the last big-scale part and I think dramatically, for your purposes, you could consider it the end.

I must tell you that it is not thought to be the right time to tell this story. That is what my superiors say to me. I personally feel that it would not harm security if it were told and I support what you are doing. I will go back and ask again. A close friend is the man who is looking after and guiding Casey, the new head. I will put your arguments to him.

It is a peculiar life. One is not allowed to tell anyone what one is doing. But that is part of the professionalism. Sometimes it would be pleasant to be recognized for the work one has done—and the real power one has. I have been told that if I was part of the regular army, I would be a general. But there are good times. For example, when the American ambassador is summoned to see the Shah and he comes into the room to find you already there having tea. Those times make up for everything. Much of the spirit of those days has been lost. The work now is all a matter of clerks gathering information. There are very few people who can go out and actually do something. The operation of which we have been talking was one of the last active attempts to do something, to behave like a strong power instead of just saying we are.

Interview conducted November 12, 1983

Bibliography

Alia, Ramiz. *Our Enver*. Tirana: 8 Nëntori, 1988.
Amery, Julian. *Sons of the Eagle: A Study in Guerrilla War*. London: Macmillan, 1948; reprint, Tirana 2002.
_____. *Approach March: A Venture in Autobiography*. London: Hutchinson, 1973.
Atherton, Louise. *SOE Operations in the Balkans: An Introductory Guide to the Newly Released Records of the Special Operations Executive in the Public Record Office*. London: PRO Publications, 1997.
Bailey, Roderick. "Smoke without Fire: SOE and the Communist Conspiracy Theory." In *Albanian identities: Myth and History*, edited by Stephanie Schwander-Sievers and Bernd J. Fischer, 143–156. London: C. Hurst, 2002.
_____. *The Wildest Province: SOE in the Land of the Eagle*. London: Jonathan Cape, 2008.
Bethell, Nicholas William. *The Great Betrayal: The Untold Story of Kim Philby's Biggest Coup*. London: Hodder and Stoughton, 1984.
_____. *Betrayed*. New York: Times Books, 1985.
_____. *La grande trahison: Le plus gros coup de l'agent Philby*. Paris: Flammarion, 1985.
_____. *La missione tradita: Come Kim Philby sabotò l'invasione dell'Albania*. Milan, 1986.
_____. *Tradhëtia e madhe: Historia e patreguar e grushtit dërmues të Kim Filbit*. Tirana: Progresi, 1993.
Bland, William, and Ian Price. *A Tangled Web: History of Anglo-American Relations with Albania (1912–1955)*. Ilford: Albania Society, 1986.
Boyle, Andrew. *The Climate of Treason: Five Who Spied for Russia*. London: Hutchinson, 1979.
Burke, Michael. *Outrageous Good Fortune*. Boston: Little, Brown, 1984.
Butka, Uran. *Lufta civile në Shqipëri, 1943–1945*. Tirana: Drier, 2007.
Corke, Sarah-Jane. *US Cover Operations and Cold War Strategy: Truman, Secret Warfare and the CIA, 1948–1953*. London: Routledge, 2007.
_____. *Operacionet e fshehta dhe strategjia e Luftës së Ftohtë e SHBA, 1945–1953*. Tirana: Globus R, 2010.
Davies, Edmund Frank. *Illyrian Venture: The Story of the British Military Mission to Enemy-occupied Albania 1943–1944*. London: Bodley Head, 1952.
Dear, Ian. *Sabotage and Subversion: Stories from the Files of the SOE and OSS*. London: Arms and Armour, 1996.
Dedijer, Vladimir. *Jugoslovensko-albanski odnosi (1939–1948): Na osnovu službenih dokumenta, pisama i drugog materijala*. Zagreb: Borba, 1949.
Dorril, Stephen. *MI6: Fifty Years of Special Operations*. London: Fourth Estate, 2000.
_____. *MI6: Inside the Covert World of Her Majesty's Secret Intelligence Service*. New York: Free Press, 2000.
Elsie, Robert. *Historical Dictionary of Albania*. Lanham, MD: Scarecrow, 2010.
_____. *A Biographical Dictionary of Albania History*. London: I.B. Tauris, 2013.
_____. *Historical Dictionary of Kosovo*. Lanham MD: Scarecrow, 2011.
Fielding, Xan. *One Man in His Time: The Life of Lieutenant-Colonel NLD (Billy) McLean, DSO*. London: Macmillan, 1990.

Fischer, Bernd. *Albania at War, 1939–1945*. London: Hurst, 1999.
Grose, Peter. *Operation Rollback: America's Secret War Behind the Iron Curtain*. Boston: Houghton Mifflin, 2000.
Hamilton-Hill, Donald. *SOE Assignment*. London: William Kimber, 1973.
Hamm, Harry. *Albania: China's Beachhead in Europe*. London: Weidenfeld and Nicolson, 1962.
Hibbert, Reginald. *Albania's National Liberation Struggle: The Bitter Victory*. London: Pinter, London and New York: St. Martin's Press, 1991.
_____. *Fitorja e hidhur: Lufta nacionalçlirimtare e Shqipërisë*. Tirana: Lidhja e Shkrimtarëve, 1993.
Howarth, Patrick, ed. *Special Operations*. London: Routledge and Kegan Paul, 1955.
Hoxha, Enver. *The Anglo-American Threat to Albania: Memoirs*. Tirana: 8 Nëntori, 1982.
_____. *The Titoites: Historical Notes*. Tirana: 8 Nëntori, 1982.
Kaba, Hamit. *UNRRA në Shqipëri 1944–1947*. Tirana, 2000.
Kasneci, Lefter. *Steeled in the Heat of Battle: A Brief Survey of the History of the National Liberation War of the Albanian People (1941–1944)*. Tirana: Naim Frashëri, 1966.
Kastrati, Sebastian. *Rezistenca antikomuniste shqiptare në vitet 1945–1955: Mbresa*. Shkodra: Camaj-Pipa, 1998.
Kemp, Peter Mant Macintyre. *No Colours or Crest*. London: Cassell, 1958.
_____. *The Thorns of Memory: Memoirs*. London: Sinclair-Stevenson, 1990.
Knightley, Phillip. *The Master Spy: The Story of Kim Philby*. New York: Alfred A. Knopf, 1988.
Kühmel, Bernhard. *Deutschland und Albanien 1943–1944: Die Auswirkungen der Besatzung und die innenpolitische Entwicklung des Landes*. Inauguraldissertation zur Erlangung des Grades eines Doktors der Philosophie in der Abteilung für Geschichtswissenschaft der Ruhr-Universität Bochum. Bochum, 1981.
Logoreci, Anton. *The Albanians. Europe's Forgotten Survivors*. London: Victor Gollancz, 1977.
Lucas, Peter. *The OSS in World War II. Albania: Covert Operations and Collaboration with Communist Partisans*. Foreword by Fatos Tarifa. Jefferson, NC: McFarland, 2007.
MacIntyre, Ben. *A Spy among Friends: Kim Philby and the Great Betrayal*. New York: Crown 2014.
Mangerich, Agnes Jensen. *Albanian Escape: The True Story of U.S. Army Nurse behind Enemy Lines*. As told to Evelyn M. Monahan and Rosemary L. Neidel. Lexington: University of Kentucky Press, 1999.
Nerguti, Halil. *Jeta ime për Shqipërinë dhe mbretërinë e saj*. Tirana: Studiu Alba, 2003.
Neuwirth, Hubert. *Widerstand und Kollaboration in Albanien, 1939 1944*. Albanische Forschungen, Bd. 27. Wiesbaden: Harrassowitz, 2008.
Oakley-Hill, Dayrell R. *An Englishman in Albania: Memoirs of a British Officer, 1929–1955*. Edited by B.D. Destani. Introduction by Colonel David Smiley. London: Centre for Albanian studies, 2002.
_____. *Një anglez në Shqipëri: kujtime të një oficeri britanik, 1929–1955*. Tirana: Koçi, 2006.
Page, Bruce, David Leitch, and Phillip Knightley. *Philby: The Spy Who Betrayed a Generation*. Introduction by John le Carré. Harmondsworth: Penguin, 1969.
_____. *The Philby Conspiracy*. New York: Doubleday, 1968.
Pearson, Owen. *Albania in the Twentieth Century, a History. Volume III: Albania as Dictatorship and Democracy: From Isolation to the Kosovo War, 1946–98*. London; I. B. Tauris, 2006.
Peebles, Curtis. *Twilight Warriors: Covert Air Operations Against the USSR*. Annapolis: Naval Institute Press, 2005.
Philby, Harold Adrian Russell (Kim). *My Silent War*. With an introduction by Graham Greene. London: MacGibbon and Kee, 1968, reprint, London: Panther, 1969.
_____. *My Silent War: The Autobiography of a Spy*. Introduction by Phillip Knightley. Foreword by Graham Greene. London: Modern Library Paperback Edition, 2002.
_____. *Lufta ime e heshtur: Autobiografia e një spiuni*. Përkthyen Sokrat Gjerasi dhe Jorgji Qirjako. Tirana: Onufri, 2004.
Puto, Arben. *From the Annals of British Diplomacy: The Anti-Albanian Plans of Great Britain During the Second World War According to Foreign Office Documents of 1939–44*. Tirana: 8 Nëntori, 1981.

Quayle, Anthony. *Eight Hours from England*. London: Heinemann, 1945.
____. *A Time to Speak*. London: Barie and Jenkins, 1990.
Smiley, David. *Albanian Assignment*. Foreword Patrick Fermor. London: Chatto and Windus / Hogarth Press, 1984.
____. *Irregular Regular*. Norwich: Michael Russell, 1994.
Sulzberger, Cyrus L. *A Long Row of Candles: Memoirs and Diaries, 1934–1954*. New York: Macmillan 1969.
Tilman, Harold William. *When Men and Mountains Meet*. Cambridge: Cambridge University Press, 1946.
Tomes, Jason. *King Zog: Self-Made Monarch of Albania*. Stroud: Sutton, 2003.
Vickers, Miranda. *Albania: A Modern History*. London: I. B. Tauris, 1994.
Williams, Heather. *Parachutes, Patriots and Partisans: The SOE and Yugoslavia, 1941–5*. London: Hurst and Co., 2003.

Index

Abdullah, Hakik 56
Adams, Alan J. 7
Aegerter, Elizabeth 86
Agaj, Daver 85
Agaj, Mirteza Haxhi 84
Airie, Terence 122
Aldridge (Aldiss), Jessica 54–55, 132–133, 135, 138
Alexandrov, Alex 61
Ali, Përparim 124–125
Alia, Çaush 85
Aliko, Turban 111
Allen, Darby 29–30, 51–55, 91, 163–164, 173–174
Allen, Dennis 103
Alushi, Shaqir 83
Amery, Julian 10–11, 23, 38–40, 65, 69, 72, 94, 96–98, 106–108, 114–115, 117–124, 140–141, 147, 150–152, 154–156, 161, 165, 167, 176
Andoni, Vasil 22–24, 39, 65, 69, 77, 110
Angles, John 123
Angleton, James Jesus 26
Arapi, Gjin 48, 50
Asllani, Xhemal 125
Athenisiades, Bodosis (Bodosaki) 16, 19
Attlee, Clement 118
Averell Harriman, William 175
Azizaj, Aziz 112

Baddeley, John 120
Baftiari, Shukri 83
Bajo, Sejdi 84
Bajraktari, Muharrem 11, 23–24, 63, 67, 83–84, 93, 100
Bajrami, Hysen 56
Baker, John 166
Balili, Qemal 83
Balluku, Beqir 111
Bamfield, Mario 123
Barclay, Sam 26, 31–32, 53, 90, 165, 168
Bardha, Sami 124, 144, 146

Barraclough, John 154
Basha, Murat 83
Bateman, Charles 119–121
Beatty, Chester 21
Bedell Smith, Walter 175, 177
Belmonte, Nina 123
Berisha, Rexh 45–47, 51, 130
Bethell, Nicholas 5, 154
Bevin, Ernest 19–20, 103, 118
Binieri, Rapo 69
Black, Howard 167
Blackburn, Jimmy 132–134, 137, 163–164, 173
Blake, George 171
Bobinski, Zbigniew 34
Bodsaki see Athenisiades, Bodosis
Boxhall, Eddie 150, 154
Bradvica, Halil 113–114
Briggs, Charles 123
Broad, Philip 115
Brocklehurst, Charles 116–117
Bromell, Bill see Brummel, Bill
Brooman-White, Dick 14, 39, 106, 119–122
Browning, Robert 136
Bruce-Lockhart, John 168
Brummel, Bill 28, 31
Bukmiri, Faik 112
Burgess, Guy 25, 103, 137, 166–167, 169–170
Burke, Michael (Burke, Mike) 24, 35, 61, 69, 88–89, 106, 122, 167
Butka, Petrit 124

Caccia, Harold 16
Cadell, Captain 141
Çami, Skender 82
Ceci, Niko 111
Cenaj, Asllan Zenel 46
Cenaj, Ramazan (Ramadan) 44–51, 89, 130
Çeprati, Muço 126, 145
Chiang Kai-shek 20

Churchill, Sir Winston 21, 31, 63, 115, 137, 160
Ciastula, Ludwik 34
Cohen, Kenneth 167
Collins, William (Bill) 52, 142, 145, 147, 156, 158
Cowgill, Felix 167
Cromwell, Oliver 21
Çuli, Hetem 126

Daci, Selim 49–50, 59, 81, 85
Daci, Xhetan (Cetam; Gjetan) 49, 59, 81, 85
Dalipi, Ramazan 56–57
Daliu, Sali (Dalliu, Salih) 57–60, 81, 85
Damani, Selim 121
Daquari, Lucio 123
Dauti, Ago 76–77, 109, 125
Davidson, Basil 151–152, 155
Davies, Peter 51–52
Deakin, Bill 122
De Gaulle, Charles 20
De Neufville, Lawrence 61
Dennys, Rodney Onslow 60–61, 167, 168
Dervishi, Ferid 159
D'Estaing, Giscard 102
Deva, Xhafer 69
Dilo, Jani 61, 68, 75, 111, 125, 142, 145, 148
Dine, Fiqri 84
Dobrusha, Medi 126
Doko, Mustafa (Doko, Muça) 125–126, 142, 145–146
Domi, Shahin 47, 51
Doshishti, Hysen 86
Dosti, Hasan 24–25, 39, 41, 63–64, 69, 161, 176
Dulin, Roland 61
Dulles, John Foster 41
Durham, Edith 63
Duro, Fadil 126
Dyke, Gordon 164, 173
Dzierzynski, Felix 26

184

Index

Eden, Anthony 116–117, 119–120, 155
Elezi, Cen 83
Elizabeth, Princess 64, 158
Elliott, Nicholas 107, 167–168
Elliott, William (Elliott, Bill) 115
Ermenji, Abas 14, 23–25, 63–65, 75, 77, 87, 120–124, 141, 147, 150, 154, 161, 176
Ermenji, Baki 126
Eyre, Jim 152, 155

Farouk, King 87, 124
Franks, Louis 115
Franz Joseph, Emperor 14
Frashëri, Abdyl 62
Frashëri, Mehdi 64, 83
Frashëri, Midhat bey 1, 14–15, 22–23, 62–63, 65–66, 68–70, 72, 75, 87, 106, 108–111, 120–122, 127–128, 159–160, 167
Fritchey, Clayton 159
Fuller, Hod 37–38, 40, 43, 91, 167
Fundo, Llazar 107

Gaba, Betas 80
Gaba, Haki 63, 74, 76–79, 112, 125
Gardiner, Ava 167
Geraldine, Queen 71–73, 86–87, 123, 150
Gerhart, Alan 61
Gervishi, Bardhyl 74
Gjergji, Ndue 49
Gjikola, Pjetër 48, 50
Gjoka, Muharem 86
Gjura, Adem 49, 57, 59, 80–81, 83–85
Gjura, Rexhep 85
Gjura, Shaban 83, 85
Gjuta, Zenel 47, 50
Goga, Gaqi (Gogh, Gaqo) 45, 58, 69, 82, 84, 86, 122–124, 127, 129–130
Goga, Koca 39, 41
Gordon-Lennox, Victor 106
Gougy Bey 86
Graf, Clare 86
Grant, Alistair 8, 10, 52, 78, 110, 125, 135–136, 142, 146, 148
Gregory, Dino 26, 90
Gurabardhi, Ali 86

Hajdari, Qazim 83
Hall, Virginia 108
Harcourt, Bill 115, 153
Harding, Lord 16
Hare, Alan 13–14, 17, 64–65, 79, 115, 117, 119–124, 141, 145, 151

Harriman, William *see* Averell Harriman, William
Hasler, Col. "Bunny" 51
Hasluck, Margaret (Hasluck, Fanny) 116
Hay (Hill), Eileen 27–28, 30–32, 55, 168
Heath, William 153
Herbert, Auberon 150, 161
Herbert, Mrs. Aubrey 122
Hibberdine, John 37, 40, 86, 99, 105–106, 120–123, 138, 154
Hibbert, Reg 92–93, 116, 134, 140–141, 152, 154–155
Hill, Eileen *see* Hay, Eileen
Hitler, Adolf 21, 44, 82
Hito, Muharrem 125–126
Hoare, Sir Reginald 22
Hobbs, Godfrey 119
Hoda, Adem 73
Hopkinson, Henry 121
Howard, Alfred (Alf) 8–10, 52, 132, 148
Hoxha, Enver 1, 3, 4, 42, 45, 62–63, 67, 74, 82, 94–95, 96–102, 108–109, 114, 117–118, 133–134, 137, 140, 147, 150, 154, 161–162, 177
Hoxha, Qazim 85
Hoxha, Sima 81
Hoyar-Miller, Derek 103
Hyseni, Baki 76, 109

Imeri, Mustafa 83
Inglis, Sir John 156
Isufi, Hysen 111

Jakova, Asim 25, 112
Jashari, Isuf 83
Jebb, Gladwyn 103
Jellicoe, George 21, 102–104
Jellicoe, Sir John 102
Joanna, Queen 87
Joyce, Robert (Joyce, Bob) 103–104
Juba, Veli bey 162

Kadeli, Pjetër 50
Kalinski, Fouli 166
Kapaj, Safet 111
Karamesinis, Tom 165–166
Këlcyra, Ali (Klissura, Ali) 14, 62
Kelly, Jeffrey (Kelly, John) 142, 156
Kelly, Ned 52, 55
Kemp, Peter 16, 20, 40, 93, 99–100, 105, 108, 122–123
Kennan, George 103
Klissura, Ali *see* Këlcyra, Ali
Klugman, James 140, 151–152, 155

Koka, Gjergj 50
Kokla, Tefiq 126, 145–146
Kola, Bilal 90, 128, 156
Kola, Halit 156
Koliqi, Ernest 66, 69
Konica, Arif 82
Konitza, Mehmet 63
Korpowski, Boleslaw 34
Kosova, Tati, Prince 86
Kota, Nuçi (Kotta, Nuçi) 23, 39, 41, 121–122
Kotta, Koçi 121
Krahelski, Bogdan 34
Kruja, Mustafa 67, 69
Kryeziu, Ceno 86
Kryeziu, Gani 99, 100
Kryeziu, Said 11, 14, 23–24, 39, 41, 50, 66, 89, 106–107, 120–123, 127, 129, 153
Kuka, Ahmet 109, 111–112
Kuka, Bido 76, 78, 109, 111
Kupi, Abas 1, 10–11, 13–14, 16, 18, 23, 39, 41, 63, 66, 83–87, 99, 101, 106, 108, 114–119, 121–124, 127, 141, 144, 147–148, 150, 152–156, 159–161
Kupi, Petrit 119
Kushova, Neki 84

Laci, Xhemal 82, 84–85
La Motte, Madame 123
Last, Tommy 121
Leach, Colonel 100
Leak, Philip 115
Leatham, John 27, 53, 165, 168
Lee, John 24–25
Leib, Joseph (Leib, Joe) 35, 37, 42, 44, 69, 88–89, 133, 137
Leka, Imer 85
Lepenica, Hysen 63, 110–111, 124, 133
Lepenica, Sami 63, 110–111, 133
Lightner, Al 61
Lindsay, Frank 38, 40, 44
Lirioni, Ahmet 145
Lis, Michael 93, 97
Listowel, Lady 117
Lita, Kadri 83
Lita, Ziber 83
Little, Ron 8, 52, 158
Lleshanaku, Alush 67
Low, Robert (Low, Bob) 14, 17, 20, 23, 26, 35, 38, 87, 108, 121, 123–124, 167, 177
Lufi, Llesh 48, 50
Lusha, Qazim 83
Lyall, Archie 106, 122
Lyall, John 24–25

MacLean, Donald 103–104, 169
MacLean, Sir Fitzroy 21

Index

Macmillan, Sir Harold 11, 115–117, 120–121, 153
Mainutaj, Dev 111
Major, Bill 149, 153, 156
Makarios, Archbishop 18
Malëshova, Sejfullah 3
Maloki, Miftar 47, 51
Malushi, Safet 112
Mançe, Zeni 124–126
Mangelly, Thomas 69
Manukaj, Demer 81
Mao Tse-tung 20
Marinovitch, Ana 123
Martin, Dekenzy (Martin, Gjaklin) 82
Masaryk (Mazaryk), Tomáš 16
Matjani, Hamit 71, 87, 89–90, 112–114, 131, 178
Matuka, Ramiz 111
McCargar, Jim 38, 40, 165, 176–177
McCloud, Eric 120
McCloy, John 61
McLean, Billy 10–11, 13, 16–17, 23, 25, 37–39, 62, 65, 69–70, 86, 94–96, 98, 106–107, 114–115, 119, 140–141, 147, 149–150, 152–153, 161, 165–166
McLean, Henry 166–167, 170
Menzies, Sir Stewart 170
Messare, Kemal 86
Metternich, Klemens von 18
Mihailovic, Draža 20, 97–98, 100
Milmo Helenus 170–171
Minor, Bob 120–121
Moglica, Midhat 113
Muço, Sefër 124
Muggeridge, Malcolm 106, 168
Muja, Ali 51
Muja, Hysen 47, 51
Mullin, Stanley 157

Nasser, Gamal Abdel 14
Ndoi, Gjok 49
Ndreu, Mehdi 83
Neli, Bajram 86
Nerguti, Halil 45–47, 51, 59, 81, 127
Nerguti, Hysen 47, 51
Newman, Anthony (Newman, Tony) 134, 144
Niarchos, Stavros 16, 166
Nicholls, Col. G.C. 160
Nicholson, Brigadier 106
Nika, Ahmet 47, 50–51
Nitze, Paul 104
Northrop, Anthony (Northrop, Tony) 126, 131, 144
Norton, Clifford 120, 166

Oakley-Hill, Dayrell 151, 160, 165, 167–168

O'Brien, Bill 163
Odey, George 7–9
Ohri, Irfan 114
Oldfield, Maurice 154
Onassis, Aristotle 16

Page, Bruce 107
Pali, Zef 23, 50, 69, 89, 108, 110, 121–122, 129
Palmer, Alan 94, 97, 132, 134
Palushi, Tefik 48, 51
Papagos, Alexander 12–13, 16, 19, 143, 146, 166
Papajani, John ("Palmer") 39, 62–64, 77, 142, 157–158
Papandreou, George 120
Peake, Charles 120, 166
Peci, Shefqet 83
Peposhi, Liman 130
Perkins, Harold ("Perks") 17, 28–30, 37, 39–40, 42, 105–107, 118–121, 123–124, 132–139, 147, 148–149, 151, 164, 169, 172, 174
Petrarovitch, Ros 123
Philby, Kim 1, 4–5, 19–20, 25–26, 29, 37, 39–40, 42, 60, 63, 66–67, 69, 72–74, 82, 86, 89–90, 103–105, 109, 119, 123, 129, 131, 133, 143, 145, 149–150, 154, 159, 164, 166–171, 174–178
Philip, Prince 64, 158
Philpots, Christopher 28, 167
Picari, Musa 162
Pipenelis, Panayotis 120
Planeja, Miftar (Myftar) 45–47, 130
Poniatowski, Count Michel 102
Power, Sir John 149, 153, 156
Prenci, Tahir 113
Preni, Qazim 86
Proda, Kamer 83

Radomira, Rexhep 90
Rama, Sadik 85
Ramis, Hysen 78
Ramsey, Ron 173
Reçi, Dalli 83
Reville-Smith, William 153
Richards, Brooks 168
Riddle, Iris 120, 166
Riddle, Richard 93, 96–97
Rodd, Rosy 123
Roderiques, Arturo 123
Rodney, Sadie 16
Rudkowski, Roman 34–35, 37–38
Rumbold, Tony 104, 120–122

Sadiki, Idriz 83
St. Oswald, Lord *see* Winn, Rowland

Salki, Ihsen 84
Salku, Hysen 56
Salwood, Frank 166
Sammy, Mona 123
Sargent, Orme 16, 117, 119, 122
Seda, Nebi 84
Seligman, Adrian 27
Selmani, Hysen 86, 112
Sewell, General 115
Shehi, Brahim Iljaz 47, 50
Shehi, Sali 83
Shehu, Kasem Daut 145
Shehu, Mehmet 1, 62, 92, 95–97, 99–100, 127, 147, 155
Shehu, Zenel 24, 71, 74, 86, 89, 113
Shute, Ben 61
Shyti, Zef 45, 47, 50–51
Simcox, Tony 93
Simeon, King 87
Sino, Abdyl 125–126, 141–146, 148
Sino, Pëllumb 125
Slocomb, Frank (Slocum, Frank) 163–164, 171–172, 174
Smiley, David 8, 10, 13, 39–40, 52, 62–64, 68, 80, 94–96, 98, 114–117, 132, 140–141, 144, 146–147, 157, 159
Smiley, Moy (Smiley, Moyra) 157–158
Smith, Jack 173
Smith, Victor 94, 97, 134
Sokalari, Xheladin 113–114
Somers-Cocks 123
Sophoulis, Themistoklis 16
Sotiri, Gaqo 83
Spahija, Miftar 84
Spahija, Nezir 83
Stalin, Joseph 3, 65, 109, 115
Stallwood, Frank 33
Stover, "Blondie" (Hover, "Blondie") 7–8, 135
Sufa, Halil 86
Sula, Naum 114
Sulo, Dervish 78
Sulzberger, Cyrus 158
Susea, Ida 123

Taku, Bedri 96
Tanef, Aposta 107–108
Temali, Ali 86
Tërpeza, Hajrulla 56
Tërpeza, Ihsen 84
Thompson, Llewelyn E. 108
Tilbury, Bill 173–174
Tito, Josip Broz 3, 15–16, 20–21, 65, 67, 86, 95, 97, 100, 109, 153, 156, 161
Tomorri, Nezir 78, 109, 125
Topliss, Cpl. John (ToJo) 7–8, 52, 148

Toptani, Abdi bey 159
Toptani, Esad 162
Toptani, Ihsan 11, 45, 64, 69, 75–77, 79, 117, 119, 121, 141–142, 145, 148, 153, 157–158, 159–160, 162
Toptani, Iljaz (Toptani, Ilia) 49, 59, 81, 85, 128–129
Toptani, Sali 162
Toroshi, Bresht 83
Tosku, Kol 49
Tozan, Lutfi 16
Turbohova, Ali 126
Tweedie, Bronson 166

Ulmer, Alfred 166

Van Fleet, General 20
Van Linden, Ida 123
Vata, Tahir 130
Velija, Ali 83
Verediki, Qerim 83
Vërlaci, Ismail 66–67
Vernoudakis, Frank 91

Verschoyle, Derek 120, 123
Victor Emmanuel, King 87–88
Vivian, Valentine 167
Voka, Hysen 47, 50
Voka, Ramadan 47, 51
Voyce, Reg 155, 165, 168

Walton, Kevin 163, 171–174
Watrous, Elliot 100, 115
Wheeler, Norman 132, 134
Whinney, Patrick 27–28, 30, 33, 40, 119–120, 123, 133, 165
White, Sir Richard (White, Dick) 169
Whitworth, Martin 164, 171
Wilkie, Captain 142
Wilson "Jumbo" 153
Winn, Rowland (St. Oswald, Lord) 101–102, 140–141
Wisner, Frank 39, 103–104, 119, 159
Woodhouse, Monty (Montague Woodhouse, Christopher) 21

Woods, Pat 8–9
Wyatt, Peter 163

Xoxe, Koçi 3–4, 62, 97–99, 128

Yatsevitch, Gratian 35–37, 44, 61, 74, 89, 168, 175
Young, George 14–15, 109
Young, Rollo 9, 52–55, 110, 148, 154, 156

Zaehner, Captain ("Doc") 8, 10, 52, 55, 75, 78, 80, 109, 125, 143, 146, 148, 150, 153, 158, 166
Zeneli, Enver 111
Zervas, Napoleon 21
Zog, King 1, 14–18, 20, 23–24, 62, 67–72, 83, 86–88, 90, 94–96, 98, 100, 112–114, 118–119, 121, 123–124, 128, 150–151, 153, 155, 158–159, 176–178

www.ingramcontent.com/pod-product-compliance
Ingram Content Group UK Ltd.
Pitfield, Milton Keynes, MK11 3LW, UK
UKHW050523150426
5217IPUK00026B/1777